Pictura Britannica

ART FROM BRITAIN

Contents

Curated and edited by Bernice Murphy

PREVIOUS PAGE: JOHN STEZAKER **EXPULSION I** 1994

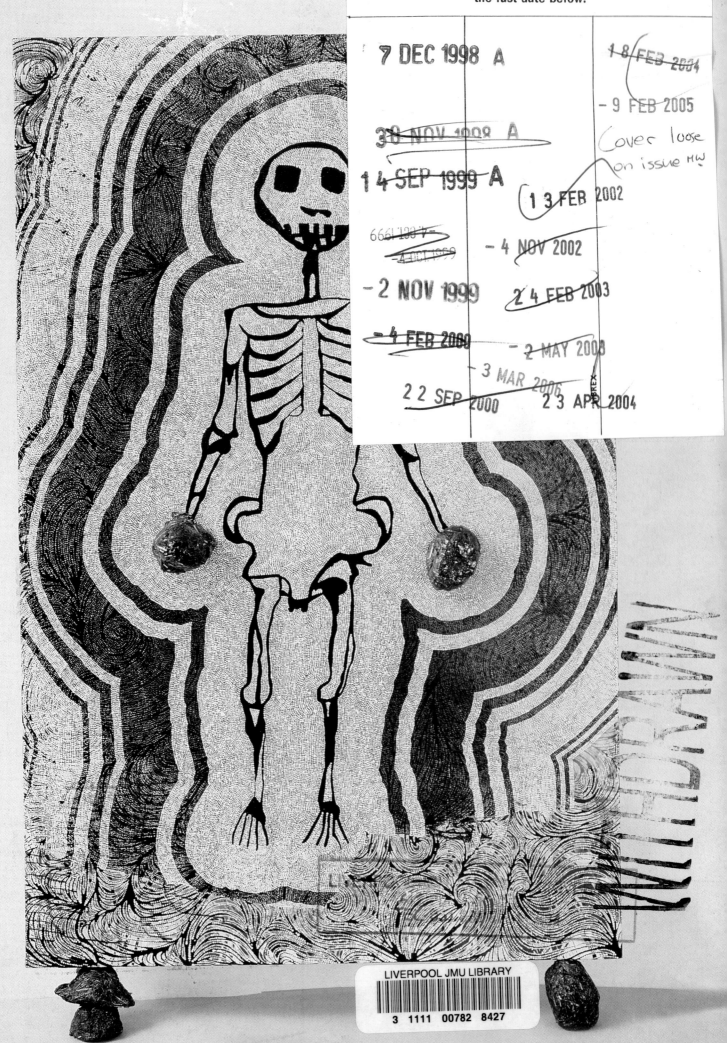

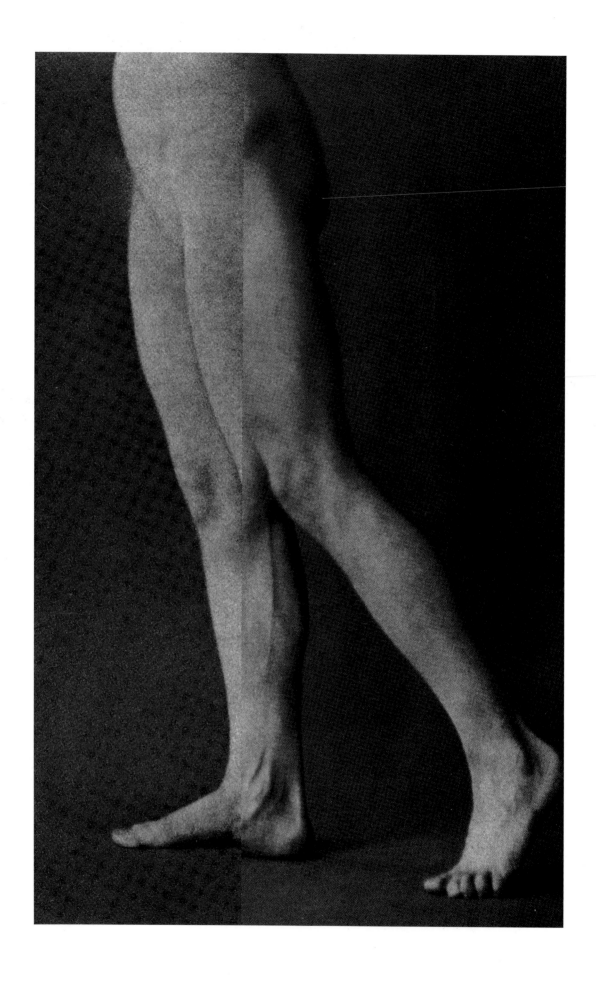

DIRECTOR'S FOREWORD

In a little more than half a lifetime Britain, Australia and New Zealand have undergone such profound transformations that in each society the shared language and parliamentary and legal systems form an armature that supports increasingly different social and cultural fabrics. Mother country and her former colonies have not only experienced the inherently natural evolution that occurs in any society; they have had different patterns of immigration, different trade relationships (Britain within the European Union and Australia and New Zealand within the Asia-Pacific region), and different responses to world and regional political changes.

It is not so long since school atlases told Australian and New Zealand children that they, and all others living in countries coloured red *were* British. Their parents bought British products, and images of Trafalgar Square and the Houses of Parliament were more immediately recognisable than images of capital cities near at hand. Their teachers might have studied in Oxford, Cambridge or London; and they taught history and geography that depicted Continental Europe as being south of the English Channel rather than to the far north of this region.

In this part of the world views of Britain remain strongly shaped by surviving memories of their own earlier provincial Anglo-Celtic society. Popular clichés and the jokes 'cousins' make at each other's expense endure, in spite of the barrage of contemporary images of British bands, drama and sport seen on television.

The present publication, and exhibition to which it relates, can only be a limited intervention in the face of such a powerful, popular intertwining of histories and perceptions. The project can neither present an overview of British art, nor can it be a definitive reflection of a society undergoing such experiential change. Like other MCA projects that have focused on developments in particular regions, this publication and exhibition address certain aspects of art practice in Britain and selected historical and contextual influences. Australian and New Zealand art audiences travel relatively frequently and devour art magazines. Through international exhibitions and through acquisitions by public galleries we are familiar with many prominent British artists. This exhibition provides the opportunity to see the work of a younger generation of British artists, and that of two older artists whose influence has been overlooked recently: John Latham and Richard Hamilton.

The Museum appreciates the contribution of artists, writers and lenders to this project. Special thanks go to The British Council for generously supporting this exhibition and publication, and for providing extensive advice and great encouragement. I am delighted that this project is part of the *new*IMAGES program, and I am confident that it will form an appropriately lively and challenging contribution to the celebrations for the 50th anniversary of The British Council in Australia in 1997.

Leon Pariossien

Director

Museum of Contemporary Art

FIONA BANNER **FULL METAL JACKET** 1996

ever pitch, the title of a recent movie on the British obsession with football, could equally describe the current state of international interest in the contemporary British art scene. With major exhibitions regularly taking place in the States and Europe (encouraging audiences and critics to concede that this phenomenon is not 'a flash in the pan' but something which deserves serious attention), it is promising to see critical interest extending well beyond Europe, into the Asia Pacific region. Given the cultural 'renaissance' Australia and New Zealand have been undergoing over the past two decades, which has involved a reassessment of their cultural and constitutional ties with Britain, and their enviable position as two of the most culturally diverse nations in the world, there would seem to be no more appropriate place nor time to stage an exhibition of contemporary British art, which explores issues of nationality, history, class and popular culture.

When we first began discussing the idea for this project with the Museum of Contemporary Art, Sydney, in 1994/5, a decade had passed since the last comprehensive exhibition of British art. In the intervening years, individual artists had been shown in different contexts, ranging from the Sydney Biennale to the Adelaide Festival, but there had been no opportunity to organise a contemporary show which would present an overview of recent developments in British art. Exhaustive research by Bernice Murphy over the course of the past two years, during which she trawled England, Scotland, Wales and Northern Ireland, supported and advised by a network of artists, curators, critics and commentators, has resulted in *Pictura Britannica*, a rigorously selected exhibition in which artists who came to prominence in the early nineties, such as Rachel Whiteread, Damien Hirst and (a little later) Douglas Gordon, are shown alongside a host of younger practitioners, many of whom are just beginning to make their mark on the international circuit. The scope and size of the show—120 works by 48 artists—represents one of the most wide-ranging and ambitious achievements yet mounted on the subject. Specific artists and works, such as Richard Hamilton's 'The citizen' have been included to facilitate the crossfertilisation of particular artistic concerns and themes, most notably those of cultural identity, competing versions of nation, contested social memory and the legacy of conceptualism.

Offering a parallel range of voices to those in the show, the various authors in this publication map out the territory, context and issues which have preoccupied British audiences during the late eighties and nineties. These writers have not been chosen to endorse the selection or to present a celebratory view, but rather to provide a critical framework in which to approach the works on show. This invaluable compendium of essays is particularly welcome at a time when so many yBa (young British artists) exhibitions have failed to produce supporting critical texts.

As an exhibition which raises important issues about aspects of British cultural, social and political life, over the course of the past decade, *Pictura Britannica* is particularly appropriate as the visual arts centrepiece of the International Festival in Wellington as well as the *new*IMAGES Initiative,

which aims to be a catalyst for new partnerships and networks into the 21st century, and celebrates the British Council's 50th anniversary in Australia. Through a series of inter-related events covering all fields of activity, from sport to trade, *new*IMAGES will, in addition to fostering links between the two countries, encourage a critical re-examination of the relationship between them. Australasian visual culture has been constructed through a diversity of influences ranging from Aboriginal and Maori culture, the legacy of the European vision of the South Pacific, and more recently the recognition of the geographical as well as cultural importance of Asia. Within this context, *Pictura Britannica* plays a crucial role - inverting the post-colonial gaze to provide an independent view of contemporary British art.

Brett Rogers

Deputy Head

Visual Arts, The British Council, London

Jim Potts

Director

The British Council, Sydney

ACKNOWLEDGEMENTS

EXHIBITION SPONSORS

The Museum of Contemporary Art is a non-profit company and receives only 6% of its income from government grants for ongoing operations. Exhibitions of this calibre would not be realised without generous support from individuals, cultural bodies and the corporate community.

Pictura Britannica: Art from Britain has been organised by the Museum of Contemporary Art in collaboration with The British Council.

It is supported by The British Council as part of the newIMAGES and The British Council's 50th-anniversary program of events for 1997.

The Museum would like to express its great appreciation to Thorn Business Services, for their generous sponsorship of all the equipment needs of the exhibition, and their enthusiastic support. We thank The Regent Sydney, QANTAS, Vodafone Mobile Gallery Guide and the Australia Council, the Commonwealth Government's arts funding and advisory body, the New South Wales Ministry for the Arts and the Australian Film Commission for their continued support.

THE BRITISH COUNCIL'S ACKNOWLEDGMENTS

We would like to thank: Jo Thornberry at Anthony d'Offay Gallery; Esther Lane at Thomas Dane Limited; Mark Sladen at Entwistle Gallery; Barry Barker and Pilar Corrias at Lisson Gallery; Bénédicte Delay at Anthony Reynolds Gallery; Saatchi and Saatchi Australia; Jenny Blyth and Sarah Rogers at The Saatchi Collection; Stephen Snoddy and Helen Simpson at Southampton City Art Gallery; The Australian Magazine; Annushka Shani at White Cube, London; Robin Klassnik and Simon Morrissey at Matt's Gallery; Ian Rogers at Momart Plc; and Sarah den Dikken, Bernice Murphy, Leon Paroissien, Louise Pether and the MCA team.

The British Council and the Museum of Contemporary Art would like jointly to thank the artists and lenders to the exhibition, whose generosity and interest have made this exhibition possible. From Australia: Queensland Art Gallery, Brisbane. From Britain: Arts Council Collection, Hayward Gallery, Thomas Dane Limited, Entwistle Gallery, Carl Freedman Collection, Stephen Freidman Gallery, Frith Street Gallery, Laure Genillard Gallery, Colin Herber-Percy, Jay Jopling, Lisson Gallery, James Moores Collection, Victoria Miro Gallery, Maureen Paley/Interim Art, Public Art Development Trust, Anthony Reynolds Gallery, Saatchi Collection, Richard Salmon, Tate Gallery. From Switzerland: Galerie Art + Public. From U.S.A.: Barbara Gladstone Gallery, New York; Collection of Vicki and Kent Logan, San Francisco. We would also like to thank those lenders who prefer to remain anonymous.

CURATOR'S ACKNOWLEDGMENTS

I have been discussing the possibility of curating an exhibition of recent art from Britain for some years now. In 1996, with the support of The British Council and the Foreign & Commonwealth Office, I consolidated my earlier research with an extensive trip through England, Wales,

Scotland and Northern Ireland. For this I thank Sir John Hanson KCMG CBE (Director-General, The British Council), Sir Roger Carrick KCMG LVO (British High Commissioner), Dr Andrew Pocock (Deputy High Commissioner) and David Fall Esq (former Deputy High Commissioner).

I am indebted to Andrea Rose (Head of Visual Arts), Brett Rogers (Head of Exhibitions) and Ann Gallagher (Exhibitions Officer), of the Visual Arts Department of The British Council in London, for their guidance and interest during this early development period. I would particularly like to thank Clarrie Rudrum (Exhibitions Officer), who inherited this project from Ann Gallagher at the end of 1996, for her commitment and enthusiasm. In addition I thank her assistants—Lizzie Carey-Thomas and Andrew Gwilliams, and the staff of The British Council Workshop in London.

I would like to acknowledge the continued support of The British Council in Sydney, and particularly to thank Jim Potts (Director), Michael Hedger (Arts Officer), Jane Westbrook (Project Director - newIMAGES) and Annette Quinn (Business Development Manager).

Most importantly, the MCA is indebted to the artists, writers and lenders to the exhibition, listed elsewhere in the publication, for making this exhibition possible through their support and insight. I am deeply appreciative of the many people who generously gave me information, guidance, and assistance in the course of my researches in Britain, and during the many phases of the exhibition's development over the last two years, especially the following: In Belfast: Liam Kelly (Orpheus Gallery), Noreen O'Hare (Ormeau Baths), Irene Orr (Northern Ireland Office of the Foreign & Commonwealth Office). In Birmingham: Elizabeth A. MacGregor (Ikon Gallery), Eva Rothschild. In Cardiff: David Alston (National Museum of Wales), Stuart Cameron (Chapter), Alison Clash (Welsh Office of the Foreign & Commonwealth Office), Chris Coppock (Ffotogallery), Dr Colin Ford (Museums and Art Galleries of Wales), Sue Grayson, Jenni Spender Davies (Oriel). In Edinburgh: Karen Crawford (Scottish Office of the Foreign & Commonwealth Office), Sarah Munroe (The Collective), Andrew Nairne (formerly of the Scottish Arts Council, now of Dundee Contemporary Arts). In Glasgow: Charles Esche (Tramway), Hilary Stirling (Tramway), Toby Webster (Transmission), Nicola White (CCA). In Liverpool: Lewis Biggs, Duncan Hamilton, Toby Jackson (all Tate Gallery), The Bluecoat Gallery. In London: Barry Barker, John Burgess (City Racing), Sadie Coles, Cubitt Gallery, Thomas Dane, Bénédicte Delay, Anthony d'Offay, Bea de Souza (The Agency), Emma Dexter (ICA), Hymie Dunn, Stephen Friedman, Laure Genillard, Lotte Hammer, Leslie Heitzman, Mrs K.E. Howard (British High Commission), Robin Klassnik, Nicholas Logsdail, Jeremy Lewisham (Tate Gallery), Victoria Miro, Simon Morrissey, Sandy Nairne (Tate Gallery), Anthony Reynolds, Karsten Schubert, Glenn Scott-Wright, Nicholas Serota (Tate Gallery), Kim Sweet (The Showroom), David Thorp (South London Gallery), Joanna Thorpe (Foreign & Commonwealth Office), Robin Vousden, Jonathan Watkins (formerly of Chisenhale Gallery, now Director of 1998 Biennale of Sydney). Also, from the USA

Barbara Flynn; from Australia: Professor Margaret Plant (Melbourne), Doug Hall (Queensland Art Gallery), Ron Radford (Art Gallery of South Australia); from Aotearoa/ New Zealand Paula Savage (City Gallery, Wellington); and the numerous artists who showed me their work during my visits to Britain.

MCA curators, Linda Michael and Lyndall Phelps, spent time in Britain during 1995-96 on Museums Australia Professional Development Grant projects. They brought back information and perspectives which are gratefully acknowledged. We also gratefully acknowledge the assistance of former MCA staff member Kay Campbell, now in Bristol.

I would like furthermore to acknowledge two concurrent projects in Sydney, also supported by The British Council: Jane and Louise Wilson's exhibition, *Normapaths*, organised by Nick Waterlow and Felicity Fenner (Ivan Dougherty Gallery), 26 June - 26 July 1997. And *Nerve - Glasgow Projects*, with eight artists from Glasgow, organised by Deborah Ely (Australian Centre for Photography), Ann Ooms (Pendulum) and Nick Tsoutas (Artspace), 3 October - 1 November 1997.

I am deeply grateful to other people whose support helped make this exhibition and publication a reality, all MCA staff involved with this exhibition, particularly Anne Dalton (Directorate Co-ordinator) for her continued support, and organisation of my overseas travel. Sarah den Dikken who first came to the Museum on an internship in March 1996 became part of this project's development; later, after her graduation from Manchester University she continued to assist me on further work in London and eventually returned to Australia for a year to act as Assistant Curator with me on this project. For her extensive professional support and continued liaison with Clarrie Rudrum in the Visual Arts Department of The British Council in London, I and the MCA are indebted to her.

A final, special thank you and acknowledgment to Hardy Jones and Brian Thompson, who supported me personally in many ways during my numerous visits to Britain—I thank them for their generosity, the resources they made available to me, and their continued good humour and interest.

JONATHAN PARSONS **HERMA** 1990

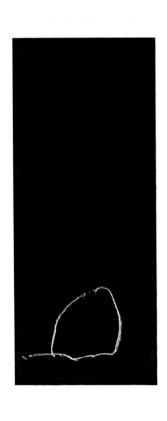

ROSS SINCLAIR *REAL LIFE ROCKY MOUNTAIN* 1996

VARIOUS SYNTHETIC MEDIA, TAXIDERMY, VIDEO, PERFORMANCE

DIMENSIONS VARIABLE

COURTESY OF THE ARTIST

'PICTURA BRITANNICA':
SCENES, FICTIONS AND CONSTRUCTIONS IN CONTEMPORARY BRITISH ART

BERNICE MURPHY

Art does not carry a passport. So what could be meant by British art?

Art from Britain has recently gained much attention, and been staged in exhibitions in many countries. The sense of newness, youth and raw vitality is regularly presented as the trademark of contemporary British art—leading to the acronym **yBa**(s) (or *young British artists*—neatly pirouetted in Kobena Mercer's essay here as *young black artists*). However actuality of some of the most interesting new art being made in the UK today is often very different from the *Vogue* styling and the *fanzine* imaging.

Most artists, understandably, abhor nationalism. Artists are generally deeply suspicious of all discussions that seek to link their work to any homogenising construction of nation, or to place the complexity of mobile contents in their work within a congealed social identity. And yet to deny all reference to structures through which nations engage with each other culturally, and through which many international projects are directly funded, would be to dissemble on crucial issues of analysis concerning the social resourcing of many cultural encounters.

To vault beyond the *national* reference to the *international* frame, implying an unsourced, unremunerated and unfettered movement of artists and works between dispersed geographic places, is somewhat specious. It would mean reaching again for a currency of exchange of values —*internationalism*—that has long been so inflated, and little related to any collateral of real local connection, as to be quite unreliable as a currency of cultural translation. Art is vitally specific and local in its materials and impulses, before it can ever attain the kind of density or referential mobility that might argue its passage into the 'universal' domain, the realm of cumulated and more commonly shared values.

For many artists, the 'national' category, rather than being irrelevant, is daily inscribed in troubling contradictions, each of them meriting resistance in different ways. The national frame represents an effort, through the conscriptive claims of citizenship, to draw boundaries around identity that are too presumptuous (federating vast differences), too narrow (segregating people within borders from those to whom they are deeply joined beyond them), or too reductive (contracting the complexity of polyform, multiple and fluctuating identities into an annealed container of statehood). Moreover the *rhetoric of national identity*, when enlisted to the communications machinery of a touristic manufacture of consciousness, soon abandons any grounded connection with actuality. Seeking to consolidate an identity around icons of place, history and difference, it evacuates the symbols of their more subtle and conflicted contents, re-presenting them as a collage of folkloric signs.

Ross Sinclair's work, *Real Life Rocky Mountain* (1996), engaged a strong critique of these difficulties. It brought together a vivid congregation of theme-parked Scottish materials in a room-installation at the Centre for Contemporary Arts, Glasgow, in Spring 1996 (unfortunately too large to imagine re-assembling for the present exhibition). In an astro-turf mountainscape environment, surrounded by fibre-glass rocks, stuffed forest animals, timber hut and a reverse-pumped waterfall, the artist installed himself in the context of a 'romanced' habitat-nationalism. With the words 'REAL LIFE' tattooed on his back, Ross Sinclair strummed and sang Scottish folk songs in daily sessions. The lyricism and evocation of the songs, recollecting events in a 'distant-present' tense, pointed up the impossibility, melancholy—and at the same time 'REAL' erasure of conflicted contents in the historical remnants mythified—through which a 'national identity' is artificially assembled.

If the dilemma of nostalgic pastiches offered as authentic identity were a matter of ridicule only, the problem would not be so irritating. However history *has* happened behind the folkloricised signs. And identification and identity *are* troublingly important issues. The complexity of contending (and excluded) histories is parodied by the depthlessness and inertia of so many of the emblematic signs of unified identity that are forced together under the rhetoric of nationalism.

Contemporary art in Britain is speaking in many contexts, and in voices from cultural backgrounds that have not gained utterance previously. As new cultural images (bearing different histories and content) appear ever more strongly across the experimental scenes of art's reception in the UK, it is difficult for criticism to cope with the unfamiliarity of some of the new materials deployed without stressing their alterity—without constantly calling attention to the itinerary of their journeys into mainstream visibility. And yet it *is* difficult, in an exciting period of transition and reformation, to avoid the stress-lines of stretched discourse that occur when vital new contents and redirected meanings are pressing forward within art, as work arises from ever more diverse cultural backgrounds and new structures of combination.

In a period of expanding and changing critique, fresh challenges of decription are exerting pressure on old thought-paths of language. For example: how to discuss new works without exoticising those parts of their contents (especially from outside the West) that seem novel, thereby artificially emphasising their passage from cultures less familiar to mainstream criticism; or, how to avoid enchaining such works' mixed contents in a politics of origin, instead of comprehending their full-bodied multiplicity (already), and liberating their energies in an inclusive dynamics of mutual becoming; and then again— acknowledging the nagging problem of the *critical temporality* within much new cultural work that deserves *not* to be ignored—how to speak of work that carries within its contents a sense of strategic difference, challenge and *agency*, in ways that do not diminish its provocative energies by instant accommodation to the mainstream, conferring another kind of 'non-recognition'.

Curator-critic Eddie Chambers provided a perspective on these problems of new stress-lines in contemporary critique in 1996, in his framing of a review of Permindar Kaur's work in *Third Text*:

PERMINDAR KAUR **UNTITLED** 1996

What references to Sikh/Indian identity and culture should we read into [Permindar Kaur's] sculpture? Or should we set such readings aside, for fear of misreading or erroneously locating some of the most powerful sculpture currently on offer to gallery-going audiences in this country? It would, after all, be relatively easy to suggest, as one commentator did several years ago, that her work 'is informed by two cultures', and that 'she may think of herself as both an Indian and a British woman'. But this type of assessment is little more than a re-hashing of the *From Two Worlds* thesis…a bizarre form of anthropology that invariably locates artists such as Kaur in neat 'half and half, neither fish nor fowl' packages. In many ways, a more plausible reading of her work would acknowledge that all sorts of 'cultural' influences (if we can speak of such things) are discernible. …The continuing temptation to ethnicise Kaur's work is apparent… We may be tempted to view…potent symbolism [in her work] as a form of literal referencing of 'identity', 'religion', 'culture' and so on. But such limited readings would leave us distinctly short-changed because such symbolism takes its place alongside (but not above, or ahead of) other equally dramatic devices in Kaur's sculpture.[1]

Kobena Mercer's essay in the present publication,[2] which opens up in different ways upon some of the issues raised by Eddie Chambers in the preceding quotation ('The challenge is to be able to theorise more than one difference at once'[3]), speaks of, and is also positioned within, a whole field of interconnected new works and writings that fundamentally change the terrain of what might be thought of as 'art in Britain' today.

One of black Britain's defining characteristics is the broad-based shift away from the essentialist views of blackness as a unitary identity fixed in the authenticity of one's origin, towards a more relational view of the plural identities constructed from the Caribbean, South Asian and African migrations of the post-war era. Because Empire brought together disparate peoples, whether as colonial subjects or as coloured immigrants, blackness in Britain has always been a more heterogeneous, composite, and hybrid affair than it is in the United States. So while the eighties' advocacy of Afro-Asian alliances under a shared signifier of blackness has become a thing of the past, a pluralist approach to the politics of 'race' and ethnicity nonetheless remains peculiar to black British perspectives in the arts.[4]

Nikos Papastergiadis's essay here,[5] pressing the issue of crisis in contemporary culture in the global domain (and including the problematic rhetoric of 'globality' itself), extends analysis into institutional frameworks for the organisation of culture. He deals with many struggles that have gone on throughout the 1980s, not only about issues of representation, but also the controlling conditions of the visibility, discussion, and reception of representations within art in the UK:

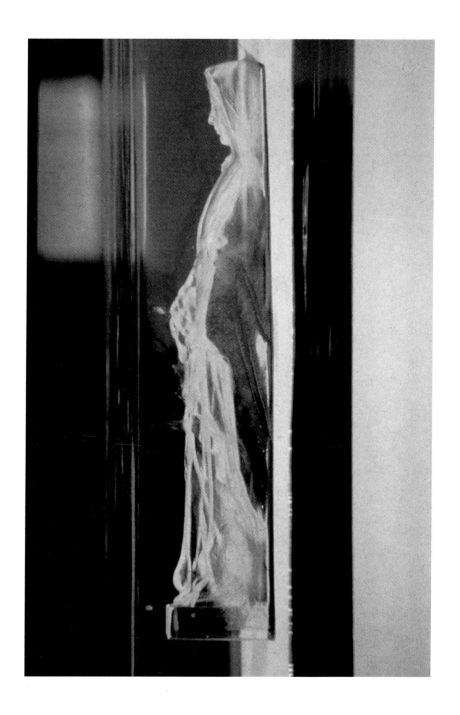

TANIA KOVATS **FATIMA** 1992 (DETAIL)

I would argue that the way the dominant institutions respond to the issues of cultural difference is also bound by their very conceptualisation of crisis. It has varied from recognition of the necessary renegotiation of existing resources to a rethinking of the very paradigms within which cultural practice is conducted. …As we witness the breakdown of the conventional models for integrating and organising the question of difference—when both universalism and particularism are seen as inadequate, or when neither evolutionism nor relativism seem satisfactory—we can then twist the level of understanding crisis: modernity is the culture of crisis. …This crisis is most palpable in the difference between the rhetoric of inclusion and the practice of participation.[6]

Meanwhile other new voices have emerged. They disclose very different temperaments and orientations. They articulate attitudes and frameworks on contemporary culture that are part of the environment in which contemporary art is thought about and discussed. For example, David Barrett was commissioned as one of the new writers invited to contribute to the catalogue of emerging artists brought together in the *new contemporaries 96* exhibition, presented by the Tate Gallery Liverpool in April 1996. David Barrett's text, reprinted in full in the present volume,[7] provides a potent enactment of a 'generational' perspective, of which he is ironically self-conscious throughout:

Somehow—who would have thought it?—we've stumbled across a milieu full of constructive possibilities. What combination of events could have produced this surprising situation?[8]

David Barrett's piece seems casually to thumb a ride from the pitch of *fanzine* celebration of a particular generation and grouping of British artists. However he demonstrates that exploiting all opportunities may also be partnered by critique, and manages to puncture a number of inflated currencies before the journey is over.

Patricia Bickers's essay,[9] expanding on an enquiry she first opened up in a Cornerhouse publication in 1995, provides the most comprehensive analysis to date of the internal dynamics, and particular occasions and exhibitions, by which British art has 'risen' recently into international prominence. This has occurred both through acts of self-assertion *from within*, as well as peculiarly self-conditioning responses along the way (which include both mocking resistance and delirious exultation), as to how British art is 'viewed' *from without* internationally.

There *is* an exciting diversity of art emerging at present in the UK. And as one explores the possible connections between various parts of the *montage* of scenes through which culture in Britain may be 'pictured' today, it is evident that many motifs from the past re-surface, and are transformed, in the ongoing contention between past and imagined futures through which contemporary art is made.

Many things that appear, change and disappear in pulsatile movements through visual imagery in British art suggest recurrent interests. These interests are linked to specific histories of ideas and images that have a long history, both in Britain itself and in the countries, peoples and cultures in distant parts of the world that it has transformed, and—most importantly for the present enquiry—itself been transformed *by*, in the intercultural engagements with many others of the world.

So it is useful to keep wondering what things might be idiosyncratic or peculiarly defined in British culture, while also holding all temptations to find national identities through art up to the most sceptical scrutiny. The present project therefore seeks to explore some of the imageries and scenes of consciousness in art being made now in Britain. Yet since the images that are strongly present in contemporary art cannot be segregated from their sources and structural connections within a wider context of the socialisation of imagery in the culture at large, some references may be made here to very disparate things.

FROM EMPIRE TO MODERN MANAGEMENT

Britain's move into the industrial revolution ahead of other European nations propelled it first into the massive changes in social life—in particular, the disarticulation of the urban from the rural—that mark the critical passage from an agrarian society into the forms of modernity, and mass-production of goods and global markets.

It would seem that the art of the late-twentieth century has moved far beyond these foundational developments of the late-eighteenth and nineteenth centuries. Yet to the degree that the encompassing structures of a cultural system move slowly and alter cumulatively—in motions that interconnect all parts and are *reiterative* as well as *evolutionary*—it is instructive to navigate the traces of past imageries and consciousness that recur, often reformulated, in the present.

At the time of the restoration of constitutional monarchy in 1688, Britain had the most enlightened structures and political institutions—for the times— among the nations of the western world. It was best equipped, relative to the specific challenges of industrial and economic development it was undergoing, to weather the political strains entailed in the change from a rural to an urban workforce. Just over three centuries later, the *political institutions* of the UK are the least altered among all the modern nations of the world; they are the most anchored in the forms and configurations of the nation's historical past.

Nevertheless contemporary British *culture* is evolving dramatically, presenting new cultural styles and volatile forms of adaptation within the lives of its urban populations that are sharply divergent from the past. The actual composition and dynamics of British society have therefore undergone the most extraordinary and far-reaching changes, leaving the political forms in which social energies must be canalised strongly at variance with the actual conditions of *lives lived*[10]

in contemporary Britain. Such a situation suggests the inevitably contrasting social forces that configure so much of the representational diversity of contemporary art in Britain at present.

Just over three centuries after the restoration of the monarchy, Britain has risen and fallen as a world empire, and has undergone the most far-reaching social transformations since it began the painful task of recovery after a punishing victory—with the Allied forces—in World War II. The UK has relinquished nearly all of its dominions and former colonies, with (after the 6 million population of Hong Kong reverted to China in July 1997) a mere 180,000 people left under British rule, across 13 restyled 'dependent territories', as the last remnants of colonial power.

Most people living in Britain today are pleased to be peacefully disengaged from imperial rule in former colonies. And indeed the British Commonwealth—now a quite warmly joined association of nation-states productively continuing evolving relationships based on a shared inheritance of British traditions—sustains some very positive and unusual ties between formerly dependent nations.

Nevertheless a fierce reminder of how potently the residues of imperial rule may be used to redirect disaffected social forces at home is to be found in the case of the Falkland Islands. It is salutary to recall what ferocity of engagement was galvanised around the seizure of these islands by Argentina in April 1982, and how completely the full panoply of state propaganda under Prime Minister Margaret Thatcher could be marshalled, in a matter of ten weeks, for the bellicose recapture of distant territory housing a colony of some 2,200 British subjects, sprinkled over 200 islands. Almost half the entire population of the Falklands was matched by the 1,000 lives lost in settling Argentina's dispute over 'Las Malvinas', and their reinstatement under a British governor.

It is also worth recalling that it was after the successful recapture of the Falklands, leading directly to Margaret Thatcher's landslide victory in the next election, that the Prime Minister set about using an unusual electoral mandate as comprehensive authorisation for the most radical changes in post-War history in the UK. The new government undertook the steady transformation (that is, frequent dismantling) of many of the structures and institutions that had long configured British public and cultural life—as is searchingly indicated in Patrick Boylan's essay in this publication.[11] Once author of the stark proposition (as Professor Boylan reminds us) that 'there is no such thing as society', Margaret Thatcher embarked on a decisive campaign of transforming most spheres of governmental and civilian life in the UK. The results were so comprehensive that 'British cultural life' has been altered in ways that may be described as not only transformational but also mutational.

Given that art is sometimes one of the last refuges of a self-conscious and critical play of representational codes (since it can work symbolically, within the interior recesses of signs—shifting, rearranging and displacing them) it should not be surprising that the effects of 'Margaret Thatcher's era' are to be registered right throughout the artistic and cultural scenes of British life of the period; nor that her manipulation of symbolic codes for state-political purposes should have been so resisted and castigated by almost all artists or cultural sector professionals active in contemporary Britain in the last two decades, quite beyond their party-political histories—in fact involving sentiments expressed across the whole spectrum of political differences.

The presence of Margaret Thatcher's social restructuring (and continuing legacies after her departure from government) casts influences across the social background of the youth and emergence of many artists represented here, and the modifications to life that occurred in this critical period of change.

> The 80s. Another ne'er-be-mentioned. That was when I grew up, and in those days there was something you could believe in, could trust in, aim for: money. But even that simple(minded) belief was lost in the darkest recesses of the deep recession. But all the ungodly shit that went on in the 80s—yes it's true that we're still up to our knees in it, though that's only because it's finally receded from our necklines.[12]
>
> [David Barrett]

The contrasts Britain lives with in the late-twentieth century—being one of the most dynamically changing, culturally and racially diverse societies in the whole of Europe, yet also sustaining social forms and institutions that trace a heritage from the Middle Ages—therefore present

some vivid dichotomies to the rest of the world. In addition, the extraordinary contemporary combustion of what can be seen by an outsider as the most starkly diverse materials of daily life evokes a great variegation in the social landscapes within and throughout Britain today.

It could be said that the very friction of contending forces and possibilities, daily negotiated, is perhaps at the heart of the vitality and volatility expressed within contemporary art in Britain.

...the panic's over now because the worst has already happened. All that we're left with is this massive fall-out which, as it turns out, is the richest of pickings for artists. It may be a kind of cultural nuclear winter for everyone else, but it's definitely springtime for young artists. Why? Because in a way it's interesting to live in a country where the government

is collapsing, where an entire ideology is falling, leaving only confusion. Without a centre, the collective consciousness has become a mass of undifferentiated peripheries. No-one really knows what is of value since all values were levelled in the 80s. And with this, artists have suddenly discovered that they are as (un)important as everyone else. The situation that we find ourselves in is the interesting time when one thing has come to an end, but where that which will replace it has not yet arrived. (Perhaps this rich sense of collapse will be dissipated by the cocksure New Labour, which is worrying, since surely we all now understand that for 'New' we must read 'Not'.)[13]

[David Barrett]

JACK & JILL

The British flag, second only to the American flag, has been an extraordinarily resilient emblem within recent and continuing constructions of each nation's culture, used not only for national identification but also drawn on frequently within the more restricted spheres of art. The British flag still appears regularly in contemporary cultural constructs —whereas the Australian and New Zealand flags are generally left by both countries' artists to purely diplomatic and formal uses.

The British flag as a fashion item was exceptionally potent in the Carnaby Street days of the 1960s. In such a context—of the cultural revivalism and triumphalism of a more positive era in recent history—the flag was treated as a sign that could be emptied out of certain contents, to be refilled and used playfully in combinations with a variety of new ones. Ironised, the flag of once-potent imperialism could be redeployed as a counter-cultural badge of new social relations. It could signify the triumph of British pop music for an emerging global youth market, replacing the world power status that had subsided over a contracting empire. Such changes, often condensed under the newly mobile marketing sign of the British flag, were emblematised by the scenes of frantic rapture attending the Beatles on world tour in the 1960s.

Mark Wallinger's work explores many subjects that relate to monarchy, class, economic divisions and social rituals that converge in British sporting histories—'I am fascinated by racing's obsession with breeding'[14]). He continues elsewhere:

There is a degree of identification inherent in all sports, but what distinguished horse-racing is the aspect of money. The sport originated because one nobleman said to another nobleman that his horse could run faster. It is the purest form of capitalism because no goods are exchanged, and in the absence of a commodity there has to be a strong sense of identification because it is simply one's hope that one is wagering on.[15]

It is through his linkage of social stratification and popular, communally involving sporting scenes, spanning class barriers but still calibrated and theatricalised by them, that various series of Mark Wallinger's work derive their representational energy.

Judith Dean's *Installation for a chihuahua: "Rough" Patriotic version with 25 options* (1995) also plays distantly on the colours of the flag, as an ironic social reference in a more conceptually derived sculpture. Meanwhile the flag may be a banner of coerced relations, depending on the ground above which it is raised. Mark Wallinger has made a radically alternative use of the flag in a work entitled *Oxymoron* (1996), which restyles the British pennant in the colours of the Irish flag.

The Union Jack's recognition as a formal construct has been given an unusually perceptual treatment in the work of Jonathan Parsons. Sewn in polyester, Parsons's 'flag' (*Cuttlefish*, 1995) hangs (literally and figuratively) from a traditional housing, suspended from the fixture that would present it to the world unfurled. However its angle of presentation already moves it into the space and height of sculpture, where it abandons its social reference to conduct a dialogue with our memories of painting, in a syntax of subtle colour relations. The representation that simulates the British flag is in fact constructed through shades of brown. Shuffling different states and identities, as both cultural sign and as artwork, this object finally works most strongly through our faculties of perception and displaced recognition.

TV DINNERS

There have now been several generations of artists weaned into 'the social' by television. They have been solicited since childhood, first, as a consumer; somewhat secondarily, as a citizen. The effects are ubiquitous.

Paul Graham's work here touches on the impact of these changes: his three photographs (*Television Portrait*[s]...: *Danny, Bristol* (1991); *Yuko, Kyoto* (1992); and *Jack, Bradford* (1989) [ill'n p. 132, 61]—from a larger series—disclose the production of a new kind of global citizen of the televisual image, a creature brought up developing the conceptual tool-kit of *watching* moving images of the world, in ever-changing sequences. Paul Graham's work uses the language of high-colour-value close-up portraiture, simulating the imagery of advertising in one direction as it also recalls older studio traditions of the painted portrait in another.

As a result of the socialising effects of television, the construction of personal and social identities has been highly modified. Distinctions between private and public, the personal and the social, are more fluid and provisional. The individual's place within society, as a consequence, is apprehended not as a journey into the social through selfhood; rather as a gradual incorporation into a pre-existent sociality of networked information and communications—operating beyond boundaries of nation or locale, pulsating globally.

...there's no idea of free will—that's ridiculous. This idea of humanism, which was initially about knowledge giving you power and giving you access to freedom. Now we *feel* we have access to these things, but they're all completely controlled, because they have to be.[16]

[Gillian Wearing]

Competing with local structures of family and kinship, the modern 'individual' is increasingly modulated by televisual education in a subtly *a-focalising* process. Individuality is rendered more porous to forces reaching beyond particular frameworks of theology, ontology and morality, in a process of constant stimulus-response moves through competing options and multiple choices.

Artists who have been fed by TV world clips, movies and advertising since infancy belong to a generation with a gut grasp and sceptical analysis of the forces making the product or staging the show.

Francesco Bonami: *You like advertising?*

Damien Hirst: I love it. I prefer it to film because it admits its own corruption.[17]

Such sceptical regard is directed not only at the commercial producers of the things people are happy to consume, but frequently towards all social institutions as well. For society's institutions, as understood through televisual experience, become part of 'the flow'[18] of social forces through the consciousness of the individual, encouraging an individuality constructed as infinitely malleable and available to a variety of contending influences, whether the occasion be the campaign launch of a politician; the doorstop interview with a sociologist, environmentalist or stockbroker; or the product launch of a manufacturer.

Moreover as political parties have taken to employing promotional tools identical to those of soap manufacturers in reaching a mass audience, it cannot be surprising that the penetration level of commitment behind many 'pitches' to the media by public figures is considered merely skin-deep. Opportunism and ground-shifts are practised daily by the country's most distinguished, and employed as survival skills.

> **Carl Freedman**: *If you were asked to work on an advertising*
> *campaign for the Tories would you agree?*
> **Damien Hirst**: It depends how much money.
> **CF**: *So you don't adhere to any particular political beliefs?*
> **DH**: That kind of integrity is bullshit. Nobody has that kind of
> integrity. Things change too much. There's no black and whites,
> only different greys.
> **CF**: *You're not a socialist at heart?*
> **DH**: I'm not anything at heart. I'm too greedy. I believe there's a
> million different ways to get to the same point. I can't dismiss
> anything.[19]

THE HAUNTED HOUSE (THE ACADEMY)
Never have tertiary art institutions been producing so many formally credentialised artists and launching them into the world at such a high level of over-heated professional expectations.

Tertiary artist education has been through two major gear-shifts in the last three decades in Britain since the Coldstream Report of the 1960s:[20] *professionalisation*; and *managerialisation*. Many artist-teachers are still inveighing against the former, which is ineradicable, and in fact has been to general advantage (many more people have a chance to be admitted to a better quality of education in the visual arts). By contrast, they should be both learning some useful lessons from, but also vigorously critiquing, the latter (especially the ideological architecture and social effects of the march and takeover of the arts by managerial culture).

The first gear-shift of art schools into professionalised education within large tertiary campuses (whether polytechnics or universities) has been so crucially transformative as to provide staggering contrasts between settings, ideas and practices of the 1960s and those of the 1990s. The second gear-shift occurred in the 1980s, though it was probably set in motion long ago—as a stealthful, but ultimately more influential companion of the first. Nevertheless the impact within the whole geomorphology of tertiary educational institutions of a forcibly adopted managerial culture has been insufficiently recognised, utilised, and also opposed.

Artists in the 1990s: Their education and values[21] published by the Wimbledon School of Art in association with the Tate Gallery in 1994, is a compilation of papers from jointly hosted seminars (in 1991 and 1992) 'on the teaching and practice of fine art, and the connections between them, in 1990s higher education'. Considering some of its contents, the title seems curiously ill-considered. It might more accurately have been titled:'The *teachers* of artists in the 1990s: *Their* education and values'. For the crises and rifts in matters of value evident throughout the papers (both within and between them) seem overridingly preoccupied with the concerns of the generation of teachers and administrators, rather than really conveying or dealing with what are palpably altered values and needs of young artists and students.

In this first Wimbledon-Tate volume (another has followed since), there are many expressions of embattled loss of confidence and polarisation about the institutional changes in artist education. For example, the Professor of Sculpture at the Royal College of Art (Glynn Williams)—one of the major voices and contributors to open discussion in the seminars—refers to the 'rampant destruction' of art courses,[22] and characterises an atmosphere of artist-teachers feeling like a hunted down species: 'Suddenly it's open season on the practitioner'. He refers elsewhere to the practitioners' role as having been crucially that of acting as the 'guardians of quality' (in this context, an ambulance-ride back to Plato).

In these and many related comments, there is a tendency to figure changes in *orientation* as a helpless loss of direction. Artist-teachers often lament on behalf of their *own* sense of loss—rather than that of their students. In so doing, they miss the opportunity to address the ways in which the life-experiences of students have already been altered fundamentally, through radical social changes that have transformed most students' attitudes to the world long before they reach entry to a tertiary art institution.

I was watching TV and listening to pop music before I ever went into an art gallery, and I am an artist. I don't know why. So doing a video for a band like Blur is normal but it seems weird to other people. When I curated the exhibition *Freeze*, everybody said to me, 'Now, you have to decide whether you are an artist or whether you are a curator.' And I said 'Why?'. There was no reason, 'Why?'. I spent all my time asking myself 'Why?'. When someone tells me I can't do something, so far I've always found out that I can. Now people ask me, 'What are you doing now? Are you going into pop videos, films, or are you going to be an artist?' I can't see the difference. I just do the whole thing. It's all art to me.[23]

[Damien Hirst]

The studio is still spoken of in the first Wimbledon-Tate papers as emblematic of history and tradition, and mentioned with a consistently directed meaning as a certain *kind* of studio: the painting or sculpture studio. It is evident that this studio has, in the late-twentieth century, continued viably. However it can also become stultifying when allied with a certain kind of social insularity. For example, Paul Huxley, Professor of Painting at the Royal College of Art:

Like most professionals, my social world is limited to like-minded people. Only rarely, say two or three times a year, do I meet that nasty question, 'Teach art? — surely not! After all what is good or bad is a matter of personal opinion isn't it?'[24]

The studio behind such a life-style is not only often socially aloof; it is also crucially segregating in its modelling of creativity, a place of isolation and singular (predominantly manual) production. Such a studio space is only one of a number of available models that might be relevant to young artists' needs, against others (places of collective and interactive production) that are equally familiar and useful sites of work: for instance, a music studio; photographic studio; film, TV or broadcast studio.

Painting no longer *belongs* to the painting studio as it once did. The old faith has been broken. Painting can be re-thought in new aspects, and even re-imagined within a broader context of a more diversified culture of visual materials, with new technologies of reproduction traversing all possibilities. Painting often serves more as a *memory* of the tradition of art, by agnostic citizens who may still work on the cumulated ideas of art's history but are no longer able to act as believers. The technologies and social experiences of late-modernity have put an unforgettable channel of new knowledge between young artists and the old ways—just as it became impossible earlier to think *only* of mural and panel paintings once the new tradition of oil painting had emerged. The new ways of creating things produce innovative ways of thinking, and it is impossible to *un-remember* the new possibilities, without opting for denial.

I always felt like a painter who couldn't paint, and I liked the way you could create this formal way of making a painting, and that I could do it for the rest of my life. I like this idea of a created painter, the perfect artist. Art without angst.[25]

[Damien Hirst]

The kinds of new studios referred to here—broadcast, sound and TV studios are of course environments for the production of culture that have come into being in partnership with managerial culture's own rise, especially in the post-War period. Nevertheless they have in numerous ways not abolished creativity, but brought new forms into existence, encouraging collaborative as well as individual forms of cultural output.

Hirst is acknowledged to be amongst the most significant of a group of artists coming principally, though by no means exclusively, out of Goldsmith's College, until recently a little-known art school in South London. Rarely since the legendary 1960s when the famous pop artists of London including Blake, Kitaj, Hockney, Jones and others emerged from the Royal College of Art more or less simultaneously, has there been such excitement—a sense of something genuinely new arising. ...

Naturally there are always leaders, those who begin the dialogue, ask new questions, and Damien Hirst is definitely such a leader. He is capable of arousing jealousy and even resentment, an artist who is also an impresario—not only a painter himself— but generously (quite untypically for a creative artist) also of the art of many others. Indeed, he was first approached principally as an impresario, an organiser of other artists, in a series of now-legendary exhibitions and manifestations in East London around 1988-89. *Freeze* was the best known, taking place in an old warehouse in the shadow of the spectacular property and financial boom and ultimate collapse that was centred in the old docklands of the Thames, east of the old city of London.[26]

Marcelo Spinelli: *You were the curator of* Freeze, *a now-famous exhibition of student work held in an abandoned warehouse in East London. How did the show come about?*

Damien Hirst: It's very difficult making that kind of work that a lot of the people at Goldsmith's were making, and as an artist you need an audience in order for what you're doing to make sense. I had seen a lot of work at the college that I thought was better than what was in the galleries, but there was no way that those students were all going to get exhibitions in London galleries when they left college. That gave me the incentive to find a building and do it. And if you're going to do something, you might as well try and do it properly.[27]

In addition to social change, the cultural backgrounds of artists emerging from British art schools have altered significantly, incorporating new influences, forcing 'tradition' to speak no longer monolingually, but to be opened up to a decentring, cross-weaving and pluralisation of voices, of multiple models of creativity:

[Permindar] Kaur grew up in an Asian family environment in England. At art school, the aesthetic ideas and forms of her Sikh family culture were unfamiliar. She attempted to synthesise her cultural background with western artistic stereotypes; a sense of community with the 'cult of the individual'. In *Glass Houses*, 1991, she used craft sources, traditionally treated with indifference in fine art teaching, in combination with sculptural sources of minimalist orientation.[28]

The historical interests of new voices, formerly silent or rendered invisible, but now active and engaged, inevitably probe old closures and open fresh ground on which to build new vocabularies of representation. These expanded conditions change the understood scope for *everyone* involved. It is not only a matter of an etiquette of addition or inclusion, but—far more important – a decisive revision of the *dramatis personae* of history itself. New figures and metaphors are *irrupted* into our consciousness, interconnecting actors and agencies in unusual ways, challenging our notions of where we have come from, the journeys undertaken that have contributed to and defined our contemporary cultural conditions, and on what grounds we may now stand, and work be made:

The inspiration for *Syrcas* has haunted Maud Sulter for many years. Politically the power of fascism in the 20th century, spiritually the re-memory of the holocaust of slavery of the African diaspora, and personally the holocaust of the 1930s and 40s, which once again tore people from their psychic and physical homelands, robbed people of their dignity, their lives and their families.[29]

This important sense of a 'haunting' within history is alone insufficient. It has to be transformed into a specifically directed use of language to function *within* art; to force open the gaps in the representational codes through which 'history' has been constructed and expressed, in order to change history itself, to articulate new consciousness in new forms.

And so Maud Sulter (of Scots and Ghanaian background) has worked at occluded dimensions within the existing visual constructs that already functioned historically—as within a tradition of visualisation. Incorporating additional, specifically feminist, scrutiny as to the eclipsed roles of women within historical representations, Maud Sulter has worked to prize open what was deflected and not expressed within the existing codes, creating in the photographic medium a new 'actor' (a child), to perform within the *caesurae* (or gaps) of what is depicted. She has introduced a new presence and agency within a system of representation already created by an earlier visual artist (the German photographer, August Sander):

The aesthetic springboard to *Syrcas* is twofold. The writings of Primo Levi…and the photographs of August Sander were crucial to the development of the work. …What fascinates Maud Sulter about Sander's magnum opus [ed.: a photographic portrait series intended to represent the social order in Germany in the 1920s/30s] is the wide inclusion of people of African descent (and of course many portraits of 'Persecuted Jews'), in particular the *Zircus* series, Köln (1926) . …[showing a] man of African descent in *Zirkusleute vor dem Zelt (Circus people in front of a tent)*.[30]

One of the most substantial installations of Yinka Shonibare recently, entitled *Victorian Philanthropist's Parlour* (1996), is a work not only of postcolonial critique, but of humour, fantasy and imaginative suppleness. Having spent his life between Lagos and London, Yinka Shonibare's work contributes to the opening out of subtlety on questions of critique and imaginative projection. He presses beyond the simplistic presumption that processes of identification will always move to take up single positions or exclusive currents of affiliation. (Why shouldn't a child of the African diaspora explore the imaginative position and accoutrements of all parties in the theatre of colonial relations — instead of adhering to the contestational vantage-point of the oppressed?)

Shonibare's works have extensively explored the history of socialising and migratory influences that accompany (and acculurate) many of the textiles and ceramics associated with colonial trade and exchange of goods in the days of European colonies in Asia and Africa. Textiles in particular, such as batik, while often worn in new contexts (such as Africa) as affirmative signs of indigenous identity, have in fact been introduced along tradegoods-routes from distant places (such as Indonesia), as part of a long history of inter-cultural flows and transfers.

In Africa the fabric has the allure of imported goods which are made in Europe, while in Europe itself the vibrant texture connotes exotica. In another twist, other West African textiles, such as kente cloth from Ghana, are now appropriated in popular fashions among young black people in the Diaspora. In other words, you may already 'belong' to communities that you previously did not know existed.[31]

[Kobena Mercer]

I am actually producing something perceived as ethnic, in inverted commas…but at the same time the African fabric is industrially produced, and given its cultural origins my own authenticity is questioned. …Just imagine being a primitive, a proper primitive that is. A primitive that is beyond civilisation, a primitive in a state of perpetual indulgence, a primitive of excess. I think I would really enjoy that. Here too I can be a kind of urban primitive: a kind of back to nature cliché with a twist. Oh how I long to be ethnic, not just ethnic, but authentic ethnic.[32]

[Yinka Shonibare]

YINKA SHONIBARE *VICTORIAN PHILANTHROPIST'S PARLOUR* 1996 (DETAIL)

REPRODUCTION FURNITURE, FIRE SCREEN, CARPET, PROPS, AFRICAN FABRIC; DIMENSIONS VARIABLE

COURTESY OF THE ARTIST AND STEPHEN FRIEDMAN GALLERY, LONDON

Yinka Shonibare has utilised batiks in many ways, including as the basis for paintings stretched on frames [ill'n p.135]. In this context, Shonibare has incorporated batik as both a formal 'ground' and expressive structure through which to confront multiple systems of representation simultaneously (the forms of batik, the language of abstraction developed in the West, and the incorporation of a kind of 'urban indigenous' mark-making that has evolved through the international diffusion of artists like Keith Haring and Jean-Michel Basquiat, and the subcultural diasporic 'black' styles which they both helped to evolve.

A very different artist who is also interested in the social itineraries of textiles and their convertible relationship to painting is Louise Hopkins. Her works are more thoroughly a kind of conceptual painting, in which there is a consistent disinclination to rely on any materials or processes that do not serve her critical interests in art's boundaries. Her reverse-fabric and reverse-process paintings, made on the rear side of printed floral cotton, carry a commentary on the continuing deflections of nature within culture, and the complex journeys painting must make today to keep finding ways out of the entrapment of its past history. The exceptionally subtle perceptual effects achieved in Louise Hopkins's works may belie the complexity of the self-questioning itineraries of their making.

The issue of multiple acculturating influences is also strong in Chris Ofili's works, who—like Yinka Shonibare— plays across a range of cultural styles of marking, from cultures lying outside the West, to the painting styles of Western modernist history, and indeed synthetic cultural furnishings in domestic interiors. Chris Ofili, also of Nigerian background (like Yinka Shonibare and Rotimi Fani-Kayode), has abundant styles of painting, drawing and mark-making, in which some of his most haunting works have been tiny, carefully built-up portrait heads.

POP, GRAPHICS AND ADVERTISING
Turning to other scenes of contemporary art, where visual art crosses into the wider structures of pop culture and music, or graphics, fantasy products and advertising, the conditions of production and reproduction are accelerating all the time.

The painting of Richard Wright seeks to establish itself in odd sites and places, in ambiguous conditions of execution and imagery that elide its status as fine art, often seeming instead to push towards applied art or design. Sometimes incorporating emblems that swim between logo-forms and arcane symbols or product designs, Richard Wright's paintings are often wall-applied, incorporating large zones of flat unmodulated colour, as if by an industrial painter or sign-writer.

The industrially produced forms of popular culture (for example, toys or knick-knacks) are also incorporated as the basis of works by other artists here. Richard Patterson's carefully abstracted blow-ups of the figure of a motorcyclist, rotated through space in different versions and all thrillingly energised in vibrant colour (*Motocrosser III*, 1995), represent a kind of urban cavalry hero. Kerry Stewart's creation of monumental-style figures in synthetic materials deploys a

31

KERRY STEWART *MONSTER* 1995 (DETAIL)

PAINTED FIBREGLASS, 183 TALL

COURTESY OF THE ARTIST AND STEPHEN FRIEDMAN GALLERY

of productivity. Art often struggles to distinguish itself, to compete with the ecstatic confusion and throb of the wider culture itself. David Barrett again:

> Art, it seems, is going the way of British pop: younger bands, higher praise, less time at the top. Everything is new and it's always the new-big-thing. Yeah, it leads to instant burn-out, but—as the editor of NME once asked—who ever said it was about careers anyway? One problem of this, though, is that fashion then becomes the dictator as to how long an issue can be sustained in the public eye, so whatever progress can be made in an 'in' era, like multiculturalism was, will be lost as soon as the issue is no longer 'fresh'. Fashion, by definition, can sustain nothing but itself, which means that as trends turn over faster, less will actually change—save for the packaging. Every generation will be the first generation, or as Tricky succinctly put it: 'Brand new, you're retro.'[33]

'JACK, PHONE YOUR MUM'
(note on the message board of an artist-run space)

Young artists generally reject, or find simply irrelevant, the nostalgic modes of high cultural criticism or elegiac social critiques of their forebears. What distinguishes most younger British artists from the preceding generations from which their teachers were drawn, is a sense of inescapable (but also productive) location within the circumstances of their own collective socialisation in a communications-society. Damien Hirst, like many other contemporary artists represented here, is emphatic about the changes that savage all pretensions to individuality in imagery now. Significantly, he focuses his sense of change (and emphasis) on the audience rather than the author:

counter-formal language of simple, 'punched-out', stamped or loosely modelled forms. She favours a direct 'gestalt' in her figures, simply presented, eschewing the nuances or lineage of 'fine art'. Her images could be derived from the fairground, plastic toys or filmic effects, as she deliberately seeks to hold the psychological recognition of her work within the domain of mass-socialised experience.

In comparison with just two generations ago, we live in a more complex world of competing systems of social stimulation, where 'post-production' may be as crucial an element to a work's realisation as any inaugural drawn plan or sketch. And so the inherited sequences (taxonomies) of production in the *bottegha* or *atelier* sites of art's long evolution in the West have been re-arranged, interpellated and spliced with many other, quite disparate sites and kinds

Today there are better ways to communicate to an audience raised on television, advertising and information on a global level.[34]

Many artists have opted for film as a medium, including Hirst himself recently, with a new work for the group exhibition, *Spellbound*, dealing with artists and film—which included Douglas *Gordon's 24-hour Psycho* and Fiona Banner's *Apocalypse Now!* [a text-work]—at the Hayward Gallery, in 1996. Damien Hirst commented on the mixed reception his first film-work received in *Spellbound*:

I am an artist. I put things in art galleries, and the film is one of those things. But it's also a film, which is confusing, but I like that. People didn't really like it because people expect you, according to your reputation, to be able to make a perfect film, while in reality you have to learn a whole new visual language. People didn't know how to approach it because they couldn't decide whether to treat it as art or film. If it's art, it's great. But if it's a film, it's not really as good as *Apocalypse Now*. ...

The only difference between art and film is that art can be cheap and film is fucking expensive.[35]

FIONA BANNER
THE NAM 1996

Artists today might choose to work in social zones of production that are still ideologically shunned by those who preceded them: for example, using the technologies of market research, product advertising, journalistic interview, or TV mini-series-style production on videotape—though what will distinguish their use of these, in all the best cases, will be critical strategies of analysis, re-interpretation and transformation. This is instanced in the forms and content especially of Sam Taylor-Wood, Gillian Wearing, Georgina Starr, Gary Perkins, Fiona Banner, Critical Decor, Yinka Shonibare, Kerry Stewart, and many other artists here. A critical art, even when using the broadest social tools, will not simply extend the status quo; it will analytically reflect upon and transform various aspects of its functioning.

I like to alter people's perceptions because that's the way I live my life. This explains why I enjoy the ambiguity of their response. And that's why I'm an artist and not a politician. If I wanted people to get exactly what I was saying, I'd stand on a soapbox. Art's an excuse for a conversation, and conversation is what changes things. I really don't think the world will change if people are so struck dumb by art that they go home speechless. Personally, too, I don't want to go to an art exhibition and be shocked into silence. I much prefer going to the pub afterwards and talking about what I've seen.[36]

[Douglas Gordon]

Artists have absorbed information in new contexts that have shaped their consciousness. They have constructed their pictures of the world—indeed constructed 'the world' itself—in modes of intake and consciousness distinguished by 'flow', 'channel-switch', 'game-change', 'program failure', 'sound byte', 'synthesiser', 'multiple tracking', 'video loop', 'CCTV', 'set-up', 'network link' and 'melt-down'. In consequence artists' thinking has been shaped as much by an 'editing' consciousness, across a great range of cultural forms (many of them quite ephemeral), as by impulses towards the manufacture of discrete or unique objects.

Indeed this editing consciousness, previously presumed to be a mode of passivity, is itself linked to new kinds and intensities of 'social productivity', rather than an exclusively manual production of carefully made, unique things. Breadth and speed of intake of streams of information, in a continuum from the audio to the textual to the visual, are now crucial survival skills, stimulated from infancy in a modern city. They have inevitably modified the human creature we call *homo sapiens*—not yet in form, but certainly in consciousness—and had their impact on the cultures we associate with our existence.

Francesco Bonami: *Do you believe there is a big difference between the art world and the music world?*

Damien Hirst: Yes, the music world is a pile of shit and the art world is fantastically free. Basically in the music world the people who are the furthest away from creativity have the most control, which is totally stupid. The people who make the decisions about what we listen to should be the bands, and they are at the bottom. If you look at the contracts they have to sign, it is ridiculous. ... 'You can't change style.' So if the record company is primarily interested in money, why are they so stupid? They

don't realise that if the Beatles had signed a contract like that in 1962, they would never have become the Beatles nor made all that money.[37]

Sam Taylor-Wood has made a series of works incorporating unidentified people on multiple video-screens, disconnected but juxtaposed in 'real-time' sequences, their random actions or words variously juxtaposed, crossing-over, dissociated or fused. Her recent film work, was one of the strongest pieces in the Corderie section of the XLVIITH Venice Biennale (July-September 1997). Sam Taylor-Wood alluded to some of her structural principles of *montage* and counter-effect in discussing the development of her film, *Method in Madness* (1994), for which she employed a method actor:

But in the end I wanted to make something else, so I put on a sound track that changes the whole feeling of the film. I used a track from the Beastie Boys' album *III Communication*. It's very jazzy, soft, mellow. So you're watching this intense thing going on but listening to soft music, and you begin to think, 'I don't care, just shut up, will you?' The juxtaposition makes you aware of how you're being desensitized to the emotion on the screen.[38]

The languages and structural concepts of different media (histories and styles) now cross over and coalesce. Sam Taylor-Wood's experience with film and video can also be seen as an insistent influence behind her skilled use of the horizontally stretched landscape-format photograph, like repeated frames re-presenting a long tracking shot; or a film-still worked up as an historical *tableau*—(*Wrecked*, 1995)—

CATHERINE YASS

STARKMANN LTD 1992

PHOTOGRAPHIC TRANSPARENCY, LIGHT BOX

215 X 180 X 30

COURTESY BERNHARD STARKMANN

machines and the acceleration of external stimuli in a modern metropolis); and effects from *within* (the Surrealists' interest in the subterranean layers of human thinking through Freud's theorisation of the entities of the *subconscious* and *unconscious*). However these forms of attention, and their legacies throughout modernism, have been foundationally altered by the critical recognitions of a post-modern consciousness—of the supersession of the *hyper-real* of post-modernity—a kind of *meta-modernity*. The metropolis has become a place not only of intensified appearances, but also of the merging and dissolving of identities:

In London, you get everything, and you'll always feel that this is a place where you can disappear.[39]

[Gillian Wearing]

New forms of roving attention, multi-tuning and absorptive sensibilities have developed, in response to overlapping, networked, continuum flows, from the home to the street, from shopping malls to video-game parlours to pubs and clubs (with 'time-out spaces'), to anywhere on the planet where communications links provide the traffic possibilities of a communications interface.

The twinned-other of self-immersion and *disappearance* within the anonymity of the metropolis, of course, is the experience repeated seductions of intensified *presence*—images of ordinary people looking famous for a moment (or simulating it—in advertising); or others projected to a level of hyper-fame, the identity

presenting a 1990s photographic version of the temperament of Caravaggio's realism and dramatic lighting, but actually based on the picture-plane frontality of Leonardo's High Renaissance *Last Supper*.

Another artist using photography who makes considered use of both the *tableau* format and historical memory of earlier genres in painting is Catherine Yass—for example, her luminously coloured 'still-life' works dealing with institutional interiors [ill'n p. 111, rear cover]; or her group-portrait of the identities composing the new 'corporate patron' of contemporary art—(*Starkmann Ltd,* 1992).

SUBJECTIVITY

Early modern art focused upon new forms of reality and their transformative effects on human consciousness: effects from *without* (the Futurists' sense of the speed of engine-powered

35

that Andy Warhol was first to understand and re-work so comprehensively: that of the *celebrity*. Not only emperors and popes achieve world fame today; but astronauts, hi-jack victims, terrorists, politicians, salesmen, broadcasters and football players. Artists can do so also, if they understand the networks and the particular ways in which images may ambush our memories through a sudden clashing of expectations, or unsettling of constructs.

> Antony Gormley (*Turner Prize winner of 1994*): Hirst is the most visible, energetic artist of his generation. His is an extraordinary, ever-changing body of work which challenges preconceptions of what art is and what it should talk about.
>
> Waldemar Januszczak (*Art critic and arts commissioning editor, Channel 4*): He's the most influential artist working in Britain by some way. He has cut through the bullshit and he has become utterly unmissable. ...
>
> Sarah Wilson (*Courtauld Institute*): He's managed to crack the system. He's deeply interesting in a peculiar way. He seems to be preoccupied with death and medicine—one of the few artists who try to tackle those subjects. ...
>
> David Mellor, MP (*Former secretary of state for National Heritage*): Hirst is a squib, and in a few years he will be found to be a damp one.[40]

The current generation of artists has been influenced by social forces that have targeted it relentlessly as the most economically empowered youth in history, able to activate its own currents of social change through its collectivised habits as a consumer.

This promotes a more fluid individuality, ever-shifting in options and preferences, in interaction with a social environment of constant change:

> I think people modify their opinion the whole time.[41]
>
> [Georgina Starr]

Echoing an increased lateral attentiveness induced by new media forces, and the appraisal of contrary information simultaneously, the social construction of *subjectivity* reveals marked changes. Individual consciousness is presented differently:

> I started thinking that what's happening inside my head is far more interesting than what's happening outside it.[42]
>
> [Georgina Starr]

Gillian Wearing also acknowledges how advertising and television shows have not only impacted upon, but worked to shape (even fictionally augment or displace) a sense of personal history:

> I'm interested in people more than I am in myself, maybe that's what it is. ... Some idea of your family life comes from advertisements, so you feel in a way that even your own history seems to have been altered.[43]
>
> I think my most important influence has been documentaries. I really enjoyed the 1970s 'fly on the wall' documentaries that were made in Britain. There was a program called 'The Family', where they were in someone's home and filmed the family. Video was still fresh then, and these programs felt very spontaneous. Now people know the mechanisms.[44]

The work of Georgina Starr, Gillian Wearing, and twins Jane and Louise Wilson [ill'np.36], especially, disclose the sedimentation of contemporary consciousness shaped by television as a medium: a consciousness engorged by TV's relentless recycling of the whole history of 'film' as 'the movies'; the fluctuating *montage* of clips, scenarios, types, stars and styles liberally redistributed to successive generations between the products, news, game-shows and ads.

Francesco Bonami: *Why has art not got such a big audience as films and music?*

Damien Hirst: Maybe art is too threatening. People are incredibly visually educated, they don't even know how well educated they are about films. The amount of films that people watch is so big, but they don't realize how much they know about it and how it works. If people would see as many art exhibitions as they have seen films, they would know a lot about art. This visual intelligence that everyone has got from films is used in advertising to sell things to us.[45]...

Francesco Bonami: *So the music world is shit. What about the movie world?*

Damien Hirst: Same thing as Hollywood. The art world is fantastic, you can have so much fun. ...There are regular moments in the art world where something has been invented and no-one knows if it's good or bad. How fantastic is that?

Francesco Bonami: *So, why are people in the art world so often depressed if it's all about freedom?*

Damien Hirst: Because they can't admit to themselves the secret that they want to be famous, and they resent not being famous.[46]

Gillian Wearing's work in the present project is derived from a *Time Out* advertisement that has moulded its title: *Confess All on Video. Don't Worry You Will Be in Disguise. Intrigued? Call Gillian* (1994) [ill'n p.125]. It presents respondents to her actual advertisement in a variety of masks and wigs in the video-piece that resulted. What they relate frankly about their ordinary lives has an uncanny double-effect. The voices of the subjects are direct, even 'confessional' (and the contents of their stories often socially startling to the middle classes!). However the intimacy of each narrative is dramatically distanced behind a coloured latex face-mask, a vividly dissociating, bizarrely assumed *persona*. Each subject, though informal and particular, is also anonymous and enclosed. What links them is the structure of the work, the artist's recognition of their common social enactment within a kind of carnivalesque theatre of urban fugitives.

Georgina Starr has also made works using people whose contributions have been gained through the marketing tools of a communications society—the advertisement, the opinion survey and the interview. Both artists are fascinated by the productivity of social fantasy and fictionalised identities, and the vastly greater access to *self-representation* (through video) and momentary public attention (through television) by ordinary *voiced subjects* in the modern world.

The possibilities of validating new forms are extensive: of free-play, posture, gossip, nostalgia, disguise— all aspects of both living improvisation and 'killing time' (the actual title of a work by Sam Taylor-Wood). These are the

have wanted to record themselves being wacky in their own homes; this is the 'true them'. But they're doing it in private. I'm sure a lot of people have done a lot of dancing in their bedrooms, but taking that fantasy and putting it somewhere that's alien to that fantasy—that's where you can start questioning. ... It's like editing life. Nothing would ever be interesting in its real state. ... There's elements of humour and there's humility as well. I'm interested in every emotion being part of the work. ... Subtly being on the outside, or being different is the most interesting thing, because the person looks like they have access to both worlds.[48]

very qualities derided by artists of a previous generation as allied to the low-grade and 'empty' aspects of a popular television culture. Yet it is precisely the same aspects that are embraced with a redirected intent by many current artists: as disclosing the shaping influences on the consciousness of everyone (for instance—Sam Taylor-Wood; the Wilson twins; Mark Wallinger); or as valid forms of mediatised interpersonal action, revealing the actual flow and recirculation of the social productivity of desire (Georgina Starr; Gillian Wearing). These artists are aware that their works play against the grain of 'art'. But they are also precisely conscious of the rapid shifts of situation, of the switch button that flips the 'take' into another mode—into re-play, recontextualisation and review.

For instance, Gillian Wearing frequently uses other people and social settings as her medium, and also incorporates herself. In one work she located herself in a typically 'low-culture' shopping mall for a videopiece that seems to challenge the social autism projected through many inner-city urban spaces—in a single-monitor piece called *Dancing in Peckham* (1994).[47] Her commitment to the social as her subject is quite explicit and sourced:

You've seen on Video Diary and Video Nation people acting silly in their own homes—and that's since camcorders have come out. People

Georgina Starr has evolved elaborate moving-image and site-specific works involving combinations of herself as a fictional character, herself as a fantasy character *interacting* with ordinary people within an openly structured work, or herself playing multiple characters within a tightly structured, pre-filmed video work. She most relishes elaborating these possibilities so that the forms overlap and demarcations dissolve, when she can use combinations of all modes, including props and *in-situ* installations—as in her solo room-installation at the Tate Gallery in 1996. Through variously intermixed social voices and conjectured identities, through slices of real-life or real-time augmented by 'acts' and make-believe, new spaces of existence are opened for the most 'unauthorised' creativities of ordinary citizens (who have seen more moving images and slices of others' lives than in all of human history that has preceded them).

...the events and moments that I'm showing are so familiar to anybody. They're not bizarre; they're things we all do. I've just highlighted them and given them a space where they can be contemplated. ... If I weren't an artist but I was doing what I was doing, there'd be nowhere to put the products of the activity. I use the umbrella of art to give it a place.[49]

INTER-SUBJECTIVITY

Subjectivity in the works of such artists is not represented as separate selfhood, as the identity of an individual emblematically detached from the crowd, but rather of performative interconnection:

> I think of the public as a whole rather than as individuals.[50]
> [Georgina Starr]

Georgina Starr and many other artists in this exhibition—especially women—deal repeatedly with the representation of a *performative self*, one interfaced with many cultural systems, adjusting, altering, rearranging them in a continual process of feedback.

With Georgina Starr and Gillian Wearing, art can take up right on the pulse of instant entertainment. A socially expansive, interactivity of selves is disclosed as the new social condition of mediatised relations. Personal identities are what you make of them, or may project or change, from moment to moment.

> I wanted to take a simple idea and see how it becomes something else if you multiply it by different interpretations. I'm tapping into people's fantasies, or their projections.[51]
> [Gillian Wearing]

Memory is not a conduit to fixity, or certainty of self, but an ongoing activity of constant reformulation and revision. These works suggest altered states of existence and changing models of socially viable reality: in a communications world, already overstuffed with things, people are now increasingly making ephemeral products of their own consciousness. Their focus is on interacting *with* the world rather than producing completed objects to exist finitely *in* the world. More provisional sensibilities are evident —permitting multiple and contradictory interpretations simultaneously. Veracity may no longer be appealed to as an external referential scale or system. There need be no authoritarian override to principles of consistency. The productivity of *recapitulating fictions* may be valued against, or even beyond, the closure of putative 'truths'.

Georgina Starr's work [ill'n p.38] often tensions the elements of specific inter-personal situations, involving random meetings, imagined identities or quite arbitrary and ephemeral encounters. Her works could be seen to present a world of modified social relations, or the ever more widely distributed and transitory social experiences of late modernity. The structural components of her work are suggestive of this world of transition: having a party alone; a videotape of oneself crying; a work-scenario evolved through distorted memory of a cherished movie seen in childhood; conjecturing a man's identity without meeting him; the setting up of appointments or rendezvous through advertisements.

New social forms are appearing in art that originated in the tabloids: dating services; solicitation of relationships through advertisement; forms of temporary alliance versus the older structures of kinship; relations that cross through metropolitan networks, blurring social demarcation and breaching received borders. The interview is often a useful tool. Many forms assumed by works disclose people's narratives or improvisations cross-threading, creating a projective screen of inter-subjective possibilities.

When I was younger, I always believed that another reality existed behind the surface of the screen. I wanted to use this childish idea as a device to move the viewer around the space and to avoid the traditional cinematic 'fixed perspective'. ... As a teenager, any girl or guy can sit in their bedroom and run and rerun a video of their current obsession and watch the whole thing in slow-motion. This is not an academic exercise. This is about sex. This is about a human drive of real desire to see what shouldn't be seen... It's like being taken from the academy to the bedroom, and then ending up somewhere else altogether.[52]

[Douglas Gordon]

There is an ethic of more reflexive tolerance and social generosity behind these and other works of popular interchange, a different productivity of social effects. They suggest an ecology of recyclable meanings rather than the quest for 'authentic' identities or novel and 'unique' things: a permeability of structures that are networked rather than closed; an expansiveness of a more ephemeral and participatory social consciousness; an accommodation of constant change and improvisation, of the aleatory play of ordinary social desires.

The works of many contemporary British artists therefore present adaptive models of inner-urban experience—emerging from the very social streams that have undergone the massive restructuring and transformation of working-class life in the UK since World War II. Against a popularly disparaged sociality of 'mindless mass consumption'—a condescending presumption of social torpor by their forebears—an alternative modelling of experience has emerged strongly.

Artists of the kind discussed here figure an individual experience that is not separate but inter-socially defined. They create contrastive fictions that return spectators to a recognition of their own experience, of the vital nexus between personal history and socially produced interpretation. It is this modelling of random convergence and disjunction between individual cartographies *within* an accepted realm of the social, including traditions that continue from vaudeville and music-hall forms of entertainment, that such artists are committed to explore. They share a revocation of the idea of the autonomy of the individual.

For these artists, the supersessions of the social in a late-modern, communications-driven society are so comprehensive as to make any romantic regress into autonomous selfhood a futile illusion.

PLURAL IDENTITIES, DECENTRED SUBJECTIVITIES

Of course artists are also moulded in sites other than cities—sites that include potent mental spaces, that are acculturated and historicised through diverse processes of (ever-reconstructing) memory and socially mutating experience. Artists whose personal histories cause them to draw on various cultural backgrounds, outside the West, also work through languages of recent modernist art that are entirely within the Western canon—in other words, extending the inter-crossing streams of the languages of art that are available to all in a world of ever-more complex interchange internationally. London is now one of the richest cities for such interchange—in both the making of work, and also of its discussion.

At many other levels [Permindar] Kaur's work plays with the visual languages of Minimal and Conceptual art, refracting them with her own highly personalised concerns. …Kaur carefully filters the cathartic function that her art practice clearly provides for her through a sophisticated engagement with the Modernist tradition.[53]

A potent symbol of the richness of inter-cultural discussion in Britain now, the journal *Third Text* is one of the most important vehicles in the world for dealing with new critique from many non-Western vantage-points, and a vital conduit for Asian, African and trans-Atlantic 'black diaspora' voices. It significantly emerged in London, in the 1980s, and has still no equivalent in the United States. Elsewhere Stuart Hall has provided a vital intellectual stimulus for years in the UK: as teacher and as Director at the Centre for Contemporary Cultural Studies in Birmingham, and more recently as a re-directing force (utilising his own Jamaican background to push the ground of cross-cultural meaning) in broadening cultural studies and inter-cultural critique in Britain.

Homi Bhabha has been one of the finest intellectuals in the world in the theorisation of modernity, interculturality and 'otherness' in literature (and more recently, expanding his references to art). Meanwhile it was at the ICA (Institute of Contemporary Arts) and in an Anglophone context recently—rather than in Paris or in French—that the Martinican-French (later African-based) psychoanalyst and revolutionary writer, Frantz Fanon, received the posthumous homage of a *Festschrift* exhibition and symposium in 1995.[54] At the symposium[55] Stuart Hall, Homi Bhabha, Kobena Mercer and others gave papers (later published in a volume dedicated eponymously to Frantz Fanon).[56]

Rich bodies of work and discussion have emerged in Britain, instantiating the complexity of current critique (which cannot be trivialised as merely conditioned by cultural origins) within works of visual art.

Kaur's position is free from…the belief that an essence of a central self exists; this notion belongs exclusively to a single cultural space with which she feels only partial involvement.[57]

Permindar Kaur adds,

'It's very difficult to make statements about particular things. Issues about race and colour are very complex now. In my recent work there is no longer direct polarisation between two distinct cultures. …The work still contains questions concerning identity but on a more subtle level.' With the unsticking of national, cultural and linguistic identities in this increasingly nomadic world, we need a different way of thinking about differences…[58]

STEVE McQUEEN *STAGE* 1996 (STILL)

BLACK & WHITE 35MM FILM

COURTESY OF THE ARTIST AND ANTHONY REYNOLDS GALLERY, LONDON

Where history and difference *do* come into play is at the point of recognising how unsurprising it is that many new artists are emerging with a great range of cultural skills and awareness about the complex *corroboree*[59] of codes attending visual representation in the contemporary world. They are frequently drawing on personal histories and cultural traditions that lie beyond the West, and working in a sophisticated domain of contradiction, multiplicity and crossover. This is not to be confused, however, with a merely accommodating *addition* to mainstream traditions—which would be to mis-understand the ethical force of such works as seeking to *change the mainstream*, to regenerate, alter and radically expand the re-nutritive resources within what we understand to be *tradition* itself.

Steve McQueen's work to date discloses an emphatic preference for the medium of film, but in a compressed style of intense reflection and tight montage. Steve McQueen's film-works, sometimes employing a 'black-and-white style' but shot on colour film (prior to the recent move into vivid colour for his presentation in Documenta X), has derived from a dense embedding of the 'subject' of each work—or segment of work—in the histories of dramatic representation in earlier film and photography.

In compacted scenes and tight sequences, camera angle and viewpoint are intensified to the greatest possible degrees as structural means. However McQueen also deploys camera angles as a metaphoric language about 'vantage-points' and 'connections' (or structural dissociation)—culturally, sociologically, historically—of the subject-histories of representation that swim behind the 'identities' (black/black; black/white) that he juxtaposes in his films.

Steve McQueen calls up our deeply acculturated vocabularies of vision, which he re-structures in the way he composes his work. Having gained a steadily increasing audience since his inclusion in the 1995 group exhibition at the ICA, London (*Mirage, Enigmas of Race, Difference and Desire*), McQueen's work has employed a penetrating analysis of how our 'cultural viewing selves' are extensively socialised through our watching of television, movies and moving-image productions of reality.

Meanwhile Permindar Kaur's work moves in different directions of more psychological mnemonics:

Kaur's work relentlessly plays on our feelings of vulnerability, and effectively questions our attitudes towards power. She obliges us to reconsider our notions of childhood and adulthood, of the protector and the protected; what is safety, where are we safe, what demons or calamities might overwhelm us? What protects us and what might harm us? She obliges us to consider these questions by re-presenting domestic objects that we have learnt to identify with 'home' and the protection afforded by 'family'. ...[W]hat can protect us? What are we to be protected from? The unwelcome gaze? The potentially fatal blow? Most disturbingly, do we need or do we seek protection from ourselves?[60]

MAT COLLISHAW
INFECTIOUS FLOWERS II 1996/97
ZOSTER OF SUPRAVICULAR DERMATOMES

NATURE

Nature is explored through fragmentary images, echoing streams of thought that run deep in British culture historically. First, there is the tradition of natural science and the pre-eminence of forms of empirical investigation in Britain's contribution to an experimental scientific culture, on which both modernity and technological progress have been based. Second, there are continuing legacies of the once powerful Calvinist tradition of respect for the natural world and its blessed 'descent' from the divine, combined with an unremitting drive for its domination and exploitation.

Carl Freedman: *Do you see yourself as a humanist?*

Mat Collishaw: I'm mourning the loss of humanism. There's nothing didactic about it. I'm not taking a moral stance. I'm sidestepping all that and saying look at the incredible richness, beauty and texture of this fucked up world we live in. I think before anything changes we first have to reflect on how we live. ....

Up until my teens I was a complete believer in God. I was brought up completely religiously with the idea that everything is spiritually endowed. And then you realise that's not the case. And in place of that you're then faced with the idea that you've evolved from a monkey. You're robbed of your whole spiritual side and left without much to go on. ....

Within this process of looking there is a desire to overcome an isolated way of seeing things. To bring things together in such a way that they throw light on one another. Things which may seem at opposite ends of a spectrum but are still somehow connected.[61]

British culture's deep historical investment in rural life, and the predilection for the contours of 'natural' landscape, yielded a national fondness for the meandering contour, in contrast to the geometry and formality favoured repeatedly for the design of gardens in Europe. Such a deeply entrenched set of preferences yielded the framework of the English landscape garden, a landscape designed (often with the most careful labours) to maintain an illusive fealty to the idea of the natural.[62] This long-standing and ever-reconstituting tradition was maintained despite—or in reality, directly spurred by—Britain's leading role in industrialisation and mass-production globally in the nineteenth century. The legacy of the fatally ruptured nostalgic ideal of 'country life', and a frustrated quest for intimacy with nature, still breaks across many scenes of consciousness in contemporary British art.

Marcelo Spinelli: *That makes me think of your digitally manipulated images of flowers with animal fur. Do these images address our separation from the real world?*

Mat Collishaw: Yes. They're about how we experience flowers living in a metropolis like London. They're all flown or driven in, and we just get little corners of the natural world in the shops on every street. It becomes a kind of freak show when the whole of your environment is generated artificially with little bits of

AN ANIMAL OF NEW

HOLLAND, ENGRAVING

AFTER GEORGE STUBBS

73/4 X 95/8,

HAWKESWORTH'S

VOYAGES VOL III 1773

A FAMILY OF NEW SOUTH

WALES ENGRAVINGBY

WILLIAM BLAKE AFTER

GOVERNOR KING 71/2 X

63/8 FROM JOHN

HUNTER'S HISTORICAL

JOURNAL 1793

the natural world as a kind of decoration. The freak show's intensifying because of our ability to genetically manipulate these plants for commercial use. ...There's something incredibly strange and vulgar about the perfection that's been reached with these things.[63]

The endemic frictions between nature's humiliation, technology's progress, modernity and religious thought were conflated in one of the most undying images of Romantic poetry, William Blake's 'dark satanic mills'. However instead of sinister projections across the natural world of factories and chimney stacks marking once-rural horizons in Britain, the forms of discontinuity in the late-twentieth century occur more ambiguously, even seductively. For example, Mat Collishaw's lightbox images of mutant flowers (Infectious Flowers II, 1996-97) are bizarrely beautiful in their contradictory fusion: petals miscegenated with animal fur; the culminating moment of a full bloom uncannily ulcerated by signs of disease.

Frequently using the medium of photography and moving images, Mat Collishaw has evolved a body of work through which he explores the tenacity of our preoccupation with nature. It persists no matter how much the idea of 'the natural' is haunted by ever more mortifying instances of our distance from any reliable indications of nature's order and presence in our lives. It is as though nature is a nagging spectre of human cultural memory, stalking our apprehension of an ever more artificially constructed world.

George Stubbs figures directly and indirectly as a source for a number of artists represented here—for example, Mat Collishaw's illuminated photocopy works based on Stubbs's horses, Antonious, a horse belonging to his Grace the Duke of Grafton and the Marquess of Rockingham's scrub, with John Singelton up 1990 [ill'n p.109]; and Mark Wallinger, Half-Brother (Exit to Nowhere—Machiavellian) 1994-95, [Ill'n p.56]. Wallinger's interest in Stubbs focuses on the subject of aristocratic life and horse-breeding—and its continuing imbrication in the later working-class culture of horse-racing. An earlier painting by Wallinger was an equine 'portrait' of a racer that was in a direct line of descent from a stallion painted by Stubbs.

The earlier connections of major artists of the eighteenth century in the orchestration of scientific 'evidence', and subsequent instrumentation of vision (with the aid of art) in the whole enterprise of colonialism and Empire, touch on particular links with Australia. For an engraving after Stubbs, based on sketched material brought back by a topographical draughtsman from the colony of New South Wales, was one of the earliest formal images to be circulated in Europe of an Australian kangaroo; meanwhile an engraving by William Blake, similarly derived from early sketches, was one of the earliest representations of an Aboriginal 'family' so-called.

Andrea Wilkinson, working on a miniature scale, presents an intricately shaped topographical profile of a rolling natural landscape, modelled in turf and wall-mounted on a fluorescent perspex ledge (*Green Range*, 1994) [ill'n p. 144-145]. Working also with subtle perceptual effects, the work suggests a great deal with an almost extreme modesty of materials and minimum of means. As fellow-artist Hadrian Piggott has observed of Andrea Wilkinson's work, it conveys a sense of 'the fragility of our tenure on the earth'.[64] A second work by the artist—tiny cutout wall-pinned figures, derived from a photographic record of people's actual position along a street—registers a similar fragility (and scrupulous observation) in the social sphere. Bethan Huws is another artist who manages to circulate compressed energies in the tiniest 'gestures' towards making, crafting, and cultural form, in her miniature rush boats—of which one is included here: *Y cwch* (1983-97).

Jordan Baseman's sculptures suggest an emphatic shift in the frames of reference, from ruptures within the natural world to deep and menacing fissures within the social order. Human propensities to manipulate the world have moved from the botanical and geological spheres to more startling interventions in the realms of biological and social relationships. Cat's and dog's teeth are moulded into acrylic dentures (*Based on a True Story; Based on Actual Events*, both 1995 [ill'n p.127]). A poetic wall sculpture simulating a possible butterfly-image turns out to be made of mouth braces, pins and wisdom teeth on closer inspection in *Up, Up and Away* (1995). A man's shirt on a hanger has been re-sewn with child-size cotton sleeves—it is combined with the necktie of social conformity but also sprouts a fine 'collar' of human hair (*Call me Mister*, 1995).

There is a barely-submerged register of frustration of the ego's free possibilities of expansion in Jordan Baseman's work. Through a series of immediately registered, often poetic images, his sculptures hint at implacable anxieties created by the tyrannical demands of the regulation of desire, as human beings are harnessed into social submission and conformity. They also hint at the imperfectly adjusted results of coercion in childhood that are carried forward within the lives of society's adult members.

However 'the natural' in English tradition can be re-framed radically by filtering it through quite contrary screens of cultural memory, as in the late Rotimi Fani-Kayode's work (d. London, 1989, aged 34). In Kayode's framework (drawing on traditions outside the West—specifically Yoruba culture in Nigeria), nature is not linked to the conjunction of science, rationalism, positivism and a divinely ordered universe, but is intercrossed with other modes of thought. Kayode emphasises the confluence of the body, psychological arousal and religion in many African cultures—and the transcendent transformation possible when these strands are ecstatically fused.

Kayode employed, within his later work, what Yoruba priests and artists call the 'technique of ecstasy', where concepts of reality are distorted or disrupted to produce ambiguous meanings.[65]

Once again: it is important to consider Fani-Kayode's work in its synthesis of *multiple* cultural traditions — which emphatically overlap and include the West — rather than seeking to demarcate his work across any spurious divide of alterity (or *otherness*). Working with his partner, Alex Hirst, Kayode 'produced a body of work that is a celebration of hybridity and cultural diversity across the boundaries of race and desire'.[66] Kayode was specifically and strategically aware of the uninscribed, 'negated' position of homosexual desire within 'Third World' cultural expression:

> Both aesthetically and ethically, I seek to translate my rage and my desire into new images which will undermine conventional perceptions and which may reveal hidden worlds.[67]

In the works involving reversing uses of African masks (playing against the grain of Western historiography, while also taking advantage of the 'fullness' of art's specific and layered allusions to particular styles and 'moments' of

sensibility), Kayode breaches orthodoxies of representation in both Western and Yoruba traditions equally. He unsettles aspects of intimate assumption within both cultures of visualisation. Through surprising re-combinations and intensification, Kayode estranges many elements from each other internally, in a critical achievement of *simultaneous re-translation*.

THE BODY

Another thematic strand that emerges through this project is the increasingly diverse but proximate presence of the body as a continuing subject in visual art. Putatively the primary site of subjectivity, the body is also one of the most ambiguous constructs of social and cultural formation.

The body as a socialised subject (and even a subject of forensic control or medicalised objectification) appears in the work of several artists. Douglas Gordon has extensively drawn on medical records or film footage recording subjects under actual study by clinical research in a number of works.

> A lot of what I do is about looking at a familiar subject in a slightly different way. I work in a mixture of film, text and other information. The stripper piece I put on at Oxford used Sixties film transferred on to video, shown in slow motion. It was on two screens, one the right way up and one the wrong way, running slightly in and out of sync. Viewers were never quite sure it was the same image. The video explored notions of time and expectation and, on a very simplistic level, it was a challenge for people to turn themselves upside down.[68]
>
> [Douglas Gordon]

Meanwhile John Stezaker's split-image works reconstruct old photographs of naked bodies posed for study within several scopic regimes of objectification: anatomical studies, medical formulations of 'the normal', studies of motion, and the investigative studies of the human form in the art studio 'life class'.

The theme is more indirectly present in the case of Christine Borland, though it is a focal interest of other works of hers in the last few years. In a number of different works (imaginative investigations or reconstructions) Christine Borland has been preoccupied by forensic objectifications of the body, and has made particular use of criminological records or constructions of individuals for the purposes of social regulation, control, scientific surmise, or even resolute ostracism. There is a 'trace' of these interests in her shoes with bullet-holes in the present exhibition.

Hermione Wiltshire has dealt with many aspects of the body: for example, fluids (a major installation in the *The British Show 4* (1995-96), entitled *Seamen II* (1994) involved a scattering of tiny photographic images across the floor depicting erect phalluses, all encapsulated behind 'ejaculatory' droplets of clear glass). In the present project a small wall-mounted sculpture, *AAAGH…!!* (1996) — again encasing a photographic image behind a transparent capsule — reveals an open mouth as a cavernous aperture to an invisible, divorced body. Whether attached to an agitated torso or acting as a chamber for air, it is impossible to do more than conjecture around the abbreviated image. It shuffles ideas in a split-second of viewing the open mouth:

from cosmetic effects, to muscular convulsion, to primal scream. Tania Kovat's *Virgin in a Condom* (1992) is a multiple work, poetic and potent with social tension. It condenses a range of social questions within Catholicism that are as historically resonant and nagging as the sculpture is tiny and smooth in its caul of latex — a haplessly secular, apotropaic emblem of modern times!

Rachel Glynne's elongated *Long Hair Dress Shirt* (1995), made of human hair and with teeth enclosed, works both in the social sphere of recollection and the phantasmatic sphere of archaic psychological association (and sometimes dread). Gary Perkins's *Cleanliness next to Godliness* (1995) does not treat the body directly, but creates an environment for dealing with its washing and wastes. The details of the micro-bathroom, constantly under surveillance by CCTV cameras, suggests not only the regulation of the individual body in daily rituals of cleansing, but more encompassing restrictive regimes within the social body-politic, of which this small environment is an allegory.

If Richard Hamilton's painting, *The citizen* (discussed further below) deals with what we might call the politicised gaze, focused on the human body of a Republican prisoner incarcerated and radically objectified as socially separate, Rotimi Fani-Kayode's imagery treats the subtleties of the *acculturated* and *historicised gaze* that we bring as spectators to works featuring the nude human form in other modes of depiction. His photographs strongly feature black male bodies, in a particular combination of elements that incorporate many forms of cultural inscription, refusing any

CHRISTINE BORLAND **HOME-MADE BULLET-PROOF VESTS - COTTON WOOL AND JEWELLERY COLLECTION** 1995

simplistic discourse of racialised singularity. However Kayode absorbs so many nuances at once within an image, and recasts them, that his works belong within new streams of representation. They are so self-consciously multiple in their sources, and cross-threading in their directional movements and expression of cultural meaning, as to be called *hyper-culturalised* images.

The 'natural' body of Kayode's *Milkdrinker* contests any simple classification of *the natural* within the Western scopic domain of *the nude*—a nakedness rendered for the contemplation of a detached (though not disinterested) gaze. The beauty of form is not rendered simply within the distancing regime of aesthetics; rather, the body is actively apprehended in movement, locating the figure within a social theatre of bodies, mutually engaged, and visually active as part of daily social intercourse. In addition, of course, Rotimi Fani-Kayode draws on Robert Mapplethorpe's work, but often to counterpose that body of work with a different cultural address. While sharing the homo-erotic impulses that propel so much of Mapplethorpe's representation, Kayode subtly contests many currents within Mapplethorpe of exoticism and reductive sexual objectification, especially concerning the rendition of black male bodies cruised by a predominantly white gaze.

Kayode incorporates allusions from Caravaggio to Cubism, reversing the vantage-point of certain 'actors' or 'imageries' within the art of the West. In particular, his images deconstruct both the 'Primitivising' aspects of modern art's early history, from the Fauves to the Cubists and Surrealists; and the 'Orientalising' traditions of documentary photography, when Westerners treated African subjects; in addition, he is fully conscious of African-directed uses of the same tradition.

In each case, Kayode takes motifs or subjects that are represented within art, but according to the frameworks of others that excluded these subjects' sense of *agency*. He restores to such subjects an alternative agency on a wider stage of human inscription: a *pluralised history of cultures*, and diversities *within* and *between* cultures. Rotimi Fani-Kayode thereby alters the history of representation itself.

THE SOCIAL ORDER
Margaret Thatcher's offhand proposition to the effect that 'there is no such thing as society' (quoted in Patrick Boylan's essay) is a crucial indicator of how far her faulted sense of social relations had moved from an axis within 'citizenship'. Her dismissal of the idea of the subjects of the state as forming a vital social entity—her disavowal of an integrated *socius*—may be argued as evoking an alternative vision of unremitting, competitive individualism. Pressed imaginatively to its limits, such a vision could be construed as modelling social fission and breakdown, the erosion of cohesive common structures and a dismantling of trust in real political processes for the resolution of conflictual differences. There is much to be found within contemporary British art that in no way seeks to illustrate political theory, but nevertheless touches upon the fault-lines and effects of certain pressures within the social order.

Aspects of the social order are in fact activated powerfully in some works in this exhibition. They may be forcefully projected (as in Richard Billingham's snapshot narrativisation of his family's council flat existence and inexorable dependencies); or in Gillian Wearing's masked 'confessants' on video; or in Gary Perkins's tiny domestic interiors elucidating their socially designed contents on surveillance monitors nearby. An acerbic historical view, using other representational means, is rendered by Critical Decor—for example, *Boring Democracy* (1994); but also other works of theirs that map social structures and issues of power historically and conceptually—as is the case with *Nietzsche Piece* (1992).

Meanwhile Jordan Baseman's sculptures, already incorporated within a discussion of 'ruptured nature' within contemporary art, might (considering their punitive clues) be comprehended just as strongly as works dealing with discrepancies within the social order. All categorisations of artworks' similarities, in fact, generally reveal their alternative undertows and contrary aspects—suggesting entirely different formations, of affinity or contrast, that could just as profitably be pursued.

With regard to Richard Billingham, a particular aspect of photography's contradictory nature is forcefully embodied. It is perhaps worth mentioning this aspect of visual language, as a way of reconsidering the extraordinary 'veracity' of what these works seem to present so directly. The experience of Richard Billingham's series, *Untitled* (1993-95), more than any other photographic works in British art recently, creates a powerful hallucinatory gap of fractional

splitting, a microcosmic friction between two quite contrary things. On the one hand, we experience an almost overwhelming contract with 'the real' that they seem to guarantee through their content; on the other, there is a colliding sensation of their formal structure and artificiality. Or, to press the contradiction another way, Billingham's photographs are simultaneously eloquently disclosing and implacably inarticulate.

The photographs of Richard Billingham betray a phenomenon discussed by Roland Barthes, which is recalled by another writer in relation to Gillian Wearing's work: Jennifer Higgie figures the psychologically contradictory experience of the real/unreal of certain photography as creating an 'empathic blankness', a recognition that provides a reminder of Barthes's observation that the 'photograph cannot say what it lets us see'.[69] Seeming barely to have escaped a heartbeat from life—so starkly irruptive are the domestic contents they convy the displacement of Billingham's photographs into the scopic realm, through which we now encounter these images *as images*, also baffles our anxious efforts of envisioning what we seem to 'see'.

One of the most haunting evocations of the social order in this exhibition is to be experienced in the work of Rachel Whiteread, which builds an almost epic stillness of evacuated presence through her compellingly mute forms and textures. Her casts in plaster, resin, rubber and concrete—of spaces that have touched the surfaces and under-surfaces of ageing things, where people have walked, or lived, or sat, or been washed—have an extraordinary air of solicitude on behalf of collective social memory. Although their forms are consistently abstract, avoiding any human representation directly, Rachel Whiteread's works are densely acculturated by the traces of unspoken human presence and anonymous history.

Two works deal powerfully with the social in another realm: the multiple fractures of Northern Ireland are addressed in one case by English artist Richard Hamilton; in the other by Irishman Willie Doherty. Both deal with the baffled contradictions within all visual representations of ordinary life in such a 'Troubled' social landscape as Northern Ireland (and all constructions of it within the UK at large). However in Willie Doherty's video/voice-over work, even the natural landscape itself becomes psychologically reverberant to the impact of violent social experience and media-configured history. The televisual rendition of driving along a rural road is irretrievably linked with the idea of ambush or interception.

The dense associations figured in Hamilton's *The citizen* (the 'dirty protest' in Maze prison, projected on television as an unforgettable iteration of abjection and refusal daubed in excrement) is extensively contextualised in the essay here by Stephen Snoddy.[70] Most importantly, Stephen Snoddy's text rigorously pursues the indissoluble links of the three paintings, constituting an iconographic triptych, of which the Tate Gallery's *Citizen* picture is but one part. The relationship is far more than formally important in the interconnection between these paintings. The full measure of Hamilton's sense of tragic interweaving of all parties, and their iconic scenes of symbolic contest within the inexorable entrapment and mutual violence of 'the Troubles', can be appraised only through a precise grasp of how the three pictures—*The citizen*, *The subject* and *The state*—evolved as a unit within the artist's work.

Hamilton's work also pushes further the psychological play of interpretation around the subject of the visualised human body. Having derived the image of the IRA prisoner originally through reproductive technologies (from television footage to photography, to *re*-presentation through transfer into painting), in Hamilton's case the theme of the suffering body is transmuted into another realm, where the image absorbs the resonance of a long tradition of the portrayal of martyrdom in Christian art:

Even in an environment of total deprivation humanity will find the means of protest. Violent reaction to physical and verbal abuse must lead to an escalation of force that no prisoner can hope to benefit from. Penned in, without the presence of inanimate objects to vent aggression upon, denied the tools of hostility, an individual has only what he can make with his own body; the IRA daubed the walls of their cells with shit. …The 'dirty protest', as the British called it (in a refined play of positive and negative concepts named 'no wash' by the Irish) lasted for some five years; more than 400 prisoners were involved. …The symbols of Christ's agony were there, not only the crucifix on the neck of prisoners and the rosary which confirmed the monastic austerity but the self-inflicted suffering which has marked Christianity from the earliest times.[71]

[Richard Hamilton and Rita Donagh]

DOUGLAS GORDON *HYSTERICAL* 1995

VIDEO INSTALLATION

400 X 300

COURTESY OF THE ARTIST AND THE BRITISH COUNCIL, LONDON

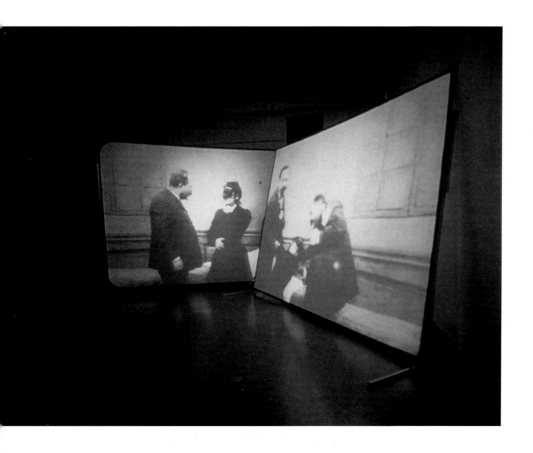

Many works by artists touch directly on these issues: photography's potential of invasive representation of others (Mat Collishaw, Georgina Starr); the social or historical classification of 'otherness' as an exercise of power relations and interpretative control (Maud Sulter, Mark Wallinger, Rotimi Fani-Kayode, Gary Perkins); the scientistic objectification— even 'medicalisation'— of the human body and behaviour in the socialisation of modernity (John Stezaker, Christine Borland, Douglas Gordon); the sentimentalisation of childhood that denies the complex sexuality and inter-personal negotiation of the child—as an already engaged, self-conceptualising and responsive 'social subject' (Nicky Hoberman).

HISTORY AS FICTION

New kinds of narrativity abound elsewhere in contemporary art. History is often conceived not as a process of discrimination grounded in factuality, but as a continual competition of plausible partialities. As authoritative voices have been contested, and institutional leaders regularly exposed as knowing deceivers, old moral verities have eroded. Even the idea of public morality itself has declined. Novel forms of boundary-testing are pursued; new styles of temporary alliance and consensual interaction are implemented, often projecting evolving aspects of a more transactionally applied ethics.

The whole idea of history as *authority*, as a mentoring force within frameworks of reason and experience for grappling with the changing conditions of the present, is decentred by much contemporary art. This is particularly so in works that most thoroughly evince the psychological impact of television, film and reproductive media, and their constant corrosions of 'the real'.

The collapsing of time in the *hyper-real*ised present tense of immanence—the desire to be orgasmically free of history, absolved of alienating anxiety, just for a moment—is a red thread running through the sensibility of many works of contemporary art:

There is a thing that I want more than anything and that I think I might never be able to have; I would love to live in the present, just to be here, now and not looking behind or into the future.[72]

[Damien Hirst]

ART AND THE MUSEUM

As art has gained ever more social presence and prominence in the forms of public recreation, there has been an accompanying rise in awareness of its historical relationship to the rise of the 'museum' in Western life and colonial institutions. Meanwhile British culture (unlike much of the world elsewhere) still adheres to the term 'gallery', which since the loss of the collection of Charles I at the behest of the Puritans in the seventeenth century, and the refounding two centuries later of the National Gallery, remains the preferred term in Britain and denotes a collection primarily of pictures. This has regrettably contracted the idea of art's expressive range to the primacy of *painting*.

A rigorous analysis of the museum's history and heritage is so widely dealt with in recent critical history and cultural discussion that its echoes are everywhere present in the critical forms and constructs of contemporary art.

Georgina Starr's *The Nine Collections of the Seventh Museum* (of which some components, owned by the MCA, are presented here) turns on the taxonomic inclinations of museums to impose orders arbitrarily across utterly disparate materials. Her work engages a strong resonance against the disciplinary habits of ethnology and ethnography. The archiving and tabulation of the materials of a temporary bedroom, while she was abroad to research ideas for a commissioned project, became the content of the work Georgina Starr finally realised for The Hague, in the Netherlands—now owned in its complete form (including the whole CD-ROM structure), by the Walker Art Center, Minneapolis, where it was shown in *Brilliant!* in 1996.

Neil Cummings's sculpture, *Detail of the Collection: Blue* (1996), works on various levels of simulation: the collection of plastic containers suggests the operation of a contemporary ethnography of use or social processes; the vitrine arrangement proposes querulously the culture of the museum, where knowledge is organised around taxonomy and display; however the whole apparatus is produced with the most informal, rough and insubstantial materials. The work gains both physical presence and social commentary through great ingenuity, and a radical economy of simple means.

In addition to the greater museum consciousness of artists generally, as a result of their theoretical studies, there are perhaps other, less obvious reasons for the continual recourse of artists to the trope of *collections* in the forms of their work. The progress of the 'heritage industry' in Britain in recent decades, as an ever more forceful presence and marketable resource in international trade and relations, has been directly counterpointed by the contraction and

regearing of publicly financed resources for cultural institutions. This is in a period, moreover, of far-reaching social and cultural change.

British culture itself, in all its contemporary forms of change, has been intensively packaged and marketed to the home and international markets *as* the British heritage industry, derived from a celebration of life-forms that are disappearing or already vanished, and bear little social inscription of the actual forms of the evolving present.

CONCEPTS/TEXTS; PRESENCE/ ABSENCE; PROCESSES/MEMORIES

The legacies of Conceptual art of the 1960s are now interwoven with other streams of contemporary practice that come from quite alternative concerns (for example, the socialisation of images through technology; moving-image cultures; non-Western forms and various genres of painting). Accordingly, many artists today inter-cross diverse strands in their practice (Ceal Floyer, Critical Decor, Fiona Banner, for example). However a more conceptually focused enquiry into the margins of art's thought, and perceptual or social presence, is also predominant in many bodies of work.

Fiona Banner's work, *Full Metal Jacket* (1996) reveals the richness of such a current condition of cross-over. Her two-panel work is one of a number she has made that have arisen through the trawling of socially and politically constructed history in the entire genre of Vietnam films. She provided one of the finest works in the Hayward Gallery's 1996 exploration of the interchange between art and film

(*Spellbound*), another work arising from the sedimentation of Vietnam movies in broad social consciousness—in this case a painstaking, handwritten, composite-text, a transcription of the action development experienced as a spectator reconstructing *Apocalypse Now*.

Critical Decor (a collaborative authorship) is achieving a range of works, in a variety of media (and some site-specific interventions), that subversively bridge some of the deepest divides in recent criticism. Having voided art of any immanent presence, body, history or status, they proceed to keep re-conjuring art's memory through case-study approaches to various critical contingencies as a way out of the casualty ward. The tragi-comic condition of art's beleaguered status, under the relentless assaults of theory and criticism, is embraced unhesitatingly—as in their exhibition in London in 1996, *Laughing in the Face of Tragedy*.

Ceal Floyer deals with extremely attenuated boundaries of art's possible intervention. She is attracted to making works which hover on the edge of self-erasure and disappearance, which only those with the most closely-tuned perception may even register as present at all. *Sold* (1996) is merely a red circular intervention, site-specifically made on a wall near another artist's painting. It has the location and emblematic inscription of art's fetishised condition as a commodity to be 'sold'; however the red mark turns out not to be a sticker but a small hole filled with red oil paint. *Projection* (1997)—an illuminated slide of a nail projected on a wall—deals similarly with the comprehensive structure within which art's 'exhibited destiny' is enclosed; it takes up

a similarly oblique vantage-point on the apparatus of presentation and display.

Some of the subtlety of perceptual discrimination in Ceal Floyer's work can be found also in an artist of entirely different persuasion—in the case of Joan Key's ineluctably subtle paintings. Her works are painstakingly made, in the oldest of building-up ways of making a painting (operationally, manually, mentally). She incorporates delicately tensioned rhythms of lexical fragments (not quite words) that introduce other suggestions, hovering on the edge of signification.

Jonathan Parsons's remarkably-made drawings work in similar channels of perceptual deliberation, where every mark builds towards a mere remainder of *un-marking*, which coheres finally as a negatively installed image. Both these artists have recourse to some of the most archaic resources of human culture's mark-making origins, while pushing their perceptions of this history, and its still-extruding possibilities, into the social and psychological spaces of the present world.

Lucia Nogueira and David Cheeseman employ a strikingly similar object—a 'Persian carpet'—as a basis for evolving quite contrary sculptures from a shared central element. Lucia Nogueira makes of her carpet an actual setting and a psychological occurrence, of 'interruption', or broken narration. Shattered glass is scattered across the carpet without apparent cause or purpose, leaving the spectator alone with an image of different states of energy, perception, and conjecture. David Cheeseman's carpet turns out to be not woven at all, but a machine-manufactured object, bearing a computer-generated image. The carpet has been radically segmented into a grid of pieces, held within an armature of glass. Cheeseman's work elucidates deep-structural comparisons between cultural systems and oppositional modes of thought, crossing a spectrum of East-West contrasts, without settling for simple polarities.

Vong Phaophanit and Anya Gallaccio are artists committed to the exploration of actual physical processes (often involving change, deterioration or even complete obliteration of form), while their works show a dramatic difference in attitudes to process itself. Anya

Gallaccio is deeply attracted to the idea of non-possession of things. Her works invariably degrade in their parts throughout their 'duration' as works—and indeed the processes of their gradual transformation (whether beginning as flowers, crushed petals, ice, chocolate or candle-flame) involve rich states of change and dematerialisation.

Vong Phaophanit, who makes works that seek to float across multiple territories of physical and cultural materials, nevertheless reveals a very different conception of nature and actual materials when contrasted with Anya Gallaccio. Phaophanit deals with various materials and cultural systems, elusively but without a rupture in transition. Whether it be tubes of 'tangled' Laotian script in neon, or processes of change or break-down: there is no conceptual break, but rather a juxtaposition of different aspects of the world, each simply brought into the presence of the other. John Frankland, working in the material of a stretched plastic membrane across architectural forms, functions elusively between painting, sculpture and spatial environment. Frankland's work pursues a conversation across different histories of art, architecture and

museographical forms. He renders his perceptions through an immensely subtle recombination of languages: ranging from minimal sculpture through to a kind of semiological abstract painting (as he stretches his skin of plastic illusively as an urban representational medium).

John Latham is included in this project to bring him into a relationship with bodies of work made by much younger artists that, in some cases, can be seen to have a parallel relationship to the experimental attitudes that have driven his work for a long period (for example, Douglas Gordon is an enthusiastic admirer of Latham). The intention is to disclose a kind of consistently experimental and category-stretching thought in Latham, which suggests the depth of his personally radical 'tradition' and commitment, pursued over decades—part of which connects him also to Conceptual art. Latham's work is the subject of a separate essay here by John A Walker.[73]

John Latham embodies a kind of experimental modelling of scientific thought and system-testing, drawing on a mobile approach to objects and materials found in the world, that represents a wide sub-soil of enterprise long

JUDITH DEAN **INSTALLATION FOR A CHIHUAHUA: "ROUGH"**
17TH CENTURY VERSION 1995

Such artists show that many of the modes of contemporary art in general—involving even social critique and video (Gary Perkins), or installational formats (Judith Dean's spatially extended series, *Installation for a Chihuahua…*)—may be carried out just as rigorously on a counter-monumental scale as in-large. They invert normal expectations of size and presence, establishing worlds of alternative productivity and processes in miniature.

THE IMPACT ON VISUAL ART OF 'CULTURAL STUDIES' IN BRITAIN

Artists working in Britain today are the direct beneficiaries of an exceptionally rich environment of cultural critique that has been slowly developing in the whole post-War period in the UK.[74] It began in a more literary context (arising out of attempts to grapple with the aloofness of the tradition of literary criticism from Matthew Arnold to T S Eliot and F R Leavis—the 'culture versus the masses' approach that these critics shared in their address to the progress of social changes with the advance of modernity). A gradual but collective effort arose against this tradition of thought in the 1960s, which sought to press beyond the confines of such criticism without entirely jettisoning its concern for intellectual integrity and a desire for moral authority.

The experience of post-War adult education teaching, rendered to those who (by definition) had not been part of any educational elect of British tradition, had a powerful impact on figures such as Richard Hoggart (author of *The Uses of Literacy* [1958]), and Raymond Williams (*Culture and Society, 1780-1950* [1958] and *The Long Revolution* [1961]). A

pursued in British art. By contrast Richard Hamilton (the other senior artist in this exhibition) brings to the project a major practitioner with axes lodged in quite different streams of art over many decades—especially the socialised conditioning of images and forms, and their implication in technologies of reproduction, social dispersal and cultural diffusion. These two artists have been included in this project because, together, they open up a network of connections that may be drawn between their own works and examples of creative commitment, and many other (even quite different) practices by young artists, ones that pick up and develop related concerns, travelling out (sometimes very fast) along multiple trajectories.

THINGS IN-LITTLE

A number of artists disclose how completely and intensely a set of mental activities can be rendered on a micro scale of delivery. Their works are not simply anti-heroic in a gesture of repudiation. More significantly, they reinstate a more open field of investigation and expanded range of structures available in art, where imagination may be applied productively (and critically) to even the smallest of things.

further vantage-point from the margins was offered by Stuart Hall (West Indian by background and an early editor of *The New Left Review*). Hall also began as a teacher, in secondary schools in England, before he became an academic and moved to become Director of the pivotal Centre for Contemporary Cultural Studies at the University of Birmingham in the late 1960s, which was a forcing-house for new critical work throughout the 1970s. He is now Professor of Sociology at the Open University in the UK.

These figures (Hoggart, Williams, and later Hall and others) engaged variously in an evolving critique that sought to breach the contradictions of leftist political commitments to social change, and 'the best that has been thought and said' (as Matthew Arnold conceived the process of value-consolidation within English literary criticism). This tradition of criticism considered lower-class forms of culture in purely nostalgic or 'organicist' terms, and avoided any sense of alternative agency or contesting vantage-point possible within the cultural description of social life in England.

The alternative critical voices rising in the 1960s led and encouraged a climate of investigation that sought to theorise concepts of distinct traditions within English rural and working-class life. The critique gradually moved on to address popular streams of tradition in urban contexts of industrialisation and mass-circulation of goods, finally giving attention to filmic social experience, reproductive technologies, televisual impact, the impact of advertising and media, and communications-based concepts of cultural diffusion.

Raymond Williams had the distinction of contributing significant works that were part of each major shift through the period of consideration (for example, *Communications* [1962]; *Television: Technology and Cultural Form* [1974]; Marxism and Literature [1977]). In *The Long Revolution*, which appeared in 1961, Williams conceived of a cumulative process of modification in British society as having been inaugurated by industrialisation, which ushered in other fundamental changes of democratisation and greater social access to self-representation that were transforming culture comprehensively over time:

Our whole way of life, from the shape of our communities to the organisation and content of education, and from the structure of the family to the status of art and entertainment, is being profoundly affected by the progress and interaction of democracy and industry, and by the extension of communications. This deeper cultural revolution is a large part of our most significant living experience, and is being interpreted and indeed fought out, in very complex ways, in the world of art and ideas.[75]

Such concepts are still relevant in the 1990s. However they involved decisively important shifts in comprehension of cultural process for the beginning of the 1960s. Stuart Hall, reviewing the impact of this work of Raymond Williams almost two decades later, judged it as a 'seminal event in English post-war intellectual life':

It shifted the whole ground of debate from a literary-moral to an anthropological definition of culture. But it defined the latter now as the 'whole process' by means of which meanings and definitions are socially constructed and historically transformed, with literature and art as only one, specially privileged, kind of social communication.[76]

Raymond Williams's formulation of a more thoroughgoing framework for understanding cultural change and its social effects — particularly new forms of relationship arising through industrialisation and mass-participation in 'the social production of everyday life' (a central theme of what came to be known later as 'cultural studies') occurred at the threshold of the explosion of cultural forms that arose through the impact of British pop music and new cultural styles in the 1960s: Liverpool, the Beatles, and 'swinging London'.

The development of a tradition of discursive cultural critique, from the 1960s onwards, may therefore be seen as a parallel force in Britain to the experimental forces in visual art dealing with 'popular culture' that arose through the Independent Group in the 1950s. The Independent Group's interest in new cultural forms and technologies linking graphic design, architecture, the movies, and an increasing range of imagery that could be called 'urban', promoted a coalescing of broadly-based visual concerns and the emergence of the phenomenon of 'Pop Art' (coined by Lawrence Alloway). These developments, which led to the establishment of the ICA in London, also involved the now-historical stimulus of Richard Hamilton's work and presence at that time.

Stuart Hall meanwhile created a crucially supportive environment for new work in cultural theory when he became Director of the Centre for Contemporary Cultural Studies in Birmingham (succeeding Richard Hoggart, who was founding Director in 1964-69). The CCCS, and the collective environment of post-graduate study that prospered there, opened up lively intellectual spaces for studies of popular cultural forms within a framework of the advancing democratisation of all aspects of social life, and a committed challenge to the precedence of 'high cultural' forms in relation to the resources and attention devoted to other forms of cultural expression.

Increasing energy was devoted to analytical work on film, advertising, popular and counter-cultural forms, shifting emphasis to the minority rather than the majority, which was codified in the work on *sub-cultural styles*. For instance the work on this theme dealing especially with punk cultural styles, by Dick Hebdidge and others, is directly traceable to the influences and the environment of the CCCS in Birmingham. Dick Hebdidge's work, *Subculture: The Meaning of Style*, which appeared in 1979, was a pivotal work[77] in this regard (even though its author revised and rejected much of his thesis about the counter-normative forces of punk culture later). Cumulatively, an expanding range of cultural critique was developed in the 1970s that turned to more excluded forms of 'othered' subjects, from outside of West-dominated discourses.

The two movements indicated here — the theorisation of popular cultural forms and their diffusion within modern society on the one hand; and the visual translation of the mass-produced materials of urban

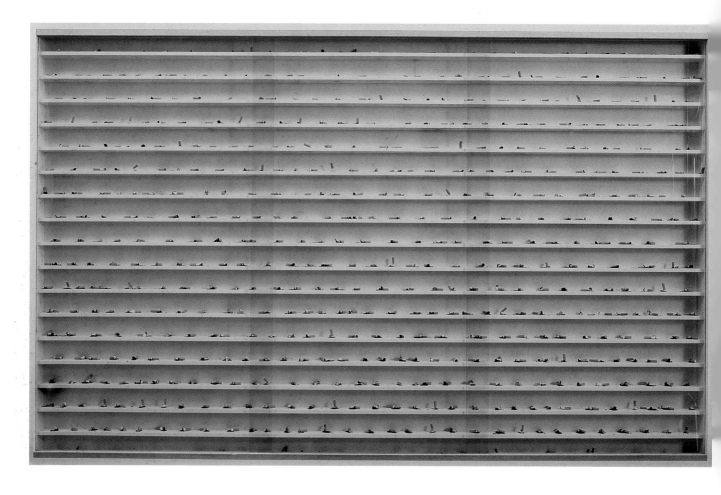

DAMIEN HIRST **DIED OUT, DEAD ENDS, EXPLORED** 1993

communications and advertising into art on the other—have jointly nourished the wide confluence of critical forces that direct attention to the socialisation of daily life in many forms in visual art in Britain at present. The interrelationship of these two streams, however, has not generally been noted or discussed in relation to the broad cultural context in which visual art is now pursued in Britain. Nevertheless it has widely conditioned what is produced.

> Art's about life, and it can't really be anything else. There isn't anything else.
> [Damien Hirst][78]

The CCCS lost its independent, postgraduate-focused status after a fierce struggle in the 1980s, and was absorbed back into more generally oriented requirements and undergraduate teaching as a Department of Cultural Studies (with the parallel demise of Sociology as a separate department) within the University of Birmingham. However the transfer of some of the key influences, personalities and publication energy (marking the leading work of the UK) to various campuses in Australia in the 1980s, suggests a wider field of common interests and inter-personal networks that have linked Australia and Britain in some mutual critical enterprises in the 1980s and 1990s.

In retrospect, it can be seen that the special course that cultural studies has taken in Britain over several decades has yielded a now-flourishing body of theory, practice, teaching and diverse applications within social discourse and criticism. It is a cumulation of work that is so particular to what has evolved in the UK in the post-War period as to merit a national rubric of description—*British cultural studies*—and a monographic account of its development[79] by Professor Graeme Turner, of the University of Queensland in Australia.

Professor Tony Bennett, who contributes an essay to the present publication, moved from Britain to Australia in 1983 (having taught in the admirably progressive Open University structure in the UK). Tony Bennett teaches today at a neighbouring campus in Brisbane, where he heads the Australian Key Centre for Cultural and Media Policy at Griffith University (Qld.), which pursues a national 'centre of excellence' focus in this field within the Australian universities structure. Two other British immigrants, John Fiske and John Hartley, who had been involved in similar enterprises in Cardiff, founded the *Australian Journal of Cultural Studies* in their new location—now 'returned to the centre from the margins', it has been observed[80], and renamed *Cultural Studies*.

It is important to stress the largely unspoken effects (in visual art circles) of this 'long march' of cultural critique in Britain, a critique that has always been powered by an agenda of experimental social thought, seeking social and political change. Its effects are everywhere present, but so diffused within general awareness as to be now largely untraceable in its particular lines of descent, in the kinds of discussions on which artists commonly draw in both their training and practice. The effects are discernible, for instance, in the widely shared orientation among British artists to a *contextual inquiry* in approaching everything that they make.

Having combined with the philosophically-based inquiries into the complex status of the art object as a mental experience—which traces, through Conceptual art, a long lineage back to Marcel Duchamp and Ludwig Wittgenstein—British artists are the inheritors today of a peculiarly rich, cross-pollinating environment, for the making and discussion of extremely diverse bodies of work. British artists, perhaps more than artists from any other single nation, or certainly in larger numbers (for Australian artists would also merit consideration in this discussion), may draw on strong critical traditions that variously intensify awareness of a number of paths of analysis within visual art, each now well developed through years of enquiry: the *socialisation* of images; the *'en-gendering'* of images (to pay tribute literally and metaphorically to the vital contributions of feminist critique to cultural theory); the *technologisation* of images; the *politicisation* of images; and the *culturalisation* of images.

Together, this constitutes a dense confluence of many streams of thought that contribute directly—more than any fashion-stylisation of street-smart energies or mythification

61

of 'youth' could indicate—to the vitality of British art at present. It is the total interaction of these influences that is behind the richness to be encountered: the traction, speed, irreverence and agency in some quarters; the polyform variety of multiple cultural imageries in others; and the quiet, speculative distance, critical undertow and social reflectiveness in yet others.

This project has sought to explore some strands of the many creativities contributing to the *montage* of images we might edit together—crossing, contending, fusing, obscuring, refiguring—of British art today. It is only through some navigation of the paths of each image, into and out of the collective *montage* they compose, that we might explore and intensify our sense of how art in Britain is 'picturing' itself so inventively at present.

Bernice Murphy (Chief Curator & Deputy Director of the MCA, Sydney) has been working internationally on exhibitions and museum-related projects since the late 1970s, when she also began to include Australian Aboriginal art in contemporary exhibitions as part of a long-standing commitment to issues of cultural diversity. She has written extensively in the field of contemporary art, criticism and museology, and is currently a member of the Executive Council of the International Council of Museums (ICOM/Paris).

NOTES

1.   Eddie Chambers, '*Cold Comfort*: Permindar Kaur, *Third Text*, London, No.36, Autumn 1996, 91-94.

2.   Kobena Mercer, 'Back to My Routes: A Postscript to the 80s', '*Pictura Britannica': Art from Britain* (Sydney, Museum of Contemporary Art, 1997), pp.112-123.

3.   ibid., p.113

4.   ibid., p.119

5.   Nikos Papastergiadis, 'Back to Basics: British Art and the Problems of a Global Frame', *Pictura Britannica*, op.cit., pp.128-145.

6.   ibid., p.131.

7.   David Barrett, *First Generation Reproduction*, first published as a commissioned essay by a young writer for the catalogue of *new contemporaries 96* (Tate Gallery, Liverpool, 1996; '*Pictura Britannica*', op.cit., pp.124-127.

8.   ibid. p.124.

9.   Patricia Bickers, 'As Others See Us', *Pictura Britannica*, op.cit., pp.65-88

10.   *Life/Live* was the pertinent title of a recent exhibition of British art in Paris (cur. Laurence Bossé & Hans-Ulrich Obrist, ARC, Musée d'Art Moderne de la Ville de Paris, Oct.1996-Jan.1997).

11.   Patrick Boylan, 'British Art in the 1980s and 1990s: The Social and Political Background', *Pictura Britannica*, op.cit., pp.147-159

12.   David Barrett, op.cit., p.124

13.   ibid., p.124-125

14.   'Turf Accounting: Mark Wallinger discusses *A Real Work of Art* with Paul Bonaventura', *Art Monthly*, London, issue 175, no.4/1994, p.5.

15.   'Blood Lines'[Mark Wallinger interv.by Sarah Curtis], *World Art*, Melbourne, no.2, 1995, pp.70-75; p.72.

16.   'Gillian Wearing. Interviewed by Ben Judd', *Untitled*, no.12, London, Winter 1996-97, p.5.

17.   Francesco Bonami, 'Damien Hirst: The Exploded View of the Artist', *Flash Art*, Milan, Summer 1996, 112-116; p.115.

18.   The televisual experience of 'flow' programming was first clearly theorised in Britain by Raymond Williams. See Graeme Turner, *British Cultural Studies*, 2nd ed. (London, Routledge, 1996), pp.57-8.

19.   Carl Freedman [interview], 'Damien Hirst', *Minky Manky*, cur. Carl Freedman (London, South London Gallery, 1995).

20.   The Coldstream Report, the basis of a major restructuring of artist education in Britain, which absorbed most art training within the new Polytechnic colleges, was delivered in 1962 [query]. Similar developments started to occur some five years later in Australian tertiary education, involving the then-new Colleges of Advanced Education.

21.   *Artists in the 1990s: Their education and values* (London, Wimbledon School of Art & Tate Gallery, 1994).

22.   ibid., p.26.

23.   Bonami/Hirst interview, op.cit., p.112.

24.   *Artists in the 1990s,* op. cit., p.71.

25.   Freedman/Hirst interview, *Minky Manky*, op.cit..

26.   Norman Rosenthal, from essay in *Prix Eliette von Karajan* catalogue, Vienna, 1995; pp.6-7. [Damien Hirst was the second artist to be awarded the Eliette von Karajan Prize for young artists, and was first suggested for the award by Georg Baselitz — a mark of his increasing recognition among artists in Europe.]

27.   Marcelo Spinelli, interview with Damien Hirst, London, 8 July 1995; printed in catalogue of *Brilliant!, New Art from London*, cur. Richard Flood (Minneapolis, Walker Art Center, 1995), p.41.

28.   José Lebreo Stals, 'About Loss But Not Childhood', *Cold Comfort: Permindar Kaur* (Ikon Gallery, Birmingham, May-June 1996, pp.4-5), p.4.

29.   Lubaina Himid, 'A Brief Introduction to the Magical World of Maud Sulter's Photoworks', catalogue essay for *Syrcas* (Edinburgh, Portfolio Gallery; for Edinburgh International Festival, 1994), p.33.

30.   ibid.

31.   Kobena Mercer, 'Imagine All the People: Constructing Community Culturally', in *Imagined Communities*, cur. Richard Hylton (Oldham Art Gallery) and Andrew Patrizio (National Touring Exhibitions), (The South Bank Centre, London, 1995).

32.   Yinka Shonibare, quoted in Kobena Mercer, 'Art That is Ethnic In Inverted Commas', *frieze*, London, no.25, Nov.-Dec. 1995, p.39.

33.   David Barrett, op.cit., p.126.

34.   From an unpublished essay by Damien Hirst *On Dumb Painting*.

35.   Bonami/Hirst interview, op.cit., pp.114,112

36.   Douglas Gordon, interviewed by Allanah Weston, *Telegraph Magazine*, n.d..

37.   ibid., p.112.

38.   Sam Taylor-Wood interviewed by Douglas Fogle, London, 1995; excerpted in *Brilliant!*, op.cit, p. 79.

39.   'Gillian Wearing. Interviewed by Ben Judd', *Untitled*, no.2, London, Winter 1996-97, pp.4-5., p.5.

40.   From article by James Hall, in the *Guardian's* pre-announcement coverage of the Turner prize, 1995 — which was awarded to Damien Hirst.

41.   'Georgina Starr — Interview: Adam Chodzko', *Tate: The Art Magazine*, Tate Gallery, London, Spring 1996, 35-38.

42.   ibid..

43.   Wearing/Judd interview, op.cit., p.5.

44.   Gillian Wearing pages from catalogue of *Brilliant!*, op, cit., p.81.

45.   Bonami/Hirst interview, op.cit., pp.114-5. .

46.   ibid.; p.114.

47.   See the reference to this aspect of Wearing's work in Gregor Muir, 'Gillian Wearing. Interim Art, London', *World Art*, Melbourne, November 1994, p.117.

48.   Wearing/Judd interview, op.cit., pp.4-5.

49.   Starr/Chodzko interview, op.cit., pp. 35-38.

50.   'Interview. Things you always wanted to do but were afraid to: Heidi Reitmaier talks with Georgina Starr', *Women's Art*, London, vol. 1, 1996, pp.12-15.

51.   Gillian Wearing pages from *Brilliant!*, op.cit., p.81.

52.   Douglas Gordon, quoted in *The Turner Prize 1996* booklet, Tate Gallery, London 1996.

53.   Piers Masterson, 'Permindar Kaur' [review of Ikon Gallery exhibition],

Art Monthly, London, no.198, Jul.-Aug.1996, p.34.

54.   *Mirage Enigmas of Race, Difference and Desire*, was an inter-disciplinary project inspired by the writings of Frantz Fanon, and in particular his influential text *Black Skin, White Masks* (first published in Paris in 1952). This book was derived especially from his experience of mental illness in Algeria, which he diagnosed as related to conditions of colonial subjection and self-exile among dominated peoples.

55.   *Working with Fanon: Contemporary Politics and Cultural Reflection* (13-14 May 1995).

56.   *The Fact of Blackness Frantz Fanon*, ICA, London, 1995 (ICA, London; inIVA, London and Bay Press, Seattle, 1996).

57.   José Lebreo Stals, ob. cit., p. 5.

58.   Nancy Proctor, 'Is Women's Art Homeless?', *make*, no. 71, London, Aug-Sept.1996, p.11.

59.   Australian Aboriginal word, meaning sacred ceremony of song and dance, involving a mixture of cultural forms.

60.   Eddie Chambers, '"Cold Comfort": Permindar Kaur', *Third Text*, London, No.36, Autumn 1996, pp.92-3.

61.   Carl Freedman [interview], 'Mat Collishaw', *Minky Manky*, op.cit..

62.   One of the most complete examples of the 'Picturesque' garden planned on these principles in Australia may still be experienced in the Botanical Gardens of Melbourne. Founded by Dr Ferdinand von Mueller in 1852; later William Guilfoyle (1873 - 1909) was responsible for the 'natural' design and introduction of Australian plants.

63.   Marcelo Spinelli [interview], Mat Collishaw pages, *Brilliant!*, op.cit. p. 27.

64.   See further comments by Hadrian Piggott on Andrea Wilkinson's work elsewhere in this catalogue, under the *Texts on Artists* section.

65.   Mark Sealy, 'A Note from Outside on Rotimi Fani-Kayode', *Rotimi Fani-Kayode 1955-89 COMMUNION* (Autograph, London, Chapter, Cardiff & Impressions, York, 1995).

66.   ibid..

67.   Rotimi Fani-Kayode, 'Traces of Ecstasy', in *Critical Decade: Black Photography in the 80s*, *Ten.8* special issue, vol. 2, no. 3, Spring 1992, p. 68.

68.   Douglas Gordon, op.cit..

69.   Jennifer Higgie, 'Gillian Wearing; Interim Art, London', *frieze*, London, no. 33, March - April 1997, p.80.

70.   Stephen Snoddy, 'From the Top of Slieve Donard...', '*Pictura Britannica*', op.cit., pp.89-99.

71.   From Richard Hamilton (and Rita Donagh), in *A Cellular Maze* (Derry, The Orchard Gallery, 1983) unpaginated; see further version for the present publication, under the *Texts on Artists* section.

72.   Bonami/Hirst interview, op.cit., p.116.

73.   John A Walker, 'Everything Equals Nothing: The Art and Ideas of John Latham', '*Pictura Britannica*', op.cit., p.100-106.

74.   A rich account of the development of cultural studies in Britain is given in the monograph on this subject by Graeme Turner (*British Cultural Studies*, 1990; 2nd ed., London, Routledge, 1996), from which much has been drawn here by way of factual background, context and focus on key figures.

75.   Raymond Williams, *The Long Revolution* [1961]; Penguin, 1975, p.12.

76.   Stuart Hall, 'Cultural Studies and the Centre: Some Problematics and Problems', in *Culture, Media, Language*, ed. Stuart Hall, Dorothy Hobson, Andrew Lowe and Paul Willis (London, Hutchinson, 1980; quoted in Graeme Turner, op.cit., p.51.

77.   Hebdidge's *Subculture* also had a pivotal effect in Australia: it was extensively used as a springboard for the lead essay in the first issue of the journal *Art + Text*, written by founding editor, then Melbourne-based, Paul Taylor; (*Art + Text* was later edited by Paul Foss, who continues as editor to the present). The first issue of *Art + Text* appeared in Autumn 1981.

78.   Quoted in Jerry Saltz, 'More Life: The Work of Damien Hirst', *Art in America*, June 1995, p.85.

79.   Turner, op.cit.

80.   Turner, ibid., p.77.

AS OTHERS SEE US
TOWARDS A HISTORY OF RECENT ART FROM BRITAIN *

PATRICIA BICKERS

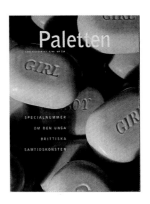

PALETTEN, NO.219, APRIL 1994,
HADRIAN PIGOTT, GENDER SOAPS,
1994, 'SPECIAL NUMBER ON
YOUNG BRITISH ART'.

Art in America's special issue on the 46th Venice Biennale made no mention of *General Release*, Britain's contribution to the off-Broadway exhibitions that many countries organised in the absence of the Aperto in that year.[1] Not so long ago, such an omission would have occasioned little comment; but today, when contemporary British art is attracting so much attention at home and abroad, it is unlikely to have been an oversight and may indeed have been a deliberate omission.

That there is a widely held perception that contemporary British art is in an exciting phase hardly needs stating. '*Brilliant!*' *New Art from London*,[2] billed as 'the highlight of the 1995 art season' and featuring the work of '22 young artists internationally acknowledged as the most exciting working today', which is due to open at the Walker Art Center, Minneapolis in October, is only the latest and most lavish of the exhibitions devoted to the work of British-based artists outside Britain. In addition to the number of individual shows that many of the artists included in '*Brilliant!*', and many not included, have had abroad, the number of group shows, in both public and commercial galleries, from Brussels to Tokyo, Lodz to Barcelona, Rome to New York, Helsinki to Istanbul, in which British artists have been shown abroad, will soon fill a modest-sized telephone directory. What is more, most of them have been initiated by the galleries and museums in the host country rather than by the British Council, once the chief conduit for contemporary British art abroad or, as in the case of *Some Went Mad, Some Ran Away* ..., curated by Damien Hirst, the exhibition was initiated by the Serpentine

Gallery but toured to Hannover, Helsinki and Chicago.[3] In addition to all this evidence of interest, one could cite articles about the British art scene with titles such as *A New Powerhouse*, or the the number of international art magazines which have published special issues on contemporary art in Britain including, most recently, *Paletten*, Sweden, *Bijutsu Techo*, Japan—arguably the most comprehensive and least prescriptive survey so far—and *Technikart*, France.[4]

In most accounts, at home and abroad 1988, the year of *Freeze*, has come to represent a critical Year Zero, a *terminus post quam*, from which everything that is exciting—hot—in contemporary British art has flowed. It was also almost a decade since the Tories under Margaret Thatcher had come to power and three years after the Heysel Stadium disaster, on May 29, 1985, when 41 people were killed after violence broke out between Juventus and Liverpool football fans during the European Cup Final, an event which, according to the *Art Newspaper*, added a new word to the Italian vocabulary: '*ooligani*'.[5] If 1988 can be said to be the seminal year, then these events seem, by general consensus, to have set the parameters within which critical discourse about recent British art, especially outside Britain but latterly, inside Britain, too, has been conducted. It seemed to me that it would be interesting to attempt to trace the development of this particular critical framework—*Freeze*, Thatcherism, football

* Though slightly altered, the first part of this text is substantially the same as that originally commissioned in 1995, by the Cornerhouse Gallery, Manchester, as No7 in its Communiqué series and entitled: *The Brit Pack : Contemporary British Art, the view from abroad*. I am grateful to the Museum of Contemporary Art, Sydney for inviting me to update it which I have done in the second part in the form of a Postscript.

ARTFORUM, VOL.XXX, NO.9, MAY

1992, ANYA GALLACCIO *PRESERVE*

(SUNFLOWERS), 1991.

hooliganism—across as wide a critical spectrum as is possible within a relatively limited space.

In 1992, a work by Anya Gallaccio, *Preserve (Sunflowers)*, 1991, appeared on the cover of the May edition of *Artforum*. It was a remarkable event for a number of reasons: the artist was young—under 30—female and British. Not so long ago, the last factor might have seemed the most remarkable. Gallaccio had not yet even shown in New York.[6] To make sense of the cover, therefore, the magazine carried an article on the new art entitled, *British? Young? Invisible? w/Attitude?*, by Michael Corris, a British-based American critic. In many ways, the article could be said to have set the tone for much of the critical and curatorial coverage that the 'new generation of British artists' has since received abroad, not just in America.

In a convincing combination of an insider's knowledge of the 'scene' and an outsider's perspective upon it, Corris conjured a picture of an economically depressed, democratically suppressed, historically obsessed and educationally regressive culture struggling to come to terms with its colonialist and neo-colonialist past. Citing sources in the *Guardian*, *Private Eye*, *Technique Anglaise*—'The early Eighties taught us that there was a market place for art'[7]— and Hofmannsthal, he asked rhetorically whether it was a 'mere accident' that this was 'the most favourable time for the individual to appear?'[8] Perceiving, presumably, a precedent in the cultural climate of Britain before the First World War, Corris

skillfully parodied the style of Vorticist manifestos, blasting, among other things: 'So much machinery to produce: *The Turner Prize*, BBC Radio 4's *Desert Island Discs*, *Domesticated Policeman (no guns)* (though in a note Corris alludes to the fabrication and suppression of evidence in the cases of the 'Guildford Four' and the 'Birmingham Six'), 'the deadly chic of Dering St' but also, 'the horrors of Hackney (more artists per square meter than any other locale in the Western world...', the amateur, humour —'quack English drug for stupidity and sleepiness'—sport and 'the years 1979 to 1990'. He blessed, among other things: humour—'the great barbarous weapon of the genius among races'—Prince Charles, *The Late Show*, 'T.W.O.C-ing' ('street talk for stealing cars: derived from a police acronym for 'Taken Without Owner's Consent' '), ram-raiding and E. But above all, he blessed Critical Decor, Rachel Evans 'brides iced into their wedding gowns', Mariko Mori, Anya Gallaccio 'one ton of Jaffa oranges spilled out on the floor of a derelict warehouse', and Hope.[9]

Leaving aside the question of the appropriateness of drawing an analogy between the Vorticists, whose proto-fascist politics are still the subject of debate, and artists working now, Corris was attempting, in these fake manifestos, to contextualise the art of this 'new generation' of 'young British artists' and thereby to provide a much-needed corrective to the prevailing critical discourse concerning contemporary British art in North America. This discourse is characterised by what he described as a tendency, 'to read the work of English artists across a narrow band of already assimilated "international" art rather than *within* the local cultural context of England', as a result of which, 'the particularities of (local) strategies and struggles remain invisible'.[10] In his attempt to establish just such a 'local cultural context' for the new art, he has fallen into another tendency, not peculiar to North American critical discourse, that of conflating the 'context of England' with that of 'London', and both with 'Britain'. It may well be true, as he quotes Karsten Schubert as saying, that '"nobody in London thinks that anything outside London is worth looking at"', but developments outside London, for instance in Glasgow, cannot be dismissed or absorbed in this way.

Notwithstanding the inverted commas Corris placed around the terms 'new generation' and 'young British artists' and the disclaimer that, 'The conceptualisation of a new generation of artists who are fixed in the ambered abundance of London is subject to a number of constraints that abrade and unsettle the normal logic of promotion and curatorial logic',[11] the article nevertheless represents Corris' bid to identify a new avant-garde, focusing on particular artists as being representative (though not including Damien Hirst, an omission that today would seem unthinkable), which he then characterises in familiar generational and oppositional terms.[12] In doing so, he follows a well-trodden route from the celebration of diversity to the identification of a dominant mode into which that diversity is eventually subsumed: British, young, invisible, with attitude.

Apparently taking his cue from Corris, the Brussels-based independent curator, Philippe Braem, curated an exhibition called *With Attitude* later that same year as part of a programme of British Art hosted by the city of Brussels in the Winter of 1992, to coincide with Britain's Presidency of the EU under Leon Brittan. Braem, however, intended the title to refer to what he described as, 'the stylish, tongue-in-cheek way' in which 'the young generation of British artists have emerged on the national and international scene'.[13] 'Stylish and tongue-in-cheek'? This is hardly what the show's title leads one to expect. On the other hand, this disjunction between the challenging title and the mild language of the catalogue text, could be said to be a true reflection of the mixture of work selected which ranged from Anya Gallaccio's floorpiece of cast-chocolate handguns—Godiva and the arms industry in sickly conjunction—to the measured elegance of Perry Roberts' canvases.

Braem, too, cited 1988 as the seminal year in which the new art emerged in what he described as an 'outburst of creativity', referring specifically to the 'Freeze' generation though, in fact, only two of the artists included actually took part in *Freeze*: Anya Gallaccio and Simon Patterson (Dominic Denis was included in the catalogue, but did not actually take part in any of the shows)—again, not Hirst himself[14]. And though the emphasis was on 'the young generation', not all the exhibiting artists could be included in that category, at least, not without some degree of latitude: Hannah Collins, Lucia Nogueira and Amikam Toren, for instance, were all established artists in their own right. In many ways, *With Attitude* was a transitional exhibition; Toren

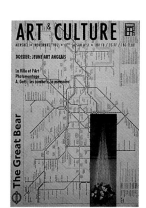

ART & CULTURE, NOVEMBER 1992,

SIMON PATTERSON, *THE GREAT*

BEAR, 1992

represented a link with an earlier show of the work of British-based artists, *Instalment—5 British Artists*, curated by Braem in 1987 as part of the *British Season* in Brussels, held at Plan K, which unlike the PLA Building which housed *Freeze*, was an authentic 'warehouse' space in a rundown part of Brussels.[15] What these apparent contradictions, or disjunctions, perhaps suggest is that there were two competing interpretations of the defining tendency of the 'new art' from Britain which Braem was unable or unwilling to resolve: that it was predominantly 'cool' and 'knowing' and/ or that it was aggressive and transgressive in character.

A similar irresolution is reflected in the immediate critical response to the 'new art' from Britain in Brussels. Though Simon Patterson's, *The Great Bear*, which appeared on the cover of the November issue of the Belgian magazine, *Art & Culture*, which devoted a special section to 'Britain in Brussels' to coincide with the exhibition, is described in the cover note as 'emblematic' of its coverage of the art of the 'new young generation', far from providing any sort of key, the work is barely discussed in the main text.[16] Written by Claude Lorent in consultation with Braem, the curator of *With Attitude*, the lead article is entitled, 'When Attitude becomes Art', and also cites 1988 as the year in which a 'dynamic' young generation emerged in London.[17] It begins by sketching in a brief (two paragraphs), introductory background history to postwar British art, focusing on the 'dominant personalities' ('personnalités artistiques hors du commun'), from Henry Moore and Francis Bacon, Anthony Caro, Richard Hamilton and David

Hockney, Richard Long, Gilbert and George and Art & Language, among others, to the 'Lisson Gallery Sculptors', and the 'next generation', including, for example, Julian Opie, Lisa Milroy and Grenville Davy[18], before launching straight into a discussion of *Freeze* and the emergence of Damien Hirst—who is finally given his due—and his contemporaries on to the scene.

However, though on the one hand the magazine takes the trouble to define for its readers, for whom there is no exact equivalent, what is meant by the phrase, 'With Attitude',[19] on the other, it singles out the professionalism, entrepreneurial spirit and general market savvy of Hirst and his contemporaries in setting up their own exhibitions— qualities that are difficult to reconcile with the idea of a generation in rebellion against the *status quo*. Indeed, whereas Corris, despite the fact that his article in *Artforum* is illustrated by works photographed *in situ* in two commercial galleries, chooses to stress that Hope, and to a lesser extent, Critical Decor, worked most successfully when they operated outside the gallery system, *Art & Culture* actually stresses the promptness with which commercial galleries in London such as the Anderson O'Day Gallery, Karsten Schubert Ltd and Interim Art snapped up some of the artists, successfully absorbing the new work into their orbit. They were quickly followed by others such as Laure Genillard and Victoria Miro. However these galleries were comparative latecomers compared with the long-established Waddingtons Gallery, Michael Craig-Martin's dealer, who signed up Ian Davenport before *Freeze*, actually during his degree show (Karsten

TECHNIKART, NO.17, MARCH-APRIL 1995; CONTENTS: 'GILBERT & GEORGE, GAVIN TURK, ANGUS FAIRHURST, GEORGINA STARR, THE PLAYLIST OF THE NEW GENERATION' AND 'THE A TO Z OF ARTISTIC LONDON' AND HEADLINE: 'LONDON: CAPITAL OF WHAT?' WITH PHOTOGRAPH OF GILBERT & GEORGE.

Schubert also signed up Michael Landy shortly afterwards). Even Anthony d'Offay (who failed to take up Hirst when he was working behind-the-scenes at the gallery), later tried to make up for lost time by including him in a group exhibition, *Strange Developments—Ten British and American Artists* in September 1992.[20]

When it comes to discussion of the nature of the work associated with the group (with the important exception of Hirst who, it is suggested, had become a star in spite, or because of, the 'morbidity' of his work—albeit 'clean' and 'sterilised' in presentation), it identifies as its chief characteristics its diversity, sophistication and conceptual base. At this point, it is worth remembering that the title of the article also deliberately invokes another seminal exhibition: *When Attitudes became Form (Works—Concepts—Processes—Situations—Information)*, held in 1969, which attempted to define the kind of art now referred to by the portmanteau term, Conceptual Art; 'When Attitude becomes Art', thus neatly encapsulates the two tendencies that both the exhibition and the article were trying to define. Indeed, the apparent contradictions inherent in both exhibition and article represent a potentially more productive approach to developments in contemporary British art since 1988 than that sketched in by Corris, precisely because of the contradictions—the 'constraints' that Corris referred to 'that abrade and unsettle the normal logic of promotion and curatorial logic'.

However, a gathering editorial, critical and curatorial consensus has swept aside these and other apparent contradictions, or more properly, complexities, in favour of a particular view of contemporary art in Britain as predominantly aggressive and anti-establishment, made by a generation of 'Bad Girls' and boys, a view that has gradually hardened into an orthodoxy that effectively excludes other possible readings. Take, for example, the recent special British edition of the French magazine, *Technikart*: the word *agressif* recurs like a leitmotif throughout: '...la jeune génération des Damien Hirst, Sarah Lucas, Gavin Turk, crée aujourd'hui l'art le plus agressif et le plus réfléchi de cette fin de siècle', and so on, and so on.[21] Gilbert and George, who feature on the cover, brandishing Union Jacks, as well as in the magazine, represent a link with the late 60s and early 70s, which is partly why they are invoked as godfathers to 'la nouvelle génération',[22] while their subject-matter—themselves, the Queen, the Horse Guards, Tower Bridge, (boys), 'les bobbies' and, of course, the Flag—aligns them with the young. Cue Gavin Turk's *Study for Window* of 1991, a fake front page of the tabloid newspaper, *The Sun*, featuring his self-portrait against the background of a Union Jack and the headline: 'Support Our Boys And Put This Flag In Your Window', recalling that newspaper's crude jingoism during the Gulf War.[23] The link with the subject-matter of Gilbert and George and with the spirit of the punk era is further emphasised: 'Aussi bien dans les sujets traités (la Reine, la presse à scandale anglaise, le malaise social) que dans l'esprit (punk, gauchiste

ARTFORUM, MARCH 1994,

VOL.XXXII, NO.7, GILLIAN WEARING:

YARD + GRO SAY DIVERT THE

DIVERTED FROM THE SERIES, 'SIGNS

THAT SAY WHAT YOU WANT THEM

TO SAY AND NOT SIGNS THAT SAY

WHAT SOMEONE ELSE WANTS YOU

TO SAY', 1992-93.

engagé, ironique), le style (collages, coupures de presse, auto-mises-en-scène), les techniques (assemblages d'objets pour la 'sculpture anglaise'), on trouve un art "so british" '. And the most 'british' works singled out by the magazine are, unsurprisingly, Turk's *Pop*, 1993 (a wax cast of Gavin Turk as Sid Vicious in the pose of Elvis after Warhol), 'Ce travail, typique de l'esprit punk agressif anglais', 'Il reprend en cela l'image de l'artiste anti-social et marginal', and Sarah Lucas' bovver-boy *Razor boots*, both illustrated.[24]

Dependence upon cultural stereotyping is hardly unique to the coverage of the visual arts. Indeed, much of the work cited in *Technikart* deliberately takes on those stereotypes, but whether it subverts them or merely reinforces them is a moot point. The kind of coverage represented by *Technikart* suggests the latter. The prominence given to Gilbert and George is also explicable in terms of cultural and, in their case, sexual stereotyping of the kind that is overtly acknowledged in the title of *Technique Anglaise* (see n[7]), one of the earliest attempts to identify what the subtitle described as, 'current trends in British art'. It is inevitable that all of us who commentate on the arts will

see what we want to see. It might be more illuminating, however, periodically to subject those precon-ceptions to more rigorous scrutiny or, occasionally, to less scrutiny. For instance, in a recent article in *Artforum* which featured on the cover

a work by Gillian Wearing from her series, *Signs that say what you want them to say and not signs that say what other people want you to say*, Jon Savage, who also writes for the style press, saw the revival of interest in 60s pop and 70s punk as arising in part from similarities between the political climate then and now, similarities which are, in fact, largely cosmetic.

Articles like these seem to confuse style with content, the look of something with its substance.[25] While it is true that many younger artists working in Britain today have expressed an affection for, or a preoccupation with, the 60s, the phenomenon may have as much to do with the fact that most of the artists concerned were born in that decade, as with any political agenda; Douglas Gordon, for instance, incorporated 30 songs from January-September 1966, the year of his birth, in his work entitled, *Something between my Mouth and your Ear*, 1994, while in *26th October*, a piece made in 1993, Henry Bond and Sam Taylor-Wood collaborated on restaging an icon of the 60s, the photograph of Yoko Ono and John Lennon lying entwined with Ono's hair spread out and a naked Lennon clinging foetally to her side, but the work is only political in that, as we have been told, the personal *is* political. On the other hand, it might with more justification be said that the fixation with the 60s and 70s on the part of editors, critics and curators has as much, or more, to do with the fact that they are reliving their own past.

The issue of class in relation to the new British art is discussed in similarly simplistic terms. Whereas Corris' only overt reference to the issue of class is buried in a brief note that merely states its importance as one of the determining factors governing membership of the new avant-garde, *Technikart* dives straight in, confidently characterising the work of Turk and Lucas, in particular, as playing specifically with '*l'esprit de revolte et de la frustration de la middle et lower-class anglaise*'.[26] The dubious assumptions underlying both articles, and much that has been written since, are that the new avant-garde is largely working class—whatever that means—and *therefore* anti-establishment in character. The English obsession with class is only matched by the obsession of the rest of Europe and America with the English obsession with class. For example, a certain degree of glee is detectable in the news item from Venice reported in *The Art Newspaper*, cited earlier; it is worth quoting in full: 'VENICE. By now Europeans [sic] have learned from English football fans that the traditional gentleman is no longer representative of his country. "ooligans" have taken over instead, and true to form, the UK included one among the twelve young artists sent over, courtesy of the British Council, to represent trends in British art at a show in the Convento di San Pasquale. This one decided to throw the hotel furniture out of the window into the canal and got locked up with another nabbed for drugs.'[27] 'Traditional gentleman'? This surely tells us more about how others see us than about how we see ourselves! This strangely old-fashioned stereotypical view is echoed in the course of a review by Neville Wakefield of Lucas' show at the Barbara Gladstone Gallery, New York: 'If nothing else, Sarah Lucas' sometimes abrasive, invariably funny art puts paid to the myth of British decorum. Delivered with the visual equivalent of a belch, Lucas' work turns the tables on her American audience, placing the dainty tea cup in the hands of those who espouse the politically correct'.

Seen in this light, Lucas represents a kind of supercallifragilisticexpialidocious-Dick-van-Dyke-chirpy-cockney-type character out of *Mary Poppins*, Hollywood's idea of 19th-century London. (Dick van Dyke, readers may recall, was an American actor whose attempt at a cockney accent was generally held to be execrable.)

However, Wakefield also offers us another key to the attraction that certain kinds of contemporary British art holds for American audiences: a certain licence denied American artists conscious of the constraints imposed by the prevailing culture of political correctness.[28] If this is indeed one it its attractions, then the more 'outrageous' the more anti-establishment, the better. The run-up to the opening of '*Brilliant!*' *New Art from London* at the Walker Art Center, Minneapolis, thirty years after it staged, *London: The New Scene*, in 1965, has seen its press machine cranking itself up to produce ever more hype, and it is instructive to highlight the buzz words, most of which can be found in the various sources so far quoted in this essay, but which have now coalesced into a single, homogenising profile of a generation of artists working in London today.

The May edition of *Walker News*, kicked off by heralding the arrival of 'Twenty-two young British artists' known for 'their aesthetically diverse, *provocative* artworks', 'united by a shared interest in ephemeral materials and unconventional presentation, a willful identification with working-class emblems as well as a *youthful, oppositional* vitality'.[29] Most, it went on to say, 'are graduates of a handful of London art schools (notably Goldsmiths College and the Slade School of

Fine Art), which have provided a fertile ground for the development of emerging artists in the late 80s and early 90s. At the end of the 80s, faced with a flattened art market and a sense that the aesthetic options that were open to them were extremely limited, these artists adopted an *entrepreneurial* attitude of collective *self-promotion* evident in such exhibitions as *Freeze* (1988), organized by then-Goldsmiths' student Damien Hirst and held in a *rundown warehouse* on the Surrey Docks of East London. A seminal event in this history, *Freeze* demonstrated the independence, self-reliance, and intense *professionalism* of these young students'.

By the Autumn, new press releases were sent out in the form of a fold-out double-sided poster, one side of which contained a combination of images and texts that when folded, showed on the front a black-and-white reproduction of *I'm Desperate*, one of the images from Wearing's series, *Signs that say what you want them to say...*, overlaid by a headline proclaiming: WALKER WELCOMES BRASH BRITS FOR FLASHY BASH! Inside, one of the texts now reads: 'Twenty-two young British invaders are set to storm the Walker Art Center when *'Brilliant!' New Art from London* premieres. Witness work by a new generation of artists from the land that brought you *Sid and Nancy*, Chuck and Di, fish and chips, Hugh Grant and *Cats*. Gritty, funny, and *in-your-face*, *'Brilliant!'* begins with a bang: a preview party with hot art, cool people, and cold beer. Bring a friend and an attitude and join the party with more Soho than so-so. (Dress to suggest your favorite Brit and you could win a smashing prize!)'. And as a permanent record of the event, a 'fanzine-type magazine' will be published that 'will serve as the exhibition book'.

Does any of this hype matter? Perhaps not. It is only a problem if the sheer weight of it begins to distort the way the work is seen. Would Rachel Whiteread have been included but for the hype surrounding *House*? An internationally recognised sculptor, included in Documenta IX, represented in most major museums and collections and widely regarded as continuing a British tradition of sculpture, Whiteread hardly fits the profile promulgated in these press releases.[30] It will only become a problem, as they say of movie stars, when the actors in this scenario begin to believe the hype or, in other words, when we begin to see ourselves as others see us and make, or curate, work accordingly. An example of this process at work was *Minky Manky*, an exhibition held at the South London Art Gallery in 1995, curated by Carl Freedman, who was, according to the catalogue, also 'responsible for *Modern Medicine* and *Gambler*' (co-curators Billee Sellman and Damien Hirst, seem to have been written out of this particular script). This attempted reprise of *Freeze* was greeted enthusiastically chiefly by those who did not get to see *Freeze* back in 1988.[31] Miren Jaio, for instance, reviewing the exhibition in the Spanish-language magazine, *Lapiz*, singles out the 'scatalogical irreverence' of the work in the show, and attributes to it a political agenda, seeing in it a reaction, for example, to the Government's *Back to Basics* campaign ('vuelta a "los valores básicos" '). He makes the by now obligatory reference to 'the enormous influence' of musical culture in the work—'mod, punk, rave'—especially to the importance of the connection between rock artists and Hirst, the 'artistic phenomenon of the decade: artist, curator, publicist' and 'friend of certain illustrious rock personalities ('el fenomeno artístico de la decada: artista, comisario, creador de publicidad y, como buen aficionado al formol, amigo de ciertas momias ilustres del rock'). And, as though in final validation of the work, he points to the continued irritation it causes readers of *The Sun*, an assumption that belies a die-hard modernist position that assumes that the popular press and 'avant-garde' art must necessarily be at odds.[32]

Like most reunions, *Minky Manky* tended to disappoint. How much longer can artists, many of them commanding high prices for their work and most of them now in their thirties, be supposed to conform to this essentially rebellious adolescent role? There is another danger, too. While the Press in Britain is beginning to take the same line as its counterparts abroad, as witness this recent headline from one of the 'respectable' broadsheets: 'BRILLIANT BAD BOYS OF THE GALLERIES Jake and Dinos Chapman are nasty and disgusting, or intelligent and inspired. Pay your money, take your choice',[33] there are signs of a backlash. Allan Schwartzman, in his coverage of the 1995 Venice Biennale for *Artforum*, already sounds jaded: 'Finally, *General Release*, a show organized by the British Council to present the work of yet another group of young British artists, includes a video image of a pair of twiddling thumbs—a fitting image for an art scene passing time while waiting for clarity, a whole generation of artists inching forward, fearful of making a mistake.'[34]

The 'backlash factor' may also be why *Art in America* decided to ignore the 'Brit Pack' in its special Venice issue.

POSTSCRIPT

When the concluding paragraphs above were written, *'Brilliant!'* had not yet opened in Minneapolis, so that many of the questions posed and fears expressed, in the light of the relentless barrage of press releases issued by the Walker Art Center, had to remain unanswered and untested. The opportunity afforded me by Sydney's Museum of Contemporary Art to write this postscript not only allows me to address them now, but also to reflect on, and update, the more general aim of the original text, which was to attempt to trace the development of a particular critical discourse within which recent art from Britain has been framed (I use the word advisedly, both literally, in terms of a 'framework', and metaphorically, in the sense of the deliberate incrimination of innocent parties).

To begin with the *'Brilliant!'* show itself, the Private View confirmed the worst fears of cultural, if not racial, stereotyping of the kind that, had they been directed at some other racial minorities, would have been actionable. The clichés included extras dressed in joke shop costumes supposedly representing British Bobbies—*Domesticated Policemen (no guns)*— (actually more like Keystone Cops) and Horse Guards who handed guests tins of Altoids™. *Altoids?* No one I spoke to from among the British contingent at the Opening, or since for that matter, had ever heard of them. Like Glen Grant™ whisky and Lipton's™ tea, these throat pastilles, as the slightest enquiry would have shown, clearly belong to the kind of 'genuinely British' products that are manufactured specifically for the export market. In fact, Altoids™ are actually manufactured in the United States.

Perhaps my failure to appreciate these shenanigans merely betrays a lack of the much-vaunted British sense of humour—'quack English drug for stupidity and sleepiness' or 'the great barbarous weapon of the genius among races' —providing further evidence of the truth of Wilde's oft-quoted observation that Britain and America are 'separated by the same language'. Worse, perhaps it represents a failure on my part to recognise the same kind of 'interplay between stereotype and its ironic embrace', that according to the catalogue, characterises the work in 'Brilliant!'.[35] Nevertheless, at the risk of appearing humourless and dull-witted, the question still remains: how could the weight of this kind of hype fail 'to distort the way the work is seen'? With hindsight, Whiteread for instance, who will be representing Britain at the Venice Biennale this year, looks even more out-of-place in this context than she did back in 1995. And what of Steven Pippin, whose work has been described as a benign form of boffinism more appropriate to the garden-shed than the gallery: where does his work fit in? And the painter, Alessandro Raho: how can his pallid portraits be said to be 'gritty, funny and in-your-face'?

It could be argued that none of this hype has anything to do with Richard Flood's basic curatorial premise or with the exhibition itself. After all, Press Departments have their own remit. However, in this case, the publicity seems to have taken its cue accurately from the curator—and worse was to come. No, not the Brit punk lookalike contest but the catalogue, or rather, the 'Exhibition Book', a 70s-style underground magazine printed on cheap paper, an hommage to Jamie Reid and the Sex Pistols, that featured on the cover a black-and-white photograph of the aftermath of the IRA bombing in the City of London in 1992, emblazoned in pink and white with the words, 'Brilliant!' New Art from London. Whatever the merits or otherwise of the work upon which it is based, Mat Collishaw's, IRA Bombing, Bishopsgate, London April 10, 1992, its use as a cover is questionable both in terms of taste—imagine for a moment a photograph of the Oklahoma Bombing in the United States emblazoned in pink and white with the words 'Cool!' New Art from Oklahoma—but, much more importantly, in terms of what it suggests about the exhibition's agenda. It is one thing to observe similarities between the products produced by Sarah Lucas and Tracey Emin's shop, in particular the t-shirts, and those of Malcolm McLaren and Vivienne Westwood, but quite another to equate their aims and then to characterise these as somehow 'working-class'.[36] The equation of 'Brit art' with punk, punk with Situationism and all three with working-class political values, made explicit in Wakefield's essay whose title, 'Pretty vacancy', deliberately recalls the Sex Pistols' single, Pretty Vacant, simply does not add up.[37] Even supposing that the working class (for whom, according to Wakefield buses were the 'preferred'—the preferred, mind you— means of transportation in the late 60s!) is, or has ever been, an undifferentiated mass with shared political values, how is Collishaw's photograph supposed to express such values? Why are those values, and thus those of the artists included in 'Brilliant!', repeatedly assumed to be anti-establishment and anti-institutional? (The Walker Art Center is an institution, after all.)

One answer may be that the work *must* be seen in this light in order for it to conform with a particular view of new British art that predates *'Brilliant!'*, one that, as I suggested earlier, dates back to Corris' 1992 *Artforum* article. The artists and their work must be made to conform to the 'British? Young? Invisible? w/Attitude?' formula even if it means bending both out of shape in order to make them fit. In a passage in his catalogue essay in which he describes the new art as an *'arte povera* of irony and ruination' Wakefield, for instance, refers to the 'material poverty of the work of this generation [which] appears to invest it with nothing more than a sort of obdurate, dumb perversity'.[38] He clearly does not know just how much it costs to fabricate one of Hirst's large formaldehyde pieces. The high fabrication costs of these works, and the difficulty of installing them, is probably why several of them, including the largest, *The Physical Impossibility of Death in the Mind of Someone Living*, 1991, belong to Charles Saatchi, aka the advertising guru (with his brother Maurice) to the Tory Party—to the Establishment, in fact. It is actually peculiarly appropriate that so many of Hirst's major works have become part of the Saatchi Collection, not only because he was just the type of collector that Hirst had hoped to attract to *Freeze*—and who in fact *did* see the show—but also because of the impact on him of the *New York Art Now* shows at the Saatchi Gallery in 1988. Hirst himself has acknowledged this, in particular the importance of the flotation tank works by arch 80s artist, Jeff Koons.[39] However, this circumstance runs counter to the main thrust of *'Brilliant!'* which, perhaps for logistical reasons, did not include one of these pieces. Neither did it focus on Gary Hume's signature, and highly sought-after paintings, the largest and most comprehensive collection of which is also in the Saatchi Collection. Instead, visitors to the exhibition were immediately confronted with a one-off, low tech, black-and-white video piece by Hume, *Me as King Cnute*, made in 1994.

Flood's essay, 'The Levellers', whose title refers to the ultra republican 17th-century English group that was regarded as subversive even by Oliver Cromwell, who suppressed them, continues the anti-institutional, anti-establishment line. He also plays the generation game, making the, by now obligatory, reference to Gilbert and George, whose work he states unequivocally, 'immediately preceded the artists in *'Brilliant!'*'. He adds, however, that 'further back and to a lesser degree', the work of David Hockney preceded theirs, and by extension, the art in *'Brilliant!'*: 'Gilbert and George manage to suggest an apocalyptic West where the flies are buzzing around a corpse that has yet to drop'.[40] Flies? A Corpse? *Now* one sees the connection with Hirst. But where does Hockney figure in all this? 'David Hockney's world is hardly apocalyptic but its depiction of lascivious anomie is no less chilling. ... The people in Hockney's pretty sybaritic sets didn't know about the dole and disease and IRA bombs that were coming to the London of Gilbert and George, but they had long lost the power to react anyway. Their poisonous passivity was symptomatic of the future they would awkwardly age into'. So, Hockney, or his subjects, are 'symptomatic' of the future and, by extension, of the art to come? One senses a connection stretched too thinly here, even more so when

Hume's colours are described as reminiscent of 'the *gelati* hues of Hockney' and Alessandro Raho's portraits as 'an odd amalgam of Hockney and Katz'—even Flood admits this similarity is only 'superficial'. As for Hirst, he is 'the natural inheritor of Bacon' (Hockney, Gilbert and George, Bacon—is there another agenda in operation here?), 'to whose work he brings an additional horror—that of the actual as opposed to the illusionistic.'[41]

.It may seem churlish to question the premises, or assumptions, underlying an exhibition that apparently celebrated new art from London. On the other hand, the prominence, not to say the pre-eminence, given this particular show in America, or at any rate in *Artforum*, makes it imperative because of the influence they can still be said to wield both at home and abroad. For instance, David Frankel, Senior Editor of *Artforum*, recently referred to the word, *'Brilliant!'*, as the 'generation-defining title' of a show of young British artists.[42] This is to elevate the taste of one man, Richard Flood, above the level of opinion to that of historical fact, one which 'defines' a generation. That *'Brilliant!' did* reflect Flood's own taste is made clear in an interview with Brook Adams in the October 1995 issue of the magazine, in which he explained his reasons for excluding artists from the exhibition, among them Fiona Rae, Peter Doig, Jane and Louise Wilson and 'the Simon Patterson group'.[43] Of the latter he said, 'Their linguistic research is very meticulous, very Reading Room of the British Museum—its just not my personal interest'. The point here is not that no such 'Simon Patterson group' exists, but that Flood freely acknowledges that the show was selected on the basis of his own personal interests. Few would object to a show selected on those terms. Indeed, when *'Brilliant!'* was first mooted most observers, knowing of his association with the Barbara Gladstone Gallery at the time of her show of British artists in 1992, assumed that it would include the kind of work that was shown then, and in fact, seven out of the eleven artists involved *were* selected for *'Brilliant!'.*[44] It is only the claim to be representing the history of recent British art—and not just the last decade, either—that has to be questioned.

Flood's concentration on the 'London scene', to the exclusion of the rest of Britain, could be said to have provided a corrective to the tendency remarked on earlier (see above, p.3), of 'conflating the "context of England" with that of "London" and both with "Britain" '. However, his definition of what constitutes the 'London scene' appears to be entirely arbitrary as evidenced in his off-hand remark to Adams, in reference to Newcastle-born Jane and Louise Wilson, 'Don't they live in Brighton?'[45] Is a London artist one who was born in London, preferably within hearing of Bow Bells? Clearly not. Then one who studied in London or one who lives in London or both? On this basis, can Bristol-born Hirst, educated in Leeds and London and who now lives partly on his estate in the country, still be described as a London-based artist? Again, questions of definition only matter because of the historical claims made for the show, both at the time and since. Thirty years earlier, when the Walker staged *London: The New Scene*, it might have been easier to contain the work under such a rubric. This is no longer the case if, indeed, it ever was.

To their credit, Laurence Bossé and Hans-Ulrich Obrist, curators of the more recent 'Brit art' exhibition, Life/Live, at the Musée d'Art Moderne de la Ville de Paris in October 1995, exactly one year after 'Brilliant!', consciously tried to avoid the exclusive approach of that show by adopting an inclusive one. This approach risked relinquishing any pretence to coherence—indeed, that was part of their strategy to reflect the 'remarkably inventive and open professional stategies' of artists in Britain. Suzanne Pagé, in the preface to the two-volume catalogue, describes the curators' punishing itinerary which took them to Belfast, Birmingham, Edinburgh, Glasgow, Halifax, Leeds, London, Liverpool, Manchester, Newcastle, Nottingham, Nailsworth and elsewhere which they pursued in order to avoid 'the usual circuits—and customary critical assumptions—in favour of the informal web of complicity (les connivences) woven by the artists themselves'. The curators also eschewed, 'the reflexes and agendas of nationalism' in favour of 'multiculturalism', including in the exhibition artists who though British citizens, come from other countries but are based in London (why London?). Pedro Lapa, in his foreward to the Portuguese edition of the catalogue that accompanied the show when it travelled to the Centro Cultural de Belém, was even more forthright on this point, referring to nationality as a 'fallacious' and much misused criterion. Finally in defiance of frontiers, including those of age, they decided to include older artists alongside those of the younger generation.[46]

This approach suggests, though it is nowhere acknowledged, that the curators deliberately set out to plan an exhibition that would be defined in contradistinction to the agenda of 'Brilliant!'. In the run-up to the exhibition, there was a sense that things were still fluid, that additions to the line-up of artists could be made at any moment—the 'live' element of Life/Live—in imitation, perhaps, of the apparently ad hoc manner of so-called 'alternative shows'. At the same time, it suggested a certain curatorial hesitancy, as if it was the 'museum experience' that was being endorsed, rather than the art. In the end, was that experience so very different from 'Brilliant!'? The promised admixture of older artists eventually came down to the somewhat arbitrary inclusion of John Latham, David Medalla, Gustav Metzger and, of course, Gilbert and George—the 'life' element of Life/Live. In their somewhat helter-skelter catalogue essay, in which the panel containing the word 'Life', from Gilbert and George's photowork DEATH, HOPE, LIFE, FEAR, is reproduced, the curators explain the centrality of these artists to the concept of the exhibition on the grounds that all the artists included in the show 'are set on bringing art and life together, on overcoming the frontiers that separate art from the rest of the world' and thus, that Gilbert and George's sub-Beuysian notion of 'ART FOR ALL', 'has never been so pertinent.'[47]

Leaving aside the highly problematical assumption that all the artists in the show are concerned with 'bringing art and life together', what is the connection of these younger artists with Latham, Medalla and Metzger?[48] The key may be the inclusion of Richard Wentworth, represented in the Videothèque section by a video based on his on-going series of photographs of people's 'do-it-youself' solutions to everyday problems, Making do and getting by; in a conscious or unconscious echo of Wakefield's admiration for the '"fuck

BIJUTSU TECHO, VOL 5, MAY 1994, 'SPECIAL FEATURE: UP AND COMING LONDON ART SCENE', WITH PHOTOGRAPH OF GILBERT & GEORGE.

it" do-it-yourself attitude' of the artists in 'Brilliant!', Pagé refers to the 'Situationist-style do-it-yourself approach' of the artists in Life/Live.[49] It is difficult to see any connection, beyond this tenuous link through Situationism, between the different generations. However, the most tenuous of all is that between Metzger, doyen of Auto-Destructive Art who gave up all art production for a period of three years, and any of the rest of the artists, with the possible exception of John Latham. It is impossible to imagine any of the 'Brit Pack' giving up art or destroying their work—unless it was to make movies or become rock stars. It seems, however, that there is a connection after all: 'Gustav Metzger' we are told, 'collects newspaper front pages about the "mad cow" crisis. Dinos and Jake Chapman create a cruelly absurd and comic hybrid world that raises the worrying question of human mutation', and of course, now one comes to think of it, Damien Hirst cuts up cows and ...But this is patently absurd.[50]

Whether or not the curators' specifically intended to distance Life/Live from the narrow focus of 'Brilliant!', the art press reaction in Paris, what there was of it, far from abandoning the 'customary critical assumptions', responded pretty much in the same vein as before. Articles like The Art of being English, clearly indicate that the curators' wider agenda has not reached all parts. However, even in this article, some reference is made to the rest of Britain, but the fascination is specifically with the English and even more specifically (despite the fact that they are represented solely by one short video, The Ten Commandments, 1995-96) with

Gilbert and George, who are saddled with the unlikely role of 'chaperones' to the new generation of avant-garde artists.[51] 'Plus hype que les Blues, plus sexy que les Marx!' proclaimed TechniKart, hailing the 'Chapman brothers' thus: 'Their first word: "fuck". Their first film: Sammie and Rosie Get Laid. Their first job: assistants to Gilbert and George. Result: Fuck Face, a wax [sic] sculpture with a decapitated head and a nose in the form of a penis...'. The link with Gilbert and George having been made, the critic makes a quick exit, handing over to Obrist who gives us a brief 'tour' of the highlights of the show. Eric Troncy, writing in artpress, avoids the excesses of TechniKart, instead, in the space of a brief review he tackles issues of nationalism in art, comparative artistic infrastructures, education systems and funding in France and Britain while trenchantly championing those artists he admires and with whom he has collabrated in the past, either as a curator or as one of the editors of the French art magazine Documents. Gilbert and George are mentioned once, in passing.[52] Elisabeth Lebovici's review in Libération, begins with a dire warning to visitors to: 'Abandon hope all ye who enter here', but as she goes on to compare the experience of walking through the exhibition to a visit to a flea market, Dante's dread words seem somewhat inappropriate. Like Troncy, she ignores the sensational stuff altogether, concentrating instead on those artists whose work she is already familiar with and who have already shown extensively in France or, like Medalla, also have some connection with the country. Gilbert and George are not mentioned once.[53]

The curators' careful strategy of focusing on other 'scenes' than London, or of broadening the definition of 'British' was entirely lost on the critic of *Die Zeit*, who focused entirely on the London *Künstlerszene*, 'nowhere in Europe do artists live in such a densely populated colony' as in the East End of London—'the horrors of Hackney (more artists per square meter than any other locale in the Western world...'). Though his account of the 'scene' is conventional—the Goldsmiths, Saatchi, yBa story is retold—he makes none of the simplistic links with the 60s made by others, noting in particular, the critical detachment from socio-political issues that marks out the younger generation of artists from the older.[54] Perhaps because the French critics are more generally familiar with contemporary British art and were not obliged to 'buy' the package that they were being offered, or for whatever reason, there was very little coverage of the exhibition and even less serious critical attention given to it. By contrast, when *Full House: Young British Art*, featuring seventeen of the usual suspects (though *not* Gilbert and George), opened at the Kunstmuseum, Wolfsburg in Germany, in December 1996, the response was extraordinary, at least in terms of volume.[55] The excitement is palpable: 'Suddenly it is here. Powerful. Loud, vulgar, carefree, playful... aggressive and ironic, indifferent and witty: the new British art.' Even the newspaper critic of the distinguished *Frankfurter Allgemeine Zeitung* wrote, 'At last we in Germany have the opportunity to see young British art' and finds it indeed, 'Young, bold, oblique, shrill, and, above all, exciting.' Berlin's *Die Welt* joins in, 'England ist hip. Mode! Filme! Britpop!' and now, last but not least, *Kunst!* 'Die "Young British Art" (YBA) ist zum trendsetter und Exportschlager geworden (and has become a popular export)'. In general the coverage is broad rather than deep, the largest coverage was that given by *Spiegel* which profiled several of the artists—the most photogenic. Overall, most of the attention, particularly by picture editors, was focused on the 'Working-Class-Portraits' of Richard Billingham (in an interesting transposition, one newspaper referred to the latter as Richard Birmingham) and the 'Genmanipulierte Engel' and 'bizarren Freak-Show' of Jake and Dinos Chapman's *Tragic Anatomies*, 1996, guaranteed to 'shockieren das Kleinbürgermillieu', the German equivalent of 'épater la bourgeoisie'.[56]

As for the intentions of the Director, Dr. Gijs van Tuyl, and curator, Veit Görner, these must be gleaned from interviews with them and from the brief bi-lingual text of the fold-out poster that did duty for a catalogue. The absence of a catalogue for both *'Brilliant!'* and *Full House* is regrettable. It suggests a less-than-whole-hearted commitment to the individual works in the show as opposed to the larger yBa phenomenon itself. It is interesting that in an in-depth interview with the Director about his overall policy for the Museum, he spoke about his approach to temporary exhibitions and to the relative freedom that exhibitions of contemporary art, such as *Full House*, permit: 'Here we are not arguing about what is art and what is not art' since we do not know what the future will be.[57] This approach may be laudable in its openness but on the other hand, it smacks of the quasi-social Darwinist approach of the Lisson Gallery's 1993 Summer exhibition, *Wonderful Life*; why invest in artists who may not be regarded as 'important' in 10 years' time? Better just to

ARTFORUM, NOVEMBER, 1996
VOL.XXXV, NO.3, GEORGINA STARR,
VISIT TO A SMALL PLANET (BEING
BLUE) 1995, VIDEO STILL

ARTFORUM, NOVEMBER, 1996
VOL.XXXV, NO.4, FEATURING A
STILL FROM DAMIEN HIRST'S
MOVIE, HANGING AROUND, 1996,
SCREENED AT THE HAYWARD
GALLERY, LONDON AS PART OF
THE SPELLBOUND EXHIBITION

show them and wait and see what the future will bring before making any commitment.

As to the *stated* intentions of the show, according to the poster-cum-catalogue, these were to present an exhibition of contemporary British art that would 'highlight the *diversity* of artistic agendas involved, stressing that the British phenomenon is not to be grasped with the aid of familiar *stereotypes* and *clichés*' (my emphasis). Aware that it has already become part of 'a complex cultural mechanism that packages the creativity of a generation under labels such as Brit-Pop, Brit-Film, Brit-Culture and now Brit-Art, giving it media currency as if it were all one homogenous product', the curators wished instead to preserve the individuality of the participating artists by, for instance, giving them individual spaces within the museum. However, the result appeared to be somewhat at odds with this praiseworthy aim; if by 'diversity' is meant any work that is seemingly 'spontaneous' ('spontikunst'), 'hip' or 'schocking', then apparent diversity quickly becomes homogeneous. On the other hand, this seeming contradiction may be the direct result of the Director's true intention which was precisely to shock the 'Kleinbürgermillieu' out of its complacency. In an interview with a local radio station he made this clear: an exhibition of work by this 'MTV generation' would not only inform audiences, he explained, but would also 'stimulate the art scene in Germany which', he added 'is somewhat

calmer', and by implication, duller. In effect, the artists are English shock troops brought over to kick some life into contemporary German art.[58]

'"Everything is brilliant", says Gijs van Tuyl, Director of the Museum speaking to the journalists in the course of the press conference for *Full House*.'[59] The local newspaper reporter who attended goes on to explain to his readers the English usage of the new 'Modewort', 'Brilliant', but without reference to *'Brilliant!'*, the exhibition. However, it is clear both from the artists selected and from the rhetoric surrounding it, that *Full House* owed much to the earlier show. As if to complete the circle, the artists singled out for the most attention by the press in Germany, Jake and Dinos Chapman and Richard Billingham—who was also the sensation of *Life/Live*—became simultaneously the focus of attention in America. In the case of the Chapman brothers, as the likely successors to Damien Hirst at the Gagosian Gallery, New York; in the case of Richard Billingham, as the latest artist based in Britain whose work has been featured on the cover of *Artforum*. In 1996/7, for an unprecedented three successive issues, the covers carried work by artists from Britain: in November it was a video still from Georgina Starr's *Visit to a Small Planet (Being Blue)* of 1995; in December, a detail of a still from Hirst's 'movielet', *Hanging Around*, of 1996, featured as part of a composite cover and in January 1997, it was an untitled photograph from 1995 by Richard Billingham.[60] If *Artforum*

ARTFORUM, JANUARY 1997

VOL.XXXV, NO.5, RICHARD

BILLINGHAM *UNTITLED*, 1995

can be said to be a major indicator of artistic trends, then the message could not be clearer: 'buy British!'

A reading of the respective articles in the magazine that refer to the artists featured on the covers confirms that the same critical framework, originally established by Corris, is still in place. David Frankel, for instance, writing about Starr, recites a litany of Englishness reminiscent of Corris' list of the damned and the blessed: 'In the shabby England of the 50s and much of the 60s, World War II did not seem so far away. Even as Swinging London, when it came was said to be thrilling the youth, people too old for it (they weren't so old really) had vivid memories of food rationing; and there was a social conspiracy to make impoverishment look not just tolerable, but jolly. These were the glory days of Butlins holiday camps, Wimpy beefburgers, and Bird's powdered custard. For me that era is necessarily evoked by a caravan, the kind of car-towed, rounded, box-like vacation home-on-wheels that Georgina Starr made the centrepiece of her Spring show at Barbara Gladstone in New York'.[61] The crucial words are 'for me'. The gap between the preoccupations of an artist of Starr's generation (the caravan is only one element of the work) and that of the writer cannot be so easily bridged. That was then and this is now.

In the case of Billingham the writer, novelist Jim Lewis, and the magazine's editors may or may not share a similar agenda. In *No place like home*, Lewis writes of his first experience of the artist's collection of photographs, entitled, *Ray's a Laugh*, in positively epiphanic terms: 'Once every year or two—and lately less frequently than that—I receive a sort of visitation of art, a visual experience unlike any other'. The attraction is partly perhaps the characters: the artist's parents, the eponymous and alcholic 'Ray' and his 'behemoth' of a mother (not named), a brother, a dog and a cat, all of whom live in 'an apartment in a lower-middle-class British housing project' (translated, this would probably read, 'a working-class English council flat') plus 'a few extras'. He likens it to a play but maybe he is thinking of a novel? The film has already been made; it is called *Trainspotting*. The analogy with the film was made in a stinging letter from a British correspondent who accuses both the writer and the artist of slumming: 'In the 60s it was essential to your cred as a British artist/rock star/novelist to cite your proletarian roots. As there are no miners/dockers/steel workers left in the resuscitated Swinging England, where do you turn to prove you're not middle class?' Billingham's success is therefore no surprise because, '... dirty realism and domesticity are oh-so-hip in the UK right now'.[63] How much more hip in the US where there is an extra frisson in witnessing the Brits exposed, putting paid 'to the myth of British decorum'?

In between these two issues was the December *Artforum*, featuring Hirst on the cover and in which invited commentators were asked to list the best and worst exhibitions of 1996. Hirst is cited four times, more than any other artist, as representing the worst, though twice as part of a group show (*Spellbound*) and the other two times for his

sell-out solo show at Gagosian. Of them all, Benjamin Buchloh's citation is the most interesting: 'It's hilarious to see ... the cultural institutions of the old nation-states desperately attempt to reclaim a share of Eurocentric cultural hegemony by bestowing their prestigious honors (such as the Tate Gallery's *Turner Prize*) on the dross of an internationalized culture industry. This year's recipient, Damien Hirst, and his riffs on the old adage of antiart from Picabia to Pop, even managed to convince David Bowie that now is the time to abandon the rock industry and contribute as an *artist* to the greater glory of the British'.[64] It seems unfair to lay the blame on Hirst for Bowie's forays into art, however, as to the first part of Buchloh's outburst, it would be interesting to turn it round: 'It's hilarious to see the cultural institutions of the United States desperately attempt to reclaim a share of the New York-centred cultural hegemony by bestowing their most prestigious honors (such as the Guggenheim's *Hugo Boss Prize*) on the dross of an internationalised culture industry...'. It seems to read just as well, or as badly, this way round.

Hirst's crime seems to be his uppitiness. Behind Buchloh's apparent anger lurks perhaps a sense of grievance similar to that which runs through Serge Guilbaut's seminal book, *How America Stole the Idea of Modern Art*, which was, of course, written from an unashamedly European perspective. Substitute the word 'contemporary' for 'modern', and the question then arises, is Europe, in particular, Britain, stealing it back? Elsewhere in the same issue, Jan Avgikos, a contributing editor to *Artforum*, provides confirmation that at least in New York, there is a fear that the centre has shifted:

'Consensus has it that the New York art world has skidded into [the] doldrums. The ubiquity of cultivated listlessness suggests that reaction against the critical strategies of 80s-style postmodern art continues to influence the market's myopic preference for low-wattage work enamoured of its own ineffectuality.'[65] This analysis is in marked contrast to the perceived energy, streetwise confidence, media savviness and all-round 'can do' approach of the Brits which is positively, well, *American*! But let one of them break away from the pack, like Hirst, and it is time to slap him down.

Is the critical drubbing that Hirst received for his first major one-person show in New York a sign of the 'backlash' that I referred to before? If so, how widespread is it? Catherine David, curator of Documenta X, is, at the time of writing, still playing her cards very close to her chest, but one thing that has emerged is that the British presence in Kassel will be minimal. Perhaps this is an instance of 'reculer pour mieux sauter', a period of reappraisal. Now that the new British art phenomenon appears no longer to be a flash in the pan, a 60s-style bubble, it seems that the period of indulgence is over and it is time to take it seriously. It is time to take it seriously in Britain, too. Though we have begun to take responsibility for the critical discourse about contemporary art in Britain our institutions, our public museums and galleries, have barely begun to take stock of the last decade. The Hayward Gallery's *Material Culture*, co-curated by Michael Archer and Greg Hilty, is the first exhibition to attempt this, but once again, there is no accompanying catalogue.[66] Once again, an opportunity to suggest more subtle and more rigorous critical and historical approaches to the *real* diversity of recent contemporary art in Britain has been lost. It is more than time that our institutions caught up. Much as we may enjoy the trip, we should not have to travel to Brussels, Minneapolis, Paris, Lisbon, Wolfsburg and now Sydney, to see ourselves as *others* see us.

Meanwhile, the Brit art, Brit pop, Brit film bandwagon rolls on regardless. In 1966 *Time* magazine designated London the 'Swinging City'. Thirty years on, *Vogue*, *Newsweek* and, most recently, *Vanity Fair*, have discovered that 'London swings again!'. The cover of *Vanity Fair* featured Patsy and Liam, draped in the Union Jack, 'the reigning couple of swinging 90s London', the John and Yoko of the 90s while a twenty-five page special pull-out section covered the London music, architecture, food and fashion 'scene'. (The fashion section ran a colour feature on the 'blueblood beauties', four aristocratic models got up in joke shop Horse Guards' busbies... If there is one thing more hip than the so-called working-classes, it seems, it is aristocrats letting their hair down.) In the art section, Damien Hirst is photographed with actor, Keith Allen, who not only appeared in *Hanging Around* but, like Bowie, has 'assisted' in the making of one or more of the 'spin' paintings and Alex James, bass guitarist with Blur, for whom Hirst made a pop video. Ironically, the most obvious analogy here is not with 'swinging London' of the 60s but with Warhol's factory days in New York.

My grateful thanks to Hymie Dunn of The British Council for her kind assistance in providing me with press material, and to Andrew Wilson, critic, curator, and Assistant Editor of *Art Monthly*, for casting his eye over my text.

Patricia Bickers is a London-based critic and art historian, editor of *Art Monthly* and teaches art history and theory at the University of Westminster.

NOTES

1.   Marcia E. Vetrocq, 'The Birthday Biennale: Coming Home to Europe', *Art in America*, Vol.83, No.9, September 1995, pp.72-81 and p.120.

2.   *'Brilliant!' New Art from London*, is at the Walker Art Center, Minneapolis, October 22 - January 7, 1996

3.   The Kunstverein Hannover, the Nordic Arts Centre, Helsinki and the Museum of Contemporary Art, Chicago.

4.   *ARTnews*, Vol.93, No.7, September 1994, Jeff Kastner, 'A New Powerhouse', pp.146-153; the cover carried the legend: 'Britain's feisty new avant-garde'.

Special issues: *Paletten*, No.219, April, 1994: Cover: Hadrian Pigott, *Gender Soaps*, 1994 (the texts, however, are mostly by British-based writers including Liam Gillick, Andrew Wilson); 'Special Number on Young British Art'; *Bijutsu Techo*, Vol 5, May 1994, 'Special Feature: Up and Coming London Art Scene', cover photograph of Gilbert & George; *Technikart*, No.17, March-April 1995; cover headlines: 'Gilbert & George, Gavin Turk, Angus Fairhurst, Georgina Starr, the playlist of the new generation' and 'the A to Z of artistic London' and headline: 'London: Capital of what?' Cover photograph of Gilbert & George.

5.   *The Art Newspaper*, No 50, July - August 1995, p.2

6.   Later that year she was included with 10 other artists from Britain in a show curated by British collector, Clarissa Dalrymple, at the Barbara Gladstone and Stein Gladstone Gallery, New York; the other artists were: Lea Andrews, Keith Coventry, Damien Hirst, Gary Hume, Abigail Lane, Sarah Lucas, Stephen Pippin, Marc Quinn, Marcus Taylor and Rachel Whiteread.

Liam Gillick's contribution was a photobook that was an

independent work rather than a catalogue.

7. *Technique Anglaise: Current Trends in British Art*, edited by Andrew Renton and Liam Gillick, Thames & Hudson, 1991; the remark cited was made by Andrew Renton in the 'Discussion', p.37.

8. Michael Corris, 'British? Young? Invisible? w/Attitude?' *Artforum*, Vol. xxx, No. 9, May 1992, pp.106-110, p.106.

9. 'Critical Decor' is the name adopted by David Pugh and Toby Morgan who have collaborated since 1990. Rachel Evans' *All things nice*, 1988, is a self-portrait in and 'iced' dress. Anya Gallaccio's *Tense*, 1990, one ton late Valencia oranges, was shown in the 'East Country Yard Show' at the South Dock, Plough Way, London, May 31 - June 22, 1990. Both Gallaccio and Evans were selected by Andrew Renton for '*The Times* London's Young Artists', at Art London '91, Olympia, April 18 - 21, 1991. '*Hope* is an acronym formed by the union of the first two letters of the surnames of Georgie Hopton and Simon Periton, who began to collaborate in 1988 when both were students at St Martin's School of Art, London', ibid., p.110.

A more structured version of this kind of index of the zeitgeist can be found in the catalogue for *General Release*, which has an appendix containing an art and social chronology for the years 1990-95.

Since the time of writing, the surviving members of the so-called 'Guildford 4' and the 'Birmingham 6' have been released.

10. Corris, op.cit., p.107.

11. ibid., p.106, and n[1].

12. It does seem a particular trope of discourse about 20th-century British art to trace its development and history in terms of generations. I discuss this phenomenon in more detail in, 'Grande-Bretagne: vitalité oblige, La sculpture britannique: générations et tradition' ('Generations of British Sculpture: the British Sculpture Tradition'), *artpress*, Eng/Fr edition, No.202, May, 1995, pp.30-39.

13. Quoted from the black and white fold-out catalogue-cum-press release published to coincide with the show; unpaginated. The artists included were: Lucia Nogueira, Espace Artère Sud; Jordan Baseman; Glenn Brown; Amikam Toren; Dean Whatmuff, Galerie Guy Ledune; Perry Roberts; Tessa Robins, Galerie Etienne Tilman; Dominic Denis; Anya Gallaccio; Simon Patterson, Galerie Rodolphe Janssen; John Blakemore, Hannah Collins, Annette Heyer, Espace Photographique Contretype; Jem Southam, Centre d'Art Contemporain.

14. The names of the artists who took part in *Freeze*, which was held at the PLA Building, Security Gate 16, Plough Way, Docklands, London SE16, between August 6 and September 12 (the dates on the official invitation) are, in alphabetical order: Steven Adamson, Angela Bulloch, Mat Collishaw, Ian Davenport, Angus Fairhurst, Anya Gallaccio, Damien Hirst, Gary Hume, Michael Landy, Abigail Lane, Sarah Lucas, Lala Meredith-Vulja, Stephen Park, Richard Patterson, Simon Patterson and Fiona Rae. Strictly speaking, there were three *Freeze* exhibitions, each with different groupings of the artists listed above. *Freeze Part III*' took place during an extension of the original exhibition period.

15. The building was not, as is often assumed, a warehouse; it was an empty administrative block that belonged to the Port of London Authority (PLA); cf., 'Capitalising on the evacuated hopes of a decade, *Freeze* and subsequent warehouse shows, in the spirit of McLaren, détourned otherwise useless space left stranded by the collapse of the property market.' Neville Wakefield, 'Pretty vacancy', in the catalogue for '*Brilliant!*' *New Art from London*, 1996 pp.9-12, p.11.

The keynote exhibition of the British Season was a rather sedate affair, attended by HRH Prince Charles, entitled: *Viewpoint: l'Art Contemporain en Grande Bretagne*, 18.12.18 - 31.1.88 and including, for example, three of the 'Lisson Gallery Sculptors': Edward Allington, Richard Deacon and Anish Kapoor, as well as Antony Gormley, Ian Hamilton Finlay, David Nash and Alison Wilding, among others. Among the painters were Ian McKeever and Christopher Le Brun, David Tremlett and Boyd Webb also took part. A full list of the participating artists is included in the catalogue, *Viewpoint: l'Art*

Contemporain en Grande Bretagne, 18.12.18 - 31.1.88, Musées Royaux des Beaux-Arts de Belgique and the British Council, 1988.

16.   *Art & Culture* November 1992, pp.7-21. The magazine is now defunct. Though described recently by Matthew Collings as 'an icon of Nineties art' (Matthew Collings, 'A Guide to Invisible London', *The Independent on Sunday*, September 25, pp.32-33, p.33.), before being shown in Brussels it had previously been seen only in the exhibition, *Doubletake: Collective Memory and Current Art*, at the Hayward Gallery, February 20 - April 20, 1992 and in, *Etats Spécifiques*, curated by Françoise Cohen, at Le Musée des Beaux-Arts André Malraux Le Havre, June 4 - August 23, 1992; the artists taking part were: Henry Bond and Liam Gillick, Angela Bulloch, Angus Fairhurst, Gary Hume, Abigail Lane, Simon Patterson, Caroline Russell, Gladstone Thompson, Gillian Wearing and Craig Wood.

17.   Claude Laurent writes of, 'l'émergence depuis 1988 d'une jeune génération et de la situation particulièrement dynamique à Londres.' ibid., p.7.

18.   Actually, 'Greenwille Davy'! *Art & Culture*, ibid., p.7-8.

19.   A person 'with attitude' is defined as one who, '... se positioner en stratége attentif sur le terrain miné du marché..., s'auto-gérer en manifestations parallèles et débats d'idées..., nourir une oeuvre plastico-poétique d'un fort contenu politico-social..., defier le sens caché WITH ATTITUDE, ...élire l'emblématique pour enseigner'. ibid., p.11.

20.   Corris, Op.cit, p.110. Anya Gallaccio, for instance, showed *Lead Floor*, 1989 at the Anderson O'Day Gallery and *Preserve (Beauty)*, 1991, at Karsten Schubert.

Strange Developments—Ten British and American Artists was at the Anthony d'Offay Gallery from September 10-October 16 1992.

In an interview with Francesco Bonami in Flash Art, *published at the time of his show at the Gagosian Gallery in New York, Hirst said, 'When I was a student I had an ambition: I wanted to show at Anthony d'Offay. I never thought beyond that.''Damien Hirst: The exploded View of the Artist', Flash Art,*

Summer 1996, Vol.xxix No.189, pp.112-116, p.112.

Since the time of writing, The Anderson O'Day Gallery and, more recently, the Karsten Schubert Galleries have closed, the latter at the time of Rachel Whiteread's 'defection' to the Anthony d'Offay Gallery. Karsten Schubert, however, continues to trade.

21.   (See n⁴ above for issue reference) *Technikart*, eg., pp.20, 24, 33.

22.   An entire *Communiqué* could usefully be devoted to an analysis of the reasons for the appropriation of Gilbert and George by a whole wave of artists, curators, critics and editors.

23.   *Technikart*, pp.29 and 33-4.

24.   ibid, p.20.

25.   Jon Savage, 'Vital Signs: Gillian Wearing's Talking Pictures', *Artforum*, Vol .xxxii, No. 7, March 1994, pp.60-63. He wrote a similar article for the September-October issue of *frieze*, No.24, pp.36-7.

26.   'Theoretically, the relationships between class race and gender must be made visible, as these ultimately determine how the important questions of "membership" within a newly imagined avant garde are settled', Corris, op.cit., p.106, n¹·

27.   *The Art Newspaper*, No 50, July-August 1995, p.2.

28.   The quotation is from, Neville Wakefield 'Sarah Lucas', review, *Artforum*, May 1995 Vol. xxxiii, No. 9.

Since the time of writing it is interesting to quote from an article in the October 1995 issue of Artforum, *'Inevitably, some of the more raucous sexual and scatalogical content that characterise the new British art will be toned down for the American museum. So the Walker won't be featuring Damien Hirst's new sculpture of "two cows fucking" (for that one will have to visit the Gagosian Gallery, New York next Spring), and there won't be any multiple erections or dismembered limbs from Jake and Dinos Chapman, who are showing* Überman *[sic], a phantasmagorical vision of physicist Stephen Hawking...', Brook Adams, 'Brit Parade',* Artforum, *October 1995, Vol. xxxiv, No 2, pp.34-35, p.35.*

In fact, the 'two cows fucking' were not included in Hirst's show at the Gagosian Gallery, either.

29. *Walker News*, No. 72, May 19, 1995.

The artists included are: Henry Bond, Glenn Brown, Jake and Dinos Chapman, Adam Chodzko, Mat Collishaw, Tracy Emin, Angus Fairhurst, Anya Gallaccio, Damien Hirst, Liam Gillick, Gary Hume, Michael Landy ('who will be installing *Scrapheap Services* at a new location in the Soap Factory, a raw warehouse space on the banks of the Mississippi; the installation will be, "A fictional waste disposal company, which recycles people instead of cardboard"'). Abigail Lane, Sarah Lucas, Chris Ofili, Stephen Pippin, Alessandro Raho, Georgina Starr, Sam Taylor-Wood, Gillian Wearing, Rachel Whiteread.

Since the time of writing, Landy's work, Scrapheap Services, *has been sold to the Tate Gallery, no doubt in anticipation of the opening of the Bankside site.*

30. *House* was begun August 2 1993, completed October 25, demolished January 11, 1994. Now carefully documented in *Rachel Whiteread: House*, ed., James Lingwood, Phaidon 1995, which includes an appendix containing a list of the press coverage, pp.140-143.

It is interesting, perhaps, given Miren Jaio's comments on *Minky Manky* and the new art's relations with the press (see n32 below), to note in passing that none of the popular tabloids actually covered the story at all, not the *Daily Star, The Sun*, or the *Daily Mirror*. On the contrary, it was the respectable broadsheets such as the *Daily Telegraph, The Times*, the *Guardian* and *The Independent*—even the *Tatler*—which devoted considerable space to it.

31. *Minky Manky* was at the South London Art Gallery, April 12 - May 14, 1995. The quotation is from the introduction by David Thorp, Director of the Gallery.

32. Miren Jaio, *Minky Manky, Lapiz*, Vol. xii, No.114, 1995, pp.58-61.

'Back to Basics' was the portmanteau term used by the Tory Government for its moral campaign to promote 'family values'. The campaign backfired badly and unleashed a torrent of 'sleaze' stories in the Press involving Conservative politicians.

33. The Megan Tresidder Interview, the *Guardian*, Saturday, October 7, 1995.

34. Allan Schwartzman, 'Laguna lacuna', *Artforum* Vol .xxxiv, No. 1, September, 1995, pp.33-9, and p.106, p.106.

35. Neville Wakefield, 'Pretty vacant' in the 'Exhibition book' or catalogue for *'Brilliant!'*, pp.9-12, p.11.

36. ibid.

37. See in particular this passage:'Somewhere between these parallel legacies of the 1960s—the aesthetics of Pop and the provocational strategies of Situationism relearned through punk—lie the general impulses of recent British artists' p10.

It is odd, given the constant invocation of the pop/punk connection that Gavin Turk's piece, *Pop*, 1993, his self-portrait as Sid Vicious in the pose of Elvis after Warhol, was not included in the show.

The remark about the preferred mode of transportation occurs on p.11.

38. ibid., p.11.

39. See the interview with Andrew Wilson, 'Out of control' *Art Monthly* June 1994, No.177, pp.1-9, p.9. In the *Flash Art* interview with Bonami, cited earlier (see n20), Hirst again re-iterates his admiration for Jeff Koons:'When I look at what he [Koons] did, he gave up his own idea of himself for art, which is why he is fantastic, he went the whole way...', p.116

40. Richard Flood,'The Levellers','*Brilliant!...*', p.51

41. ibid., p.52. This is not the first time that comparisons between Bacon and Hirst have been made, however.

42. The full quote reads,'...bet she saw it and said to herself,'*Brilliant!*'—assuming she's not already trying to escape that word, the generation-defining title of the show devoted to young British artists [...] curated by Richard Flood at Minneapolis' Walker Art Center last year'. David Frankel, in

an article on Georgina Starr, 'Now you see it Now you don't', *Artforum* November 1996, Vol. xxxv, No. 3., p.72.

43.   Brook Adams, 'Brit Parade', *Artforum*, (see n[28] above) p.35.

44.   See n[6] above.

45.   see n[43] above, p.35.

46.   Musée d'Art Moderne de la Ville de Paris, October 5, 1996 - January 5, 1997. The artists represented were: Richard Billingham, Christine Borland, Angela Bulloch, Jake and Dinos Chapman, Mat Collishaw, Douglas Gordon, Mona Hatoum, Bethan Huws, John Latham, Siobhan Liddell, Steve McQueen, David Medalla, Gustav Metzger, Sam Taylor-Wood, Gillian Wearing, Cerith Wyn Evans, Leigh Bowery (posthumously), Damien Hirst, Gilbert and George, Liam Gillick, Sarah Lucas, Hilary Lloyd, Christina Mackie, Steven Pippin and Richard Wentworh. The artist-run spaces represented were: Bank, Cairn Gallery, City Racing, Cubitt Gallery, Imprint 93, Independent Art Space, Locus+ and Transmission. The magazines: *Art Monthly, Artifice, Blow, Circa, Coil, Control Magazine, Dazed and Confused, Donald Parsnip's Daily Journal, Engaged, everything, frieze, Inventory, London Psychogeographical Association, Mute, Re-action, Third text, Transcript, Untitled, Variant, Words and Pictures.* Other, unlisted, artists were included in the sub-exhibitions in the artist-run spaces.

        The preface to the two-volume catalogue by Suzanne Pagé is on pp.6-9 (English translation, pp.8-9; the quotation is from p.8.

        Pedro Lapa's (bi-lingual) foreword in, *Live/Live* catalogue, pp.6-9, English text, pp.8-9, p.9.

47.   *Live/Live*, bi-lingual essay by Laurence Bossé and Hans-Ulrich Obrist in the catalogue for the *Live/Live* catalogue, pp.8-15, English text, pp.13-15, p.15.

48.   Concerning the claim that, 'all the artists in the show are concerned with bringing art and life together', in his article on *Live/Live*, Andrew Wilson pointed out 'As Gilbert and George presciently recognised, to remake life you have to make something artificial. Art cannot be life, however much you set yourself at the heart of the work.' Andrew Wilson, 'Life v Art', *Art Monthly*, November 1996, No.301, pp.1-4, p.4.

49.   Pagé, op.cit., p.8; Wakefield 'Pretty Vacant', p.8.

50.   Bossé/Obrist, op.cit., p.14.

51.   '... l'on découvre que la jeune garde des créateurs Britanniques, chaperonnée par le couple Gilbert et Georges', Laurent Goumarre, 'L'art d'être Anglais' *ex aequo*, December 1996. I am aware that the French do not always distinguish between 'Anglais' and 'Britanniques'; I have discussed this elsewhere, Patricia Bickers, 'Crème anglaise: Un Siècle de Sculpture anglaise', at the Jeu de Paume review, *Art Monthly*, No. 199, pp.3-11, September, 1996, pp3-5.

        Denis Angus, 'La Crème Anglaise', *Techniart*, No.6, 1996, pp.42-45, p.42.

52   Namely, Angela Bulloch, Liam Gillick, Douglas Gordon and Gillian Wearing. Eric Troncy, review, *artpress*, December, 1996, No.219

53.   Namely, Angela Bulloch, Liam Gillick, Christine Borland, Mona Hatoum, Steve McQueen and David Medalla, who formerly lived in France. Elisabeth Lebovici, 'Grand déballage d'art britannique', *Libération*, October 10, 1996, p.30-31, p.30.

54.   Re: The East End, Hanno Rauterberg, 'Spontikunst im Einweckglas', :'Nirgends in Europa leben Künstler in dichter besiedelten Kolonien—'. The observation concerning the crtical detachment of the contemporary British artist is made in reference to Mat Collishaw, 'Die Kritik soll beiläufig sein, hingetaupft, ohne vorwurf an irgendwen; kein Künstler der Pariser Ausstellung zeigt die Zunge, reckt den zeigefinger oder ballt die faust. Die Gesellschaftkritik bleibt skizze. *Die Zeit* No.43, October, 18, 1996.

55.   *Full House Young British Art* at the Kunstmuseum, Wolfsburg, December 1996 - March 31, 1997; the publication is unpaginated. The artists included were: Richard Billingham, Christine Borland, Angela Bulloch, Jake and Dinos Chapman, Mat Collishaw, Tracy Emin, Angus Fairhurst, Douglas Gordon, Gary Hume, Abigail Lane, Sarah Lucas, Steve McQueen, Steven

Pippin, Georgina Starr, Gillian Wearing, Jane and Louise Wilson and Sam Taylor-Wood

56.   'Suddenly it is here...', in German the text in full is as follows: 'Plötzlich ist sie da. Voll power. Laut, ordinär, unbekümmert verspielt im Sound schräger strassenkatzen-poesie, aggressiv und ironisch, witzig und wurstig: die neue britische kunst.' Martin Jasper, *Braunschweiger Zeitung*, December 14, 1996.

Noemi Smolik *Frankfurter Allgemeine Zeitung*, January 1, 1997: 'Sie is jung, frech, schräg und schrill, und, vor allem, sie ist aufregend.'.

Kerstin Rottman, 'Full House, Happy House', *Die Welt*, January 2, 1997.

'Young British Artists: Der erfölg der jungen englischen Pop-Avantgarde', *Spiegel Extra*, December, 1996 pp.6-12.

The reference to Richard Billingham's 'Working-Class-portraits' is from, Alexander Haase, *Subway*, January 1997.

'Richard Birmingham' appears in the *Wolfsburger Nachrichten*, December 24, 1996.

'Genmanipulierte Engel' is found in several sources; 'bizarren Freak-Show' is quoted from Holger Liebs, 'Wir sind Schaulustige', interview with Jake and Dinos Chapman, die *Tageszeitung* December 17, 1996.

57.   On the Museum's policy, 'Joachim Kreiborn im Gespräch mit Gijs van Tuyl', *artist - Kunstmagazin*, December 1996.

The recorded interview with Dr. Gijs van Tuyl was reported in the *Wolfsburgur Rundblick am Sonntag*, December 15, 1996. The same remarks were repeated in Klaus Zimmer, 'Voll subjektiver Poesie und unbekämmerter Spontaneität', *Cellesche Zeitung*, December 28, 1997.

58.   Han Karweik, 'Ein Steitgespräch wert', *Wolfsburger Nachrichten*, December 14, 1996.

60.   The covers are, respectively: *Artforum*, November, 1996, Vol. .xxxv, No. 3, Georgina Starr, *Visit to a Small Planet (Being Blue)* 1995, video still; *Artforum*, December 1996 Vol.xxxv, No.4, featuring a still from Damien Hirst's movie, *Hanging Around*, 1996, screened at the Hayward Gallery, London as part of the *Spellbound* exhibition; *Artforum*, January 1997 Vol. .xxxv, No 5, Richard Billingham *Untitled*, 1995, photograph.

61.   David Frankel, 'Now you see it Now you don't', *Artforum*, November 1996, (see n[60]) pp.70-73 and 111, p.71.

For Corris, see n[8] above.

62.   Jim Lewis, 'No Place Like Home' *Artforum*, January 1997, Vol. .xxv, No.5, pp.62-67, p.62.

63.   Chris Townsend, 'Class Act', Letters, *Artforum*, March 1997, Vol. .xxxv, No.7, p.6.

64.   Benjamin Buchloh, 'Dishonourable Mention', *Artforum*, December 1996, (see n[60]) p.89.

65.   Jan Avgikos, 'Tolle house', ibid., p.104.

66.   *Material Culture: The Object in British Art in the 1980s and 1990s*, Hayward Gallery, London, April 3 - May 18. There is a *User's Guide*, with a short introduction by the curators, to accompany the exhibition.

Art Monthly has attempted to redress the balance by publishing two in-depth articles on the show: Andrew Wilson's 'Object Lessons', and Mark Harris' 'Immaterial Culture', *Art Monthly*, May 1997, No.206, pp.1-5 and 6-10, respectively.

These two articles are the latest in a series of articles that *Art Monthly* has published, following the publication of my original version of *The Brit Pack: Contemporary British Art, the view from abroad*, published in October 1995, that deal with the critical issues raised by new art from Britain; they include: Andrew Wilson, 'The Art Experience', *Art Monthly*, October, 1995, No.190, pp.3-6; Mark Harris, 'Putting on the Style', *Art Monthly*, February, 1996, No.193, pp.3-6; Simon Ford, 'Myth Making' and Michael Archer, 'No Politics Please, We're British?' *Art Monthly*, March, 1996, No.194, pp.3-9 and pp.11-14, respectively. In addition, the interview with Damien Hirst (see n[39] above) and Patricia Bickers, 'Meltdown: Anya Gallaccio interviewed', *Art Monthly*, April 1996, No.195, pp.3-8.

FROM THE TOP OF SLIEVE DONARD...

STEPHEN SNODDY

PAUL SEAWRIGHT *SECTARIAN MURDER SERIES SATURDAY 3RD FEBRUARY 1973* 'GUNMEN USING A STOLEN CAR SHOT DOWN FIVE YOUNG BOYS WHO ARE STANDING OUTSIDE THE GLEN CHIP SHOP ON THE OLDPARK ROAD. A SUSTAINED BURST OF GUNFIRE WOUNDED FOUR OF THE YOUTHS AND KILLED THE FIFTH.' COURTESY OF THE ARTIST

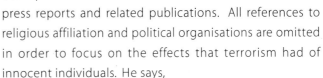

From the top of Slieve Donard, the highest peak in Northern Ireland, you can see the hinterland of Ulster, a tapestry of different shades of green, and far below the metallic glint of the Irish Sea refracts the grey-black clouds that scud in from the west. The land is so beautiful it almost seems worth all the murdering. Halfway up the mountain, below the ridge running between Slieve Donard and Slieve Commedagh, Gerry, a young Catholic with bright blue eyes, fair skin and a *Berghaus* anorak (bought at Nutt's Corner market) considered the Framework Document for peace and shook his head, 'The Unionists should talk. It's a peace document. The peace is a precious thing. But the Unionist leaders aren't interested.'

At the base of the mountain, Billy (Protestant) and his dog, a black retriever (also Protestant!) were uneasy about the possibility of being consumed into the south of Ireland, i.e. the Republic of Ireland, or Eire. He said 'Let the people decide. You shouldn't say 'No' automatically. Ian Paisley is not a good advertisement for Unionism. Talking is better than killing.'

A few yards from the summit were Victoria, a Protestant, and her boyfriend whose religion was obviously irrelevant as he was English. She pointed out, to the south, Carlingford Lough, and the Free State beyond, 'They say that, on a good day, you can see the priests fornicate with the nuns'. She smiled, signalling a joke—one can never be entirely sure in Northern Ireland. 'I wish, just once, that the Unionist politicians would say Yes.'

The Belfast-born artist Paul Seawright's *Sectarian Murder* consists of a series of photographs of places where political murders have been committed. Each is accompanied with the date on which the event occurred, and a description of the event taken from press reports and related publications. All references to religious affiliation and political organisations are omitted in order to focus on the effects that terrorism had of innocent individuals. He says,

Northern Ireland remains part of the United Kingdom, yet however similar it is in culture and ideology to Britain, it is alienated because of stark religious and political divides. These divisions have fed terrorist conflict and are manifest in the deaths of civilians from all communities. It is common for these deaths to be perceived as political by countries throughout Europe and North America. The reporting of events has led to the tacit acceptance of murder in Northern Ireland, the truth obscured by almost impenetrable political verbalisation. Real people are buried beneath the myth of armed conflict and historical attempts at justification.

This work seeks to show only a handful of victims who have no direct engagement with indigenous politics, their deaths purely sectarian but often excused as political; religious murders have become commonplace, but are given little constructive publicity by the world's media. My aim is to redress the unbalanced representation of the victim, portraying the brutality of

This is an abridged, amended and updated text based on the author's essay, 'Yes & ... No...', which appears in the Tate Gallery *Richard Hamilton* Retrospective catalogue, London, Tate Gallery Publications, 1992, pp.49-58.

RICHARD HAMILTON

FINN MACCOOL - WORKING DRAWING 1983

GOUACHE AND RETOUCHING INKS ON PHOTOGRAPH

COURTESY OF THE ARTIST

indiscriminate murder committed in the name of loyalism or nationalism. These photographs challenge the synoptic imagery that surrounds Northern Ireland, and lend a voice to the many individuals whose identity has become statistical.

The Northern Irish problem is as much a social and humanitarian issue as it is political; people must undergo a cultural and moral change, combating their ability to accept permanent division and excessive violence, before any (peace) agreement can hope to function.

What one must ask is the meaning of the opening dialogue. It seems to represent the complexity of the situation of 'the Troubles', but also to remind the reader that Northern Ireland is not some distant 'foreign' place but part of the United Kingdom. Richard Hamilton recognises these difficulties and addresses them in *The citizen*, *The subject* and *The state*. Terrorism does not just happen in Northern Ireland, and the bombs that went off at the Old Bailey and Great Scotland Yard on 8 March 1973, as one headline puts it, were to mark the 'shattering day that brought the Ulster troubles home'. The newspaper headlines: 'Suspect car closes M25 ... Mortar attack on Number 10 ... Mother's day bombing in Warrington ... suspect parcel in underground ...'[1]

For most of Hamilton's working life he has been working with images that have been sourced from the mass media, and his trio of paintings on the conflict in Northern Ireland reflects these concerns. Between 1949 and 1981, events both in Richard Hamilton's personal life and in Ireland itself had developed so as to give his interest in Irish

themes a more disturbing emphasis. It is for this reason that a particular character in James Joyce's *Ulysses* whom Hamilton had represented in 1949 now takes on a special significance.

The subject of Hamilton's *Finn MacCool - first study* (1949) is a semi-legendary figure, an Irish poet and Chieftain leader of the *Fianna*, the warrior-force from which the Fenian Society (Irish Republic Brotherhood) took their name. Organised in 1858 by James Stephens, the IRB was committed to the achievement of Irish independence through terrorist tactics and violent revolution, rather than through parliamentary or constitutional reform.

Hamilton returned to the subject of Finn MacCool in 1982, and the source of *Finn MacCool - working drawing* (1983) 'became identified, in my renewed consideration of the mythic character, with a photograph of a nationalist detainee, Raymond Pius McCartney, on hunger strike in the Maze prison in Northern Ireland'.[2] Hamilton also spoke of the 'dirty' protest when in conversation with Richard Cork: '... it's a question of jumping in when a chance offers itself, when the image itself is so compelling. You can't go out and find it.'[3]

Yet, however detached Hamilton appears to be from the realities of Northern Ireland, he makes clear his position as a viewer of 'the Troubles' in *A Celluar Maze*:

Being with Rita Donagh keeps me close to the Troubles. She was born of Irish parents in the Industrial Midlands of England. I was born in

KING WILLIAM III, GABLE END

ROCKLAND STREET WALLPAINTING,

BELFAST c1979

PHOTO: BELINDA LOFTUS

London. Our home is now in an ideal English country landscape. To be haunted by Ireland's problems may seem a little artificial. But our experience is not a rare condition: most British people feel Ireland's difficulties as a constant intrusion.

Hamilton has stated his own abhorrence of the IRA's campaign of terror, but at the same time he acknowledges the human sacrifice of the hunger strikers in the extremity of suffering they inflicted upon themselves for their principles. This dichotomy of feeling—a respect for the dignity of the protest, counterbalanced by horror at the terrible crimes committed—is a potent element in the meaning of *The citizen*. Hamilton and Donagh use the media, factually and emotionally, to construct their work, yet the distinction between their work is one of mood; it could be compared to that between different pitches of sound. Donagh's is a quiet, measured, self-reflective approach, like the softness of an echo compared to Hamilton's big-bang, raw and direct style of *The citizen, The subject* and *The state*. As Samuel Beckett once remarked, 'Alone together so much shared'; Hamilton and Donagh strike a lyrical chord and a double sense of being at once intimately close to, and at a distance from, their powerfully-charged motifs. Hamilton's identification with Ireland can therefore be seen in terms of the broad subjects of his work—contemporary history; media, technology and communication; mass culture; the iconography of modern society—but along with these he refers us to his sense of an ancient and primitive self, whereby the contemporary is interwoven with the mythic past, and the public 'secondary' media experience with the private human emotion.

In wall murals across Northern Ireland, William III (William of Orange) still rides into battle at the Boyne. These murals are associated with the commemorative summer parades by Orangemen, while the Republican wall murals often centre on notions of Mother Ireland and of a new Ireland. It is easy to dismiss both as mindless sectarian graffiti; but perhaps it is much more accurate to describe the wall mural tradition in Northern Ireland as a folk art that is omnipresent. Just as kerb stones are painted red, white and blue, or green, white and gold to mark out a territory, so the murals are part of the street iconography of Northern Ireland. Hamilton, again through the media, was to respond to the many indigenous street images he saw on television, and in a letter to the author (13 November 1991), he recalled the circumstances of his embarking on painting *The subject*. 'Having completed the painting *The citizen*, I remembered all the exposure given to the other faction. "Orangeman" seemed the natural complement to "Blanketman" so I began to research material for a companion painting. The project was given some impetus when I was invited to make a contribution to the TV series of Paintbox programmes called *Painting with Light*.'

RICHARD HAMILTON *WAR GAMES* 1991-92

OIL ON SCANACHROME ON CANVAS

200 X 200 CMS

COURTESY OF THE ARTIST

The original context for the beginning of the trio of works was the hunger strikes of 1981. On behalf of the Republican prisoners at the Maze/Long Kesh prison[4] outside Belfast, Bobby Sands went on hunger strike on 1 March 1981,[5] the fifth anniversary of the date on which the government had started to phase out special status which had existed between 1971 (when internment without trial was introduced) and 1976.

Special status meant that those prisoners who were interned (under the Special Powers Act) were treated as political prisoners and not as 'common criminals'. The hunger strike was to peak at Easter of 1981, the anniversary of the 1916 Uprising, a potent symbol of Republican resurrection. It was to be the climax in the prisoners' four-year campaign for political status. This campaign had begun with the 'blanket' protest, in which prisoners convicted of what would, in other times, be described as politically motivated offences refused to wear prison uniform, and covered themselves with the only clothing at hand—their blankets. The 'blanket' protest became the 'no wash' protest, then the 'no slop out' protest, and finally the 'dirty' protest, in which Republican prisoners smeared their own excrement on the walls, floors and ceilings of their cells. Their vow to fast to death if necessary was made in order to attain their five demands: to refrain from prison work; to associate freely with one another; to organise recreational facilities; to have one letter, visit and parcel a week; and to have lost remission time restored.

In 1992, Hamilton completed a painting on the subject of the Gulf War of 1991, in which, as the picture made clear, British soldiers participated. By showing this Gulf War picture at his Tate Gallery retrospective of 1992, it became obvious to Hamilton that his Irish diptych was incomplete without an image of the British military presence, which up to then had been in Northern Ireland for twenty-three years.

Both the government and the hunger strikers rigidly maintained their respective positions. There were few real

AERIAL PHOTOGRAPH OF H BLOCKS AT THE MAZE PRISON, 27 SEPTEMBER 1983

COURTESY OF PA NEWS

efforts to negotiate a solution. On the one side there was a simple refusal to consider concessions on any of the demands; on the other, a simple refusal to consider anything other than concessions on all five. As a consequence, the hunger strikes polarised Northern Ireland to an extent that no single event since 1969 had, or has since. Within the Catholic community the ambiguous relationship between militant Republicanism and the Catholic Church was unveiled, between ancient mythologies of blood sacrifice and the statement of Pope John Paul II, on his visit to Ireland in 1981, 'murder is murder and must not be called by any other name'. Within the Orange community, responses to the hunger strikes exposed the depth and intensity of a hatred of Republicanism, a deep-rooted fear of Catholicism, and the extent to which these factors were thought to be fused. Both communities were caged inside traditional ideologies which would not and could not be unlocked overnight. A historical twist to the situation was that it was the siege of Derry, in 1689, which had provided Protestantism with its enduring slogan—'no surrender'—when their enemies had attempted to starve the Protestant people into submission.

The Civil Rights Association, founded in 1967, was to challenge the inequalities that existed between Catholics and Protestants in Northern Ireland. On 22 November 1968, the British Government announced wide-ranging reforms. By 1969, attacks on civil rights marches widened into attacks on Catholic areas by Loyalist extremists and elements of the Royal Ulster Constabulary. The British Army had to be called in on peace keeping duties, with the first soldiers on street

patrol on 14 March 1969. They were welcomed as saviours against oppression by the Protestant majority. But they were and are also in Northern Ireland to protect the democratic right of the majority to remain within the United Kingdom, and to oppress those wishing for an Ireland united by violent means. Soon the British Army became a target of the Provisional IRA, who killed the first British soldier on 31 October 1970. Hamilton's *The state* expresses the unease of this equivocal position between *The citizen* and *The subject*. Northern Ireland is a region of dichotomy and polarity between Catholic and Protestant, Republican and Loyalist, outsider and insider, have and have not, green and orange.

Richard Hamilton's father had joined the British Army early in his teens to escape the horrors of labour in the Staffordshire coal mines; he was sent to serve in Ireland, where he was billeted with an Irish family. Compared with Stoke-on-Trent at the turn of the century, Ireland was a fairy land. For Hamilton, the salt-pork barrel by the peat fire, the characters in the pubs, the songs, the tales of heroic exploits, were all part of the repertoire of bedtime stories in his English childhood. *The state* was to refer back to Hamilton's awareness of Ireland and to his father's memories.

The familiar diptych (each canvas 2 metres x 1 metre) is employed for *The state* to further continue in visual form Hamilton's interest in issues of figuration/abstraction. Is the

93

RICHARD HAMILTON

THE SUBJECT 1988-90

OIL ON CANVAS

2 PANELS, EACH 200 X 100 CM

COURTESY OF THE ARTIST

RICHARD HAMILTON

THE STATE 1992-93

OIL, HUMBROL ENAMEL AND

MIXED MEDIA ON CIBACHROME

ON CANVAS

2 PANELS, EACH 200 X 100 CM

COURTESY OF THE ARTIST

British 'Tommy' advancing or retreating? It is likely he is walking backwards, his back covered by another soldier as the unit slowly and carefully checks out the street. The left-hand panel shows the damp climate and pervasive green hue of the beautiful Irish countryside; for the British Army patrol, not just the cityscape but also 'bandit country'. This alternative setting is just as threatening as the sniper's bullet from a roof-top. A sign says SPUDS, our national food; and the mountains of Mourne sweep down to the city—two markers of being grounded in Ireland.

The heavily armed soldiers' vulnerability is heightened by the markings applied to his face, which join with his uniform and emphasise Hamilton's continuing interest in the roles of costume and artifice in the presentation of the human image. The ambiguity of the soldier's situation is further emphasised by Hamilton's use of *trompe-l'oeil* (a familiar technique) in the treatment of the battledress, with parts of the fabric laid on the picture surface. Hamilton thus uses camouflage to camouflage camouflage. *The state* completes and conveys the remarkable power, the entrenched character of the opposing positions which underline the Irish conflict. The camouflage is beginning to wear thin.

The showing of *The citizen* and *The subject* side-by-side in London, in summer 1991, evoked in me an immense feeling of personal sorrow. It is important to view them as companion paintings (this is the only way I have viewed them, literally and symbolically), and thus more fully to understand the convictions, postures, fanaticisms and dualities which these images are about. It was noticeable that a British audience felt somewhat removed from the symbolism of the images and side-stepped the iconography of the paintings, thereby being able to discuss them only in relation to Hamilton's use of technology. It was as if the paintings called for a collective re-examination of a part of history which had become taboo. Such images correspond to a contemporary history and situation, and ask questions of the viewer's position towards the subject of these paintings. An Irish showing of the paintings would permit a more direct look, and place the work more closely in the context of political and social events. It is only the reality of the paintings that can be the subject of the debate.

The actions of the hunger strikers were beyond Protestant comprehension. They were seen by the world at large to be victims; but to Protestants, victimhood is not self-inflicted. For the ordinary Protestant takes refuge in the reason for the supreme sacrifice (as when, for example, thousands of young Northern Irish Protestants gave their lives in the trenches at the Somme during World War I) rather than in the process of the sacrifice itself. A Protestant would justify and find ways of contributing to, and living for, a country (the work ethic), while the hunger strikers chose ancient Gaelic laws of self-denial and sacrifice. It is what the historian A. T. Q. Stewart calls a 'nightmarish juxtaposition of the folk memory of Jungian psychology'; not only were the hunger strikers asserting claims to Protestants' physical territory but they were invading the Loyalist psyche.[6]

To keep the nationalist cause at the top of the political agenda and in touch with international consciousness,

Republican prisoners carry on the fight by resisting the prison regime. Maintaining the struggle within the prison is part of the psychology of 'the long war'.[7] This claustrophobic tension exists alongside the celebratory triumphalism of the Orangeman stating his claim to march the route of his forefathers.[8] *The citizen* and *The subject* are opposing images of incarceration and freedom, yet their conjunction evokes the survival-of-the-species syndrome. Each opposing side is a closed world with an unchangeable internal code of its own, impervious to the passage of time. The inflexible no-compromise stance is so deeply rooted in both communities that everything conforms to an action-response pattern which endlessly repeats itself.

The citizen and *The subject* correctly portray Northern Ireland's politics as a battle between two irreconcilable groups, with *The state* ambiguously positioned in the middle. Conforming to the two sides' intransigent stereotypes, *The citizen* and *The subject* glare at each other. One evokes a screaming silence, the other a screaming defiance. Both attract a macabre fascination through their military associations, and each signals a staunch/devout will, a stubborn intolerance and a fanaticism masquerading as nobility of cause.

In Hamilton's words,

What we had heard of the blanket protest, mainly through the propaganda agencies of Sinn Fein, could not prepare us for the startling photographic documentation on TV. The picture presented, first by Granada Television and later by the BBC, was shocking less for its scatological content than for its potency. An oft-declared British view of the IRA as thugs and hooligans did not match the materialisation of Christian martyrdom so profoundly contained on film. One became acutely aware of the religious conflict that had resulted in civil inequalities that gave a platform for IRA activity. The symbols of Christ's agony were there, not only the crucifix on the neck of the prisoners and the rosary which confirmed the monastic austerity but the self-inflicted suffering which has marked Christianity from the earliest times.

The prisoners claimed the high moral ground because their fast to death reinforced their identification as martyrs. By fusing the ancient myth of militant nationalism and heroic sacrifice with the central characteristics of Irish Catholicism —penitential fasting, atonement for wrong-doing and self-denial—we can understand the context of Father Matt Wallace's statement: '[They] were almost akin to Christ-like'.[9]

Nationalism has a power over people's minds and hearts. The defence or cause of 'a nation' is one of the few commitments for which people will kill others or voluntarily lay down their lives. The psychology of nationalism is powerfully connected to a sense of self. It is the need for people to belong to a group which is linked by culture, customs, religion and a common history. Only the collective group can give meaning and fulfilment to individuals within the group, and it is the pack instinct which is the driving force. The packs have leaders who perpetrate primitive tribal rituals by imposing strongly held convictions that one belongs to a certain human grouping. This segregation of human beings into distinct groups can be defined as a 'sense of national identity' when people find it necessary to identify themselves with a particular tribe. *The citizen* and *The subject* have this sense of national identity. They both use history as a weapon against each other. History is defenceless; it can be used and manipulated to maintain the polarisation between tribes.

Religion in Northern Ireland is a powerful early learning tool in each side's perception of the other. Childhood upbringing and shared family experience make the religious aspect of 'the Troubles' reach the deepest levels of the human psyche. *The citizen* and *The subject* convey this depth. They give a strong sense that while the individual is grounded in the world of his ancestry, his power is the collective power of the tribe.

The Orangeman is very much a fact of life in Northern Ireland. Nearly one third of adult male Protestants belong to an Orange Lodge. *The subject* in his regalia of assertive power strides out triumphantly, emphasising his supremacy. A dignified gentleman in his Sunday best, he is a staunch defender of Ulster's glorious past. *The subject* is also a 'citizen'; a citizen who loves his Queen and Country; a citizen who would die in its defence; a citizen who is obedient to the forces of law and order; a citizen who believes in the democracy of one man, one vote. *The subject* is as much about nationalism as is *The citizen*; both identify with a strong sense of self and a fanatical devotion to the same cause of defence of 'the nation': *The subject* proudly commemorating and proclaiming his 'victory' at The Boyne; *The citizen* symbolising a sacrificial martyrdom recalling a mythological past. Their meeting brings a troubled history up to the present and into the future. History in Ireland replicates itself

and, in a country where people pride themselves on their memory, the future is therefore weighed down with a sense of the inevitable, that is, there is no hope of compromise. They are mirror-images reflecting the human tragedy of using force to settle arguments, as Odysseus, in Book Nine of *The Odyssey* describes his adventures among the one-eyed Cyclopes, who are 'giants, louts, without a law to bless them'.

The citizen, The subject and *The state* are a reflection on the political conditions in which one and a half million people are forced to live in Northern Ireland. It is a situation of the impossibility of consensus. Through generations of political manipulation and intransigence, the communities have been *misplaced* by history. The younger generations have turned to political violence as a means of escape from the sectarian dilemma in which they have been put by the intolerance of their ancestors. Any interpretation of these paintings cannot dismiss the moral questions they ask; to do so is to ignore their compelling content in favour of aesthetic considerations.

Hamilton has insisted on his right to paint images of such directness that they demand a response, not an averted glance. Although everything in these works is dependent on the 'content', we have become sanitised or practised at resisting images of raw power. Yet, though we may turn a blind eye, these paintings are located in the mind's eye. We hover between not wanting to remember and not being able to forget.

Whatever judgement posterity may reach, these images grasp a painful and sorrowful reality, a sense of anger

STOP 1991

MORE THAN 2,000 CAMPAIGNERS

FROM BOTH SIDES OF THE IRISH

BORDER GATHERED IN THE

REPUBLIC, AT COOLEY, COUNTY

LOUTH, TO SPELL OUT THEIR

PROTEST AGAINST THE IRA AT THE

MURDER OF A LOCAL FARMER

COURTESY OF THE IRISH TIMES

and frustration, sadness and grief. They cast shadows upon us; we cannot be oblivious to their presence. They touch a nerve, a trapped nerve, yet by their existence they confirm a future. Regrettably, a predictable future of the zero-sum game, a Beckettian game of waiting: 'The light glitters an instant and then it's night once more' (*Waiting for Godot*). An endgame, a game over which the spoils cannot be shared or negotiated, but only won or lost. STOP.

Stephen Snoddy was Exhibitions Director, Cornerhouse, Manchester, from 1991-96, where he organised exhibitions by Rita Donagh, Edward Allington, Annette Messager, AR Penck, John Baldessari, Jochen Gerz and Bruce McLean. He was also Manchester City Co-ordinator for *The British Art Show 4*, and commissioning editor for Cornerhouse Communiqués, a series of texts on contemporary cultural issues. He is presently Director of Southampton City Art Gallery where he is developing a programme that links historical, modern and contemporary art.

NOTES

1.   See Sarat Maharaj, *Richard Hamilton*, (British Council, 1993 Venice Biennale), which weaves Hamilton, Joyce and Duchamp together.

2.   Terry Eagleton, *Work in progress, Richard Hamilton*, Orchard Gallery, Derry, 1988, p. 8.

3.   *Epiphanies*, Richard Hamilton in conversation with Richard Cork, BBC Radio 3, 1 April 1985.

4.   It is Long Kesh to Catholics, the Maze to Protestants; Derry to Catholics, Londonderry to Protestants; the six counties or the North of Ireland to Catholics, Northern Ireland to Protestants. Although both communities share a common first language, they both need what Alasdair MacIntyre describes as 'a second first language'. Padraig O'Mally, *Biting at the Grave*, The Blackstaff Press, Belfast, 1990, p.185.

5.   This was the second hunger strike, after the first hunger strike broke down during Christmas 1980. Bobby Sands joined the IRA in 1972, and within six months was imprisoned for possession of firearms; he was released in 1976; however in September 1977 he was sent to the Maze/Long Kesh, again charged with possession of firearms. He immediately went 'on the blanket' and from there onto the dirty protest.

6.   Padraig O'Mally, *Biting at the Grave*, op. cit., p. 165.

7.   I am indebted to Declan McGonagle for this information, and for many other insights through various conversations.

8.   In conversation with Richard Hamilton, he recounted how he had seen the Orange marchers clash with the RUC in 1985 on television, when their traditional marching route through 'the Tunnel' at Portadown (a Catholic area in a Protestant town) was blocked by the police because of a ban on marches likely to cause a breach of peace.

9.   *Biting at the Grave*, op.cit., p.109. Father Matt Wallace, a curate in the parish of Joe McDonnell's (one of the hunger strikers).

EVERYTHING EQUALS NOTHING:
THE ART AND IDEAS OF JOHN LATHAM

JOHN A. WALKER

Critical opinion regarding the merits of John Latham's art and ideas remains divided, nevertheless there is a significant body of opinion in Europe and the United States which maintains that he is one of Britain's most radical avant-garde artists of the post-Second World War era, that he is a figure comparable in stature to Joseph Beuys or Robert Rauschenberg. Art historians also acknowledge that he has made important contributions to such international tendencies as Tachism, Assemblages, Performance, Installation, Book and Conceptual art. The record shows that he has added terms to the vocabulary of art—for instance, 'time-based arts' and event 'structure'.

The sheer variety of art forms and media in which he has worked, the many new departures and initiatives he has pursued, and the originality of his thought, has stimulated the imagination of successive generations. Since the 60s there has not been a decade in which Latham has not influenced and/or inspired British art students and younger artists. Today, artists such as John Stezaker, Douglas Gordon and Richard Wentworth are happy to acknowledge a debt to Latham. Even his contemporary Richard Hamilton has remarked: 'We owe him'. Latham is now in his seventies, but he continues to produce new works and to fine tune his theories; thus his work remains relevant—which is why it continues to be displayed alongside that of much younger artists in mixed exhibitions such as *Material Culture* (London: Hayward Gallery, 1997). And, given the recent intense public interest in scientific theories about the origin and character of the universe, Latham's cosmological ideas are currently pertinent.

The two mixed-media assemblages by Latham in this exhibition are clearly physical constructions/art objects suitable for displaying in art galleries. However, viewers would gravely misjudge Latham's achievement and purpose if they relied on these two works alone as evidence. This is because his oeuvre encompasses films and videos, street events involving towers of burning books, performances with live actors, an ecological device, and theoretical texts, besides paintings and sculptures.[1]

Furthermore, although Latham has made numerous artefacts, the primary emphases of his art since 1954 have been on time and event rather than space and matter. Latham is unusual among British artists in having a long-standing interest in scientific theories, especially those of quantum physics, gravity and cosmology. He has developed a theory of time and structure-in-events that challenges those put forward by professional physicists and cosmologists.

Consequently his art and writings embody ideas that he regards as vital to humankind. In short, he is an artist with a message and a mission. So convinced is he of the significance of his discoveries that he is willing to address them not only to the art world but also to the Queen of England, British Prime Ministers and the Secretary General of the United Nations.

He argues that instead of thinking of the universe as consisting of solid things made from small units of matter such as atoms, we should think of it as consisting of events

made from various units of time, the smallest being defined as 'a least event', and the largest being the whole lifespan of the cosmos. Everything between the micro and the macro has different durations. Impressions of persistence and permanence are caused by events recurring. The temporal emerges from state zero or nothing (no thing), a ground that is invisible and atemporal, which religious believers call God. (This explains Latham's apparently absurd equation 'Everything = Nothing'. Thus Latham's formula 01-10 describes one cycle of a cosmos's existence: from nothing an event occurs, it repeats, but then reverts to nothing. Another cycle may then happen.) The dialectic between the two realms has been a constant theme of his work. El Greco's Christian painting *The Burial of Count Orgaz* (1586-88) inspired a relief assemblage of 1958 because of its simultaneous depiction of transient life on Earth and the eternal life of Heaven—that is, the temporal and the atemporal appear within the same picture space.

Latham believes that contradictions within present scientific theories of matter could be solved if his alternative 'theory of everything' was adopted. For this reason he has repeatedly attempted to engage scientists in public dialogues. One such encounter—*Decades Decoded*—took place at the Riverside Studios, London, in February 1990. Recently Adrian Searle, the British critic, declared that Latham's theories were 'mad'; but one wonders if critics who reach this conclusion are simply too lazy to follow the arguments put forward in such essays as *Time-Base and Determination in Events* (1972-3). In my view, Latham's theories are no more crazy than the highly speculative and

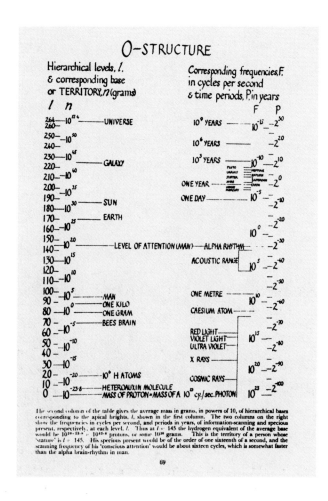

THE O-STRUCTURE DIAGRAM
REPRODUCED FROM THE BOOK
THE O-STRUCTURE: AN
INTRODUCTION TO
PSYCHOPHYSICAL COSMOLOGY, BY
C.C.L. GREGORY AND ANITA
KOHSEN (CHURCH CROOKHAM,
HANTS: INSTITUTE FOR THE STUDY
OF MENTAL IMAGES, 1959), P. 69.

non-commonsensical theories generated by scientists seeking to explain the Big Bang and Black Holes.

What such critics also overlook is that *creativity* and *visualisation* are common to both art and science — this means that art can provide cognitive insights as well as aesthetic pleasure—and that during the 50s Latham was an honorary, founding member of the Institute for the Study of Mental Images (ISMI), established with two scientists—Clive Gregory and Anita Kohsen. The content of the latter's 1959 book *The O Structure: Introduction to Psychophysical Cosmology* is crucial to an understanding of Latham's oeuvre. ISMI was an interdisciplinary endeavour motivated by a desire to overcome the dualism of mind and matter, the specialisation/fragmentation of knowledge in terms of separate academic disciplines/sciences, and the division of the world's peoples into antagonistic factions. Thus Latham's ideas emerged in association with those of certain visionary scientists with utopian ideals.

Latham's interest in scientific issues, his conception of art as a special form of cognition, and his emphasis on time rather than space, have set him apart from certain influential tendencies within modern art, in particular Greenbergian/formalist ones that sought to define painting and sculpture as autonomous, specialist practices concerned only with issues of space, colour and form, and their own identities. The hybridity of Latham's assemblages was antipathetic to Greenberg's purist aesthetic, and their stress on content ran counter to the American Critic's obsession with form. Latham met Greenberg in New York in 1961 and they crossed swords a few years later. Latham's notorious event *Chew and Still* (1966)—which involved the mastication and distillation of Greenberg's book *Art and Culture* (the documentation of the event is now in the Museum of Modern Art, New York)—was a direct riposte to Greenberg's influence, an act of resistance against the Americanisation of British art.

The presence of Latham's artefacts in galleries should not be allowed to obscure the fact that he has striven, via his contributions to the activities of the Artist Placement Group (currently named O + I, Organisation and Imagination), to transcend the gallery/museum habitat in which art is predominantly confined. One motivation behind the founding of APG in 1966 was to restore the artist's connection with the centres of power in society by placing them for extended periods within the businesses, institutions and organisations which are so characteristic of modern, bureaucratic societies. Latham undertook a placement during 1975-77 inside the Scottish Office,

Edinburgh, and produced a stream of proposals—including designs for monumental public sculptures in the shape of books—that could have helped to revive derelict industrial zones in West Lothian and Glasgow. Unfortunately, they were not acted upon.

Latham was born in the British colony of Rhodesia, Africa, in 1921 but was educated at a public school in England. During the Second World War he served in the Royal Navy and started to paint seascapes with birds or warships. From 1946 to 1950 he studied fine art at the Regent Street Polytechnic and Chelsea School of Art. In the 50s, while Tachism and Action painting were in vogue, he used a spray-gun to produce semi-abstract studies of figures with 'dust clouds' of pigment. It was while spraying paint that he had a revelation: he perceived that the white ground of the canvas could be thought of as 'state zero' and the 'quantum-of-mark' made by pressing the trigger of the spray-gun for an instant could be thought of as the trace of 'a least event'. Latham concluded that visual art was superior to language and literature because it enabled the temporal and the atemporal to be presented at once.

Then, in 1958, Latham began to make reliefs from various materials, primarily second-hand books. He was struck by the similarity of form—black marks on a white surface—between print and his 'dust-cloud' paintings. Latham appropriated books—everyday objects—and made them strange by treating them as visual/palpable things rather than as literature. His strategy was to 'reverse the function and conception and see what you get'.

Reversal also occurred in his invention of the term 'Skoob' (books spelled backwards).

Latham's first use of books may have been a matter of chance or intuition, but this hardly explains the central role they came to play in his oeuvre; nor does it account for the need to shift from the two-dimensional plane of the spray-gun paintings to the third dimension of the relief. It would appear that books served as surrogates for the human presence in nature, an emergence on the surface of the Earth: the books literally erupted from their supports. This growth and thrusting forth was mental as well as material—books as evidence of humanity's intellectual achievements over the centuries.

At first sight books were an unpromising material for a visual artist to employ, but Latham successfully demonstrated their flexibility and versatility: closed, they were as solid as planks and, placed at right angles to the picture plane, they jutted out with phallic aggressions. Alternatively, flat on their backs with their pages wired open, they evoked female vulnerability. In addition to the closed/open or hidden/visible contrast, endless permutations were possible via joining, cutting, burning and colouring. Games could also be played by obscuring/revealing titles and contents. The linguistic matter of certain books did play a role in terms of the meaning and allusions of the assemblages. Furthermore an allegorical connection was established, via titles and commentary, between the reliefs *Shem, Shaun* (1958) and the *Observer* series (1959-60) and a specific literary text—Dostoyevsky's 1880 novel *The Brothers Karamazov*—that was not physically present.

Reading a book is clearly a temporal activity, hence books exemplify linear time; the reader's repetitive act of turning pages can also be regarded as 'a recurrent event'. As part of a relief, a book's linear-time potential was negated; but Latham's tactic of cutting back the pages nevertheless served to suggest the book's temporal character by means of a strata-like exposure. Another temporal aspect of the book reliefs resulted from the possibility of painting the pages of wired-open books in different colours, and then changing the appearance of the relief by exposing different pages at different times. By using the animation technique of stop-motion to record books in different states (altered by hand between shots), Latham generated some highly original 16 mm films. Paradoxically, they were non-moving movies.

His *Skoob Films* of the early 60s depict static objects which nevertheless change their appearance as time elapses. They were intended to illustrate how the universe functions: 'Event-structure proposes a cosmology where the initial entities remain the same but display endless variation and development'. When the films are projected, abrupt changes of state occur: books open, close and alter hue. Volumes seem to have a will of their own: their behaviour appears automatic and voluntary. The books gape open and snap shut like the mouths of fish gasping for air. Although the book-mouths utter no sounds, they convey the impression of animated chatter. What the viewer experiences are constantly changing patterns of colour, ripples, rhythms and pulsations. Normally books communicate to readers via text and illustration; but in this case words have been replaced by a silent, visual language of pure colour.

In the 50s and 60s Latham's assaults on books shocked many viewers who were reminded of the Nazi book burnings of the 30s. He certainly mounted an attack on literature, language and books as emblems of learning, major religions and civilisations; but his aims were not those of the Nazis. There is something exquisitely poignant and tragic about Latham's early assemblages. They were made during the era of 'bomb culture' and CND marches, a decade or so after a World War in which Latham had fought against the menace of fascism, a war in which over 50 million died, in which the horrors of the Holocaust and the atomic bomb's devastation of Hiroshima and Nagasaki had occurred. (In retrospect, Latham's reliefs can be regarded as delayed mourning-work). Since European 'civilisation' had caused this unprecedented outbreak of violence, destruction and atrocity, was not Latham right to indict it? Was he not right to depict that 'civilisation' as a ruin, as a system dominated by logic and language which had gone terribly wrong? Perceiving that there was an intellectual crisis in both the arts and the sciences of the twentieth century, he searched for a new conception of reality.

Latham began to use thick sheets of glass in the early 80s. A series of works made from glass and books that included *The Moral High Ground* (1988) was displayed at the Lisson Gallery in October 1988. Glass is a difficult and paradoxical material: strong yet brittle; solid yet transparent. Those familiar with his event-structure writings will probably deduce that the glass sheets symbolise 0 in Latham's formula 01-10. Glass, Latham feels, is the substance which best represents state zero because

the material is the nearest one can get—perceptually speaking—to non-materiality. Duchamp's *Bride Stripped Bare by Her Bachelors, Even* is clearly the key art-historical precedent for the use of glass in modern art, and it is curious that the concept of time was associated with this work also: Duchamp referred to it as 'a *delay* in glass'.

In contrast to the coldness and hardness of the glass sheets, the book fragments also making up Latham's 80s constructions appeared warm and soft, as befits these emblems of human culture and knowledge. As previously, Latham's iconoclasm in respect of books was no mere vandalism—there was a polemical point. For instance, the volume he targeted in *History of Time* (1988) was an account of the nature of the universe: *A Brief History of Time: From the Big Bang to Black Holes* by the crippled Cambridge mathematician Stephen Hawking. (Hawking is also the subject of an amusing sculpture by Jake and Dinos Chapman).

This text—a best-seller for a scientific book in 1988—was sawn in half and then mounted on both sides of a slab of glass placed at an angle on a specially designed wooden base. Hawking's book was 'divided' in order to symbolise the divided-state conception which, according to Latham, still informed scientific accounts of the universe, however elaborate and sophisticated.

While the latter seek to describe dimensions, artists—Latham contended—work directly with them and thus have a more intimate knowledge. And since visual works of art are dimensional structures which directly embody the creative impulse informing the universe, they are more likely to be truthful than the models of the scientists which, aside from gestures towards 'the anthropic principle', have little to say about the achievements of artists.

Glass sheets divide and penetrate the books, but since they also support them, they are an essential base without which the structures could not exist. Thus Latham insists that the atemporal ground of state zero represented by the glass is as essential as the temporality of existence: only a theory which takes account of both can stand a chance of producing a holistic account.

The *Moral High Ground* was fabricated from rectangles of glass bonded together in order to simulate the V shape of a half-open book; and from a copy of the *New English Bible*, another volume entitled *Let God be True*, a fragment of newspaper with the heading 'fighting for the High Moral Ground in a Secular Society', plus a lightbulb and a cartoon of two well-known British politicians, one Labour and one Conservative. In this piece Latham ironically contrasted his own quest for enlightenment with the disciplines of religion, philosophy and politics. Since his work was built from and included the latter, his own solutions claimed a more encompassing scope and effect.

Construction Number 5 is one of a series of spherical assemblages, varying in size and hue, called *Cluster of Eleven* —first exhibited at the Lisson Gallery in October 1992. These artefacts hung from the gallery's ceiling and were perhaps the most overtly astronomical in Latham's oeuvre, in the sense that they resembled the planets of the solar system. However Latham's 'planets' looked as though massive collisions had taken place in outer space, between them and showers of books and metal objects. Oddly shaped metallic parts and damaged books projected from the interiors or surfaces of the planets. The perfection and integrity of the spheres was violated by these excrescences of human knowledge and technology, thus making vivid what humanity is adding—for better or worse—to nature.

While Latham's art and ideas have evolved over the decades, there has also been a *recursive* factor—that is, his habit of *circling back* to take up themes and forms apparently abandoned years before. This recursiveness is a sign of the underlying unity of Latham's quest: he returns again and again to the same fundamental issues of time, motivation, the cosmos and humanity's place within it.

Arguably, Latham is one of the last avant-gardists; for, since the death of Beuys in 1986, he seems to stand almost alone as an artist who produces radical, iconoclastic art, who believes passionately that art has vital social and intellectual purposes, and who is inspired by a holistic vision with lessons that—should they be heeded—would benefit all humanity.

John A. Walker has written several books and many periodical articles. A topic he has explored in some depth is the interrelationship between contemporary fine art and mass media/culture. His books include: *John Latham The incidental person—his art and ideas* (London: Middlesex University Press, 1995). He is currently a Reader in Art and Design History at Middlesex University.

NOTES

1.   For a detailed survey of Latham's work, see the monograph, *John Latham The Incidental Person—His Art and Ideas* (London: Middlesex University Press, 1995).

ART AND ITS NETWORKS: A MIGRANT'S TALE

TONY BENNETT

In his famous study of the way science works through the networks it organises, Bruno Latour accords especial importance to the role that collecting institutions play in the operation of those networks. Historically, the accumulation of objects and specimens from all parts of the world in European and American museums of natural history allowed new things and relationships to be seen. This enabled those museums to function, in Latour's terms, as 'centres of calculation', the nodal points of scientific networks through which the power of western knowledges was exported back to the colonial contexts from which the objects and specimens had initially been collected. As such, they provided those who operated them with a means of 'acting at a distance' on the procedures and frameworks of colonial science, and to do so, as Latour puts it, 'without ever leaving home'.[1]

Art galleries can be looked at in a similar light, as institutions for managing the travel of art objects. As such, they form parts of elaborate networks through which works of art flow from one context to another and within which, depending on the ways in which they are combined with other works of art and on the exhibition principles which regulate their display, they become culturally active in new ways for new audiences. In a postcolonial context, of course, these networks are no longer quite so unidirectional as they were when their primary *raison d'être* was to manage the travel of art objects from colonial periphery to metropolitan centre. Art can now move backwards and forwards with relative ease across the global networks constructed by the increasingly inter-linked world of art galleries.

This has resulted in new kinds of mobility for art objects through special exhibitions which draw on the resources of several collections to produce unique assemblages of works brought together for display in particular national or regional contexts. When, as with *Pictura Britannica*, those exhibitions are curated *in situ* by people working within the contexts in which the art that has travelled is to be received, we can see art's networks being used in relatively new ways. The pictures of Britain come to us, on terms that we have arranged for negotiating our contact with another culture. Those of us who are 'over here' can have access to art that has come from 'over there', without having to leave home, and on conditions of our own making.

GEORGINA STARR

THE NINE COLLECTIONS OF THE SEVENTH MUSEUM 1994

The pictorial memories that resonate most strongly for me from the Britain I left are those of a society still riding low on the rising tide of Tory jingoism in the wake of the Falklands armada; and of a working-class movement which, through disastrous leadership, had been fatally crippled through the historic defeat inflicted on the miners. Picturing Britain during the period since then has been an equally painful business: continuing race riots in the inner cities; the 'go slow' on Europe; beggary on the streets; the assault on the national health service and the public education system; Tory sleaze.

Yet, in a migrant country, the relations between what counts as 'over here' and what as 'over there' are not always clear cut. The relationship is a permeable one, just as the placing of 'home' is, for many, something that can remain quite radically undecided. Art that travels across these fluctuating boundaries may, for some migrant audiences, occupy many places at once or be experienced as curiously misplaced. For my part, as a British migrant, pictures of and from Britain are always ambiguously placed in this way, just as their exhibition in Australia is always spatially dislocating: they come from what was home (and might be so again) to what is now home (but not necessarily forever).

Most migrants, I suspect, feel the same. For British migrants in recent years, however, building an imaginative picture of what has been going on 'back home' from the pictures of British social, political and cultural life that circulate within the Australian media has involved a sense also of acute temporal dislocation, a sense of living in a world in which time is out of joint with itself. I came to live in Australia toward the end of 1983 and, while I have long since lost any clear sense about whether it is 'over here' or 'over there' that all things are supposed to be 'queer and opposite', the social and political trajectories of Britain and Australia over the intervening period have been decidedly and perversely antipodean in their relations to one another.

Migrants are strongly motivated to look for the best in their new countries. For 'new chums' arriving in Queensland in the early 80s this involved taking a broad view. Locally, things didn't look too good; indeed, the rampant cronyism of Sir Joh and the Nationals made Thatcherism look, if not benign, certainly a saner and more honest political creed. But the sun was rising at the federal level with the election of the Hawke Labor government which, through into the Keating years, saw the national polity pulled in directions which seemed the mirror opposite of Britain: the Accord in industrial relations; the introduction of Medicare; the 'go fast' on Asia; the big push on multiculturalism; the reconciliation process; the rapid growth of the higher education sector.

By the late 90s, however, the tides of social and political change have been reversed in both countries, so that they still run in opposing directions. The pictures from

Britain that are now beamed into our living rooms seem increasingly like messages from another world: more money for health and education; a new 'go fast' on Europe; political devolution for Wales and Scotland; an end in sight to the hereditary transmission of political power; women's rights back on the agenda; black faces in parliament.

And Australia, which had managed to dance so deftly in promoting a progressive social-democratic agenda against the tides of Reaganism and Thatcherism, is now flat-footedly out of step with the new 'new times' that are emerging from the centrist politics of Britain — and, indeed, Europe. The 'go fast' on Asia is now a confused dawdle, side-railed by 'the Pauline Hanson factor'. The reconciliation process has been shabbily tarnished by the cavalry-twill racism of a Liberal Prime Minister who cannot discern the difference between guilt and sorrow. Racial attacks are on the increase; multiculturalism seems all but a dead policy agenda. Women's issues are now about helping women get out of the jobs that aren't there any more, so that they can feel relaxed and comfortable about being back home. And non-English speaking migrants increasingly feel that 'back home' is just where the government would like to send them.

Pictura Britannica, courtesy of art's networks, brings to this now radically changed political context a still different set of pictures of and from Britain, pictures which bear the impress of the continuing traditions of dissent and opposition which characterised the 80s and early 90s. Other writers in this catalogue who were a part of the history from which this new art emerged describe the conditions which nurtured its development: the theoretical and political struggles against racism and the connection of these to postcolonial struggles; the importance of support from local and municipal councils in face of a hostile national policy context; a new internationalism in art practice; gay and lesbian politics; the influence of expanded definitions and understandings of culture associated with cultural studies; the related demands for equal and expanded rights of cultural access and participation.

These are also, of course, factors that have affected the reception of art as well as its production, fashioning new audiences and new discursive frameworks for interpreting art

MAUD SULTER
DUVAL ET DUMAS DIPTYCH
DUVAL 1993
DUMAS 1993

and reconnecting it back to the practical engagements of social and political life. These are all respects in which, however antipodean they might have been in other ways, the histories of Britain and Australia have followed related trajectories over the 80s and 90s. In spite of the changing fortunes and vicissitudes of electoral politics, there has been considerable exchange and a good deal of shared ground between the intellectual and artistic cultures of the two countries.

Not identical, of course: the new artistic practices of indigenous Australians connect questions of race and art in ways that have no British parallels. And postcolonial understandings have a wholly different turn and point to them in Australia, where the problem is not one of the empire 'striking back', but rather of striking, finally and decisively, out of empire altogether. The new forms of internationalisation associated with diasporic cultural flows are also accented differently, given the importance of Asian diasporas to Australia compared with the influence on British cultural life of the 'black Atlantic' Afro-American diaspora.[2]

However the audiences for art have been shaped by broadly similar histories—by the expansion of higher education opportunities; by critiques of earlier absolutist definitions of art in favour of relativist understandings of cultural value; and by an appreciation of the political connectedness of all art. In both contexts, new understandings of art practice—shaped, initially, in the context of social and political movements that were largely disconnected from mainstream art institutions—have since come to circulate more widely, and more regularly, via art's networks.

The art displayed in *Pictura Britannica* thus reaches us via a well-developed international network through which—via shared curatorial practices and understandings—art is able to travel across national frontiers and, at least in Anglophone contexts, to be exhibited to audiences with shared new understandings of art as a consequence of the ways in which the discursive and institutional contexts for art's reception have been reshaped over the past twenty years. However much this, its mobility *across* national boundaries, is to be welcomed, though, art still usually travels hardly any social distance at all so far as its relations to the major social lines of division *within* national societies are concerned.

James Clifford makes the same point more eloquently when, in elaborating his view that museums and the market are institutions which 'manage the travel of objects between different places',[3] he comments pointedly on those whom these networks exclude. 'For most inhabitants of a poor neighbourhood, located perhaps just a few blocks or a short bus ride from a fine-arts museum, the museum might as well be on another continent'.[4] The art that *Pictura Britannica* has brought 'over here' will still be, for many Australians, part of an 'over there'—one, however, that is socially rather than geographically remote and inaccessible, in view of the vast social and cultural distances that must be travelled to reach it.

Latour, in discussing the networks through which science organises its spheres of action, likens these to the galleries which termites construct to extend their runs out

from the central nest. In doing so, he argues that the successful application of a science always involves 'the progressive extension of a network', an enterprise that entails a certain degree of risk, and sometimes trauma, if it involves an encounter with the troubling outside world which those networks can never entirely placate. Equally, though, it can be a smooth, untroubled affair: 'when everything works according to plan,' as Latour puts it, 'it means that you do not move an inch out of well-kept and carefully sealed networks'.[5]

For Walter Benjamin, writing in the 1930s, the acid test for any artistic practice concerned its relations to the existing techniques and circumstances of artistic production.[6] Perhaps the major challenge for contemporary art—and it is a challenge for curators and audiences as much as for artists—consists in the relationship it adopts to the networks through which it circulates. At present, no matter how much it might be shaped by contemporary political engagements, the ability of art to speak and connect back into the present is limited by the social thinness of these networks. The question this poses for all exhibitions is: how far do they contribute to extending the reach of art by broadening the social reach of its networks?

This is a question for *Pictura Britannica* which only the exhibition itself, and those who go to it, can answer. Will it allow new things and relationships to be seen? Will it allow new kinds of people to see them? Will the art shaped by a culture of dissent 'over there' connect effectively with a broad constituency 'over here', where engaged criticism seems likely to become a more practised art, and one that will certainly need its networks?

Tony Bennett is Professor of Cultural Studies at Griffith University, where he is also Director of the Australian Key Centre for Cultural and Media Policy. Before moving to live and work in Australia in 1983 he worked at the Open University in Britain. The *Popular Culture* course he directed while at the Open University played an important role in disseminating the broad and relativist view of culture associated with the development of cultural studies.

NOTES

1.   Latour, Bruno, *Science in Action*, Cambridge, Mass.: Harvard University Press, 1987, p. 251.

2.   See Gilroy, Paul, *There Ain't No Black in the Union Jack*, London: Hutchinson, 1987.

3.   Clifford, James, *Routes: Travel and Translation in the Late Twentieth Century*, Cambridge, Mass.: Harvard University Press, 1997, p. 211.

4.   ibid, p. 204.

5.   op.cit., pp. 249-250.

6.   See Benjamin, Walter, 'The author as producer' in Benjamin (1973) *Understanding Brecht*, London: New Left Books, 1934.

BACK TO MY ROUTES: A POSTSCRIPT TO THE 80S

KOBENA MERCER

What a trip. From the energy and optimism around the 1981 uprisings to the despondency and despair in the aftermath of the *Satanic Verses*: the 80s were lived as a vertigo of displacement. The prevalent name for this predicament—postmodernism—has already been and gone as a best seller ideology, but as an everyday structure of feeling, the mood of restlessness and uncertainty lingers on.

It was significant that the new cultural trends of the 80s—from rap and hip hop or women's writing in the States, to black British film, fine art and photography—came from the margins, from subjects and spaces historically marginalised from the centres of power and authority in liberal society. While the loudest voices in postmodernism spoke endlessly of the end of everything, emergent voices and practices articulated a new cultural politics of difference and diversity. The post-structuralist argument concerning the decentering of the subject, theorised with such passion during the 70s, was actually put into effect during the 80s. Structures which had stabilised the consensual centre of the post-war period disintegrated into new configuration of hegemony, contestation and resistance that have had the effect of a diversification and pluralism of public space.

'Back to my Routes: a postscript to the 80s' revised and reprinted with kind permission from David A Bailey and Stuart Hall, eds., 'Critical Decade: Black British Photography in the 80s,' *Ten.8* Vol 2 no 3, 1992 (Birmingham, England).

To put it briefly, this was the context in which *True Confessions* and *Dark & Lovely* were written for *Ten.8*. Looking back, the emergence of black gay and lesbian voices on the margins of British society in the 80s was important precisely because it contributed to the pluralisation of public space. In retrospect it becomes possible to place those articles in the broader context of postmodernism: at the time, I don't think either Isaac Julien or I were fully aware that this is what we were in the process of doing. Between them, the articles speak to an emergent field of activities through which black lesbians and black gay men have expanded the range of imagined communities available in the public sphere. Or to put it another way: what was important about the way we came out over the last decade was not that we expressed a fully constituted, separate and distinct identity that was always already there, but that we actively constructed an elective community of belonging through a variety of practices, whether that was organising workshops or parties, mobilising and lobbying political structures, writing poems or making films. Black lesbians and gay men have actively contributed to the cultural and political terrain of postmodernism, not by virtue of some essentialist difference that our identities are supposed to embody; but as the result of the multiplication of critical dialogues across different political communities and constituencies.

According to the reductive calculus of categorical identity politics, we are members of a doubly or triply disadvantaged minority, displaced onto the outer limited of marginality by our deviant hybridity. This kind of thinking became instituted in the mid 80s around the Greater London Council (GLC) experiments in local socialism, in which the management of diversity and difference through

112

PICTURA BRITANNICA

YINKA SHONIBARE *HOW DOES A GIRL LIKE YOU, GET TO BE A GIRL LIKE YOU?* 1995 (INSTALLATION VIEW), INSTALLATION OF THREE COSTUMES OF WAX PRINT COTTON TEXTILES

TAILORED BY SIAN LEWIS, 168 X 49 EACH, COURTESY OF THE ARTIST AND STEPHEN FRIEDMAN GALLERY, LONDON

the bureaucratic mantra of race, class and gender encouraged the divisive rhetoric of being more marginal, more oppressed, and therefore more righteous than thou. That awful imperative of being ideologically right on was the one thing that the different social movements had in common, which resulted only in the closure of political dialogue: the whole logic of populist loony-leftism parodied the politically correct attitudes of the left. In the ruins of the rainbow coalition, the challenge is how to make sense of plurality as a political problem that is going to be around for a good few years to come. The complex field of antagonism brought into play by the Salman Rushdie affair shows that there is nothing remotely *groovy* about difference and diversity as political problems of postmodernity.

The challenge is to be able to theorise more than one difference at once: to abandon the logocentric hierarchies of binary thinking so as to enter into the over-determined spaces in between, in which relations of identity and difference are actually lived. As a half-caste negro homosexual intellectual, located somewhere in the professional-managerial class, is my marginal identity really more worthily oppressed than the homeless and unemployed white male youth who I encounter begging in the West End of London on my way home from work? Like left and right, centre and margin are merely metaphors: the question is whether or not they enable us to think through the complex terrain of combined and uneven development we each negotiate in everyday life in the struggle to get from one day to the next.

The good thing about the collapse of the grand narratives was the recognition of the end of the universal intellectual who thought he had an answer for everything. The decentering of the subject of liberal humanism—Man—revealed that the subject who had monopolised the microphone in public culture, by claiming to speak for humanity as a whole (while denying the right to representation to anyone who was not white, not male, not middle class and not Western), was himself nothing but a minority. The crisis of belief in the big ideologies of marxism and modernism needs to be back-dated to the 50s and 60s as it was the emergence of new social antagonisms, through which black people, women, gay people and other minorities found a voice, which relativised the universalist truths of the avant-garde and the vanguard party. This is to say that postmodern movements necessarily entail a politics of culture which turns on the struggle for access to democratic rights of representation, which is what the metaphors of being silenced and of finding a voice refer to.

Looking back, it was important that our efforts to find a voice involved collaborative writing. It was the feeling of collective belonging that came from our participation in the Gay Black Group in the early 80s which enabled us to give voice to black gay issues and experiences. In *True Confessions*, and an earlier article in *Camerawork* co-written with Errol Francis, such collaborations enabled a transition from I to we, which was an empowering transformation even though the process of writing was fraught with difficulty. There is always the risk of reductionism when one is positioned as a voice who speaks for a particular community because such a role can imply that all black gays are essentially the same and speak in unison. But on the other hand, I have never had much patience for that guilt-tripping rhetorical question—who do you write for? who is your audience?—because it always seemed more important to know who or what you were writing against, which in our case meant speaking out against the silence created by racism in the white gay community and homophobia in our black communities. The construction of community through critical dialogue was about creating space.[1]

For over four hundred years in Western culture, the sign black had nothing but negative connotations, to say the least. During the 80s, the central signifier or racist ideology was dis-articulated out of its naturalised meaning and reference, and re-articulated into an alternative chain of signification in which it became a sign of solidarity among Asian, African and Caribbean peoples. As a sign of political rather than genetic identity, blackness was reappropriated out of one discursive system and rearticulated into another: hence, the endless arguments about the denotation of the term arose because of the competing connotations that gathered under the same signifier. Of course this didn't just happen in the 80s, it was conditioned by a whole range of non-discursive practices which have constituted black Britain as a domain of cultural/political antagonism. Nevertheless, once seen historically, the displacement of the proper name in British racial discourse—from coloured immigrants in the 50s through ethnic minorities in the 60s to black communities in the 70s—confirms the theory that one's social identity is constructed in language, discourse and representation; that identities are not there in nature, but are socially constructed, deconstructed and reconstructed in relations to culture.

One doesn't need to accept the 70s model of linguistic determinism to acknowledge the centrality of black people's struggles over the sign as popular-democratic struggles to become subjects and agents, rather than the alienated objects, of representation. When you consider the symbolic impact of the transformation from Negro to Black across the post-war diaspora, the reason why our struggles have been so central to postmodern politics is not because we have some ontological privilege of being the most oppressed people in the world, but because of the metaphorical dissemination of black signs of the field of democratic antagonism: the extension of the desire for freedom from one site of struggle to the next.[2]

When I was an undergraduate at St. Martin's School of Art between 1978 and 1981 I was completely bewildered by the argument that the subject is constituted in language, not because I didn't understand it but because I felt emotionally terrorised by the authoritarian attitudes associated with the Althusserian avant-garde. The strangest thing, however, about the vertiginous displacements of the 80s, has been the experience of finding a voice in the language of theory while the institutions that once supported the intellectual subcultures of the British Left, especially in art schools, polytechnics, universities and other public sector institutions, have all been slowly dismantled and disappeared. Take *Screen*, for example.

In 1978, I felt its esoteric vocabulary did little to empower me, and subsequently characterised it as *Screen*-speak in the debates on Cultural identities that brought black British film workshops and avant-garde intelligentsia into dialogue in the mid 80s; by 1988, however, I had joined the editorial board and, as a specific project, co-edited an issue with Isaac Julien, in the year the organisation that published it, SEFT (Society for Education in Film and Television), was closed down by the withdrawal of funding from the British Film Institute.[3] At times it was a bad trip, but the general lesson of black negotiations of institutions lies in the issue of how to work in and against established structures and traditions. The intervention in *Screen* was important because by reinserting issues of race and ethnicity into the framework of film theory, the articles in the issue, and the debates on black cinema to which they have contributed, showed that new insights could be generated from old theories once the ethnocentric character of their universalist claims were displaced, relativised and made a little more modest.

In effect, I think this was of a piece with what black intellectual initiatives achieved in the 80s; an ecological re-cycling of elements from post-structuralist theories, once the critique of ethnocentrism had cleared enough ground for a mutual conversation. *The Empire Strikes Back* (1982) from the Centre for Contemporary Cultural Studies, was a highly influential text in this regard. As a resourceful tool box, it enabled the paradigm shift from race relations sociology to cultural studies which contributed to new forms of artistic practice in film, art and photography. The new generation of black intellectuals who were writing, such as Pratibha

Parmar, Paul Gilroy, Errol Lawrence and Hazel Carby, helped to displace the theory/practice dichotomy - they brought activist experience to bear on the production of knowledge within the academy, thus translating back and forth to create mobile frameworks of travelling theory. Edward Said's notion of travelling theory has germane connotations for artists and intellectuals of the black diaspora as our histories are about movement, displacement and mobility, whether by coercion or consent - that's how we've ended up in this strange space that constitutes our common post-colonial home, in Little England's green and not always so pleasant land.[4]

Travelling theory suggests a departure from the moral masochism of enslaving oneself to a universal master theory; an escape from patriarchal and paternalistic forms of intellectual authority that demand one's submission to the imperative of being correct and right-on. It suggests a desire, instead, to take risks by making connections between different discourses to see what works and what doesn't: the freaky deke method of experiment and collage. In retrospect this is what we were doing in the process of becoming specific intellectuals. As Isaac Julien put it: 'Territories and ideas have been explored politically through construction and reconstruction, then thrown away; if we are to change the master narratives and conventions... This does not imply that we enter into romantic ideas of black nationalism: there exist multiple identities which should challenge with passion and beauty the previously static order'.[5] We are both Foucault fans, but I wonder to what extent we were aware of translating Foucault's idea that theory is like a box of tools — 'treat my

book as a pair of glasses directed to the outside: if they don't suit you, find another pair'.[6] If cultural theory is an instrument of multiplication, I suppose that is what we were doing in the Ten.8 articles, by drawing connections between racial, gendered and sexual references at their point of intersection in images of black masculinity, in order to extend the conversation about power and ideology in particular regimes of representation.

It would be a mistake to simply celebrate the way that black artistic and intellectual practices came out of the margins during the 80s. We have to acknowledge that, if black struggles have indeed been central to the cultural history of capitalist modernity, then we are as deeply implicated in the downside of the postmodern condition as anyone else. Forward ever, backwards never; remember that slogan? Enlightenment notions of linear progress, and the desire for the centralised authority embodied in the nation-state, were integral components of black cultural nationalism. One cannot ignore the emphasis on collective belonging and empowerment that underpins religious fundamentalism among British Muslims, anymore than you can ignore what happened to the Palestinians when Zionism inscribed the return home, in 1948, for some at the expense of others. The concept of diaspora which Paul Gilroy's work has opened up has set forth adventitious lines for critical inquiry. Negotiating the cross-roads, in the cultural history of diasporic imagined communities must inevitably mean the critical examination of black people's implication in the cultural and political vicissitudes of modernity. The challenge of differences within and between black communities means that we have to move towards an acknowledgment of the everyday politics of ambivalence and indeterminacy: there is nothing inherently revolutionary or virtuous about being a black subject, because no-one has a monopoly on progressive democratic agency (to paraphrase Paul Gilroy's point that none of us has a monopoly on black authenticity).[7] Black subjects can be, and have been over the last decade, positioned in support of Thatcherism as much as anyone else. The Left did not offer much of an alternative, but the question of democratic agency cannot be reduced purely to the failure, blindness and exclusions of the British Left: black activists themselves implemented many of the official anti-racist policies that contributed to the mid 80s disaster zone around the Miner's Strike and Clause 28. The challenge of mutual criticism cuts both ways.

To follow through the question of democratic agency, we need to move towards an analysis of the contradictory identifications of which we are politically capable. This means turning the search for roots—the desire for a fixed centre of identity—into a search for routes out of the prisonhouse of marginality, to which the hierarchical ordering of difference would have us consigned, each in our own little ideological bantustan. There is nothing heroic about travelling theory: the decentered public sphere of post-modern society suggests that there is no longer any useful role for the universal intellectual who wants to save the world. On the contrary, artists, critics and other intellectual workers in the culture industry seek more modestly to make connections, to cut pathways and graft channels across the hierarchical boundaries of power that constitute the labyrinths and warrens we inhabit and dwell in, in cities like London, Lagos or Los Angeles.

To tap into the vocabulary of Deleuze and Guattari, displacing the search for roots implies turning away from the arborescent structure of dichotomous thinking, and grafting instead on to the rhizomatic movement of a centred thinking, which multiplies connections between things that have absolutely nothing to do with each other.[8] Unlike trees such as oak and pine, whose roots and radicles are organised in a hierarchical structure based on binary divisions, plants such as potatoes, strawberries, cassava and mangrove establish connections with elements in their environment through ariel roots and underground stems, thus connecting different elements that have no necessary relation with each other. In place of the search for a fixed origin, end or centre as a guarantee of one's black identity, located somewhere perhaps in mythological Africa, rhizomatic thinking invites research for routes out of the common predicaments we share here and now, not just as black Britons, but as Europeans to boot.

Travelling theory speaks to conditions of exile and displacement; it can ride in tandem with mobile privatisation, as the centripetal relations of margin and centre are stabilised by the selective incorporation of difference (where marginality, indeed, becomes a marketable commodity). But it also speaks to conditions of homelessness and restlessness in terms of a renewed commitment to theory that is motivated by the desire to

displace established orthodoxies; to keep on moving, from soul to soul, from station to station, on the dark side of the political imaginary. Diaspora is a domain of ~~discrimination~~ *dissemination* and dispersal, where seeds are scattered along diverse vectors and trajectories. You don't have to be a fan of Gardener's World to make metaphors out of a rhizome.

FOOTNOTE FROM THE NINETIES

Written in summer 1990, 'Back to My Routes' was a response to a suggestion by David A Bailey, co-editor of *Ten.8*'s *Critical Decade*, to reflect on themes from earlier contributions, such as the 1988 'True Confessions' article. It was an opportunity to take a broader view of artistic currents which had placed black Britain on the cultural map, as it were, by touching on key transformations in the social landscapes from which these diasporic interventions had arisen.

Taking a further glance from 1997, many of the essay's themes—such as the diversification of public space and the volatile character of the imagined communities who inhabit it—have acquired heightened salience in the light of new patterns of globalisation which have ensured that the vertigo of displacement continues apace. The word-play in the title was not only describing qualitative shifts in the critical outlook of black British visual artists; it was also reaching towards an understanding of trends which have internationalised the reception of black British work. Indeed, in the new internationalism of the nineties, curious disjunctures arise in the perception of black Britain at home and abroad. For instance, Henry Louis Gates Jr.'s enthusiasm for 'Black London' in a recent *New Yorker* feature highlights widespread African American interest in things black and British.[9] This is a brilliant confirmation of the generative spatial networks that constitute what Paul Gilroy calls the Black Atlantic: a fluid space of cultural exchange which cuts, leaks and flows across the boundaries of the nation-state.[10] On the other hand, however, the Union Jacks unfurled to celebrate the election victory of Tony Blair's New Labour suggest that nationalism has become more, not less, important. Hijacked by the Right since the late seventies, the flag now seems aligned with a social democratic stance—something as unexpected as seeing the staunchly Tory *Daily Mail* campaign for justice in the case of Stephen Lawrence, a young man murdered in a racist attack. Facing these contradictory currents, my impulse is to ask: how does the Britishness in British art or Brit pop relate to the beautiful chaos of the post-colonial convulsions that are also generating new forms of transnational blackness? When *Newsweek* describes the UK as one of 'the most comfortably multicultural nations in Europe,'[11] what is it about the social dynamics of ethnicity in England that makes it a place that supposedly swings? And why are my cultural studies students so worked up about the Spice Girls?

One of black Britain's defining characteristics is the broad-based shift away from essentialist views of blackness as a unitary identity fixed in the authenticity of one's origin, towards a more relational view of the plural identities constructed from the Caribbean, South Asian and African migrations of the post-war era. Because Empire brought together disparate peoples, whether as colonial subjects or as coloured immigrants, blackness in Britain has always been a more heterogenous, composite, and hybrid affair than it is in the United States. So while the 80s advocacy of Afro-Asian alliances under a shared signifier of blackness has become a thing of the past, a pluralist approach to the cultural politics of 'race' and ethnicity nonetheless remains peculiar to black British perspectives in the arts. This pluralistic outlook was crucial to the generation born in the 50s and 60s; who went to school and came of age in the 70s; who entered public visibility in the 80s, and who then began to use the polyvocal character of their experience in order to unpack the burden of being expected to speak as a minority representative. That is why I've referred to visual artists such as Sonia Boyce and Keith Piper, or Lubaina Himid and Zarina Bhimji, and film-makers and photographers like John Akomfrah, Isaac Julien and Rotimi Fani-Kayode, as post-colonial hybrids who are the flowers that flourished in the ruins of post-imperial decline.[12] The glory of the garden is such that nowadays there is a lot more strange variety creeping through the hedges.

What differentiates artists of the nineties—such as Steve McQueen, Chris Ofili, or Permindar Kaur—is that the shift away from the issue-based *gravitas* of the eighties is a response to artworld changes that have institutionalised the demand for difference. As Boyce once put it, describing this all-embracing discourse of identity: 'Whatever we black people do it is said to be about identity ... I am constantly being put in that position, required to talk in that place, never allowed to speak because I speak.'[13] Yet in the contemporary moment—in which YBAs (young black artists) such as Kara Walker in the US enjoy a mainstream visibility that is hardly marginal—even though difference is made managable as a multicultural policy object, artists have sought out aesthetic strategies that reveal happy accidents in the traffic of visual inter-culturation. This is something that has become ordinary, rather than exceptional, in global disjunctures where culture is, as Homi Bhabha observes, increasingly trans-locational and translational in character.[14]

Yinka Shonibare's source materials, in installations like *Double Dutch* (1993), unravel such an inter-cultural history. Fabrics originating in Indonesian batik, then industrialised by Dutch colonials and copied by their English rivals in the textile trade, were all made for export to African markets. Often appropriated as an emblem of authenticity, the cloth is ironically revealed to carry at least three meanings—an imported luxury, a colourful exotic fetish, or an Afro-kitsch badge of pride—none of which are intrinsic to the object, but are only acquired through its passage or *worlding* through different systems of exchange. Shonibare's stance suggests a process of *counter-normalisation* when he says,

It is normal for me to switch between cultures. I grew up speaking Yoruba at home and speaking English at school. ...I grew up watching local comedy programmes like *Baba Sala*, Australian programmes like *Skippy*, American ones like *Hawaii Five-O* etc. I listened to the music of Fela Kuti, James Brown, Sugar Hill Gang and King Soni Ade. I read Shakespeare, Charles Dickens, Wole Soyinka and Chinua Achebe at school. I am a post-colonial hybrid.[15]

Bringing Yoruba and Western elements together in an open-ended interplay between incommensurable codes, photographer Rotimi Fani-Kayode similarly inhabited such a transcultural space. But because his approach to the black male nude was bedevilled by a misleading comparison to Mapplethorpe during the early 90s culture wars, many failed to see that his aesthetic was never about identity but the ego's ecstatic loss of self in the *petit mort* of sexual pleasure. Collected in *Rotimi Fani-Kayode & Alex Hirst: Photographs* (Editions Revue Noir, Paris, 1997), we can see how his Dionysian passion deployed visual 'techniques of ecstasy' in which the mask interrupts the scopic drive so as to trans-code the universally human preoccupation with the enigmatic relation of sex and death. While it was inevitably frustrating to see black gay work caught up in the neo-conservative backlash—when Marlon Riggs's *Tongues Untied* (1989) video was demonised by Pat Buchanan in the 1992 US elections, for instance—the panic over political correctness also had the perverse effect of normalising difference. Isaac Julien's ability to play with sado-masochistic iconography while evoking slavery, as he does in *The Attendant* (1993), betokens the self-presence that pervades Topher Campbell's cheeky portrayal of photographer Ajamu in *The Homecoming* (1994), or Sri-Lankan born Sonali Fernando's praise-song to Audre Lorde in her smart and sexy film debut, *The Body of a Poet* (1995).

Watching *Ellen* come out on prime-time TV recently, it struck me that the post-p.c. settlement has not simply normalised diversity: it is part of a broader shift which has changed the very terrain of cultural politics now that multiculturalism has become a mainstream phenomenon of the marketplace. Hence, while some may celebrate black gay influences, like Julien's *Looking for Langston* (1989), in opening up approaches no longer inhibited by 'racial' anxieties—as seen in Steve McQueen's *Bear* (1993), which choreographs lines of flight to further de-territorialise the already overburdened symbolism of the black male body—others may be induced into a cultural cringe whenever identities are named as such. So what if Skin, the black female lead singer in the heavy metal band Skunk Anansie, is a dyke? Lighten up and enjoy the difference: this seems to be the message when culture and politics are subject to an ideological de-coupling—be as visible, as vocal, as different as you like, just don't make the mistake of grounding any ethical or political claims on the basis of your precious identity!

Nowhere is this dilemma more disturbingly evident than in what could be called the post-Civil Rights settlement in the US. In music, sports and entertainment, African Americans enjoy global visibility such that US popular culture *is* black popular culture: yet the loss of moral authority on the part of blackness as a floating signifier indicates a crisis of political direction that is a complete reversal of the sixties when black struggles had universalist resonance. Interestingly, Gates observed something similar on his visit to Britain. Puzzled by the passion which white youth have for jungle—the futuristic sound of dub reggae speeded-up by be-bop breaks, constructed entirely via cut-and-mix sampling that pushes digital technologies against the grain —he noticed the simultaneous escalation of racist violence and concluded, 'there you have the central contradictions of post-Thatcherite England: the growing cultural prominence of black culture doesn't mean that racism has abated much.'[16] The market has de-coupled earlier equations of public visibility and political gains, creating a precarious trade-off in which representational presence compensates for the loss of direction with regard to the pursuit of such aims as social justice. Such contradictions intensify rather than ameliorate the political, for as Stuart Hall comments, 'One of the paradoxes Thatcherism released [was to] encourage the hustling instinct. Some black kids will see an opportunity and can make it [and] at the same time there's this kind of Little Englandism [that is] racing away from difference.'[17]

In such a transitory moment, one needs a Janus-like ability to navigate the crossroads. While certain touchstone references in the 'Back to My Routes' essay now seem parochial or outdated—the photography journal *Ten.8* is sadly no longer with us and, like other cultural institutions of the Left, belongs to an era that is gone forever—there is a sense in which a changed disposition towards the past is one of the most interesting promises of the future. If multicultural normalisation now fulfills the feel-good factor for the G7

artworld, there is a unique opportunity to take a fresh look at how 'race' figures in modern British art history. From the blackfaced Al Jolson in the window of Richard Hamilton's *Just What Is It...?* (1956) or Peter Blake's pin-up of *Bo Diddley* (1964), to the Asian women service-workers depicted in Victor Burgin's image-text works of the 70s or Gilbert & George's stained-glass photo-montages of the East End, what do such images reveal of Englishness, now that we are all familiar with the post-structuralist tenet that what the Other represents is a mirror-like confirmation of the Same? Similarly, while Brit pop is largely a defensive reaction against the hegemony of black-originated dance music, what is often overlooked is that the house and techno music which came from black gay clubs in Detroit and Chicago was mostly based on African American re-appropriations of German synth-modernists like Kraftwerk. In other words, contemporary culture foregrounds the unstable energies of the cross-cultural traffic whereby the necessary fictions we call our identities are constantly being altered and detoured by the unfinished stories of inter-culturation. Forging new routes through the chaos, this quaint, medium-sized, offshore enterprise with a permanent identity-crisis (why else would it have three names—England, Great Britain, the United Kingdom—when one would do?) may yet yield some more surprises on art's long journey through the wreckage of modernity.

Kobena Mercer is the author of *Welcome to the Jungle: New Positions in Black Cultural Studies* (London and New York: Routledge, 1994), the editor of *Black Film/British Cinema* (ICA Documents no 7, 1988) and co-editor (with film-maker, Isaac Julien) of *Screen* (Vol 29 no 4, 1988). He has written and lectured widely on identity, sexuality and ethnicity in the visual arts of the black diaspora and is currently Visiting Professor, Africana Studies Program, New York University.

N O T E S

1.　　See, Errol Francis and Kobena Mercer, 'Black People, Culture and Resistance,' *Camerawork*, November 1982, which attempted a Foucauldian reading of Afro-Asian culture as sites of power and resistance. The Gay Black Group article, 'White Gay Racism,' *Gay News* October 1982, was reprinted in Jonathan Rutherford and Rowena Chapman, eds., *Male Order: Unwrapping Masculinity*, (London: Lawrence & Wishart, 1988).

2.　　On struggles over the sign of blackness see, Stuart Hall, 'Signification, Representation, Ideology: Althusser and the Post-Structuralist Debates,' *Critical Studies in Mass Communication*, Vol 2, no2, 1985.

　　On revised historiographies of the sixties from such a perspective, see my, '"1968": Periodising Postmodern Politics and Identity,' [1992] in *Welcome to the Jungle: New Positions in Black Cultural Studies* (London and New York: Routledge, 1994).

3.　　'The Last 'Special' Issue on Race?', *Screen* Vol 29 no4, Autumn 1988.

4.　　Edward Said, *The World, the Text and the Critic* (London: Faber, 1982).

5.　　'Cultural Identities,' *Undercut* no 17, 1988, p 36.

6.　　Michel Foucault and Gilles Deleuze, 'Intellectuals and Power,' [1972] in Michel Foucault, *Language, Counter-Memory and Practice*, ed. Donald Bouchard, (Oxford: Basil Blackwell, 1977) p 201.

7.　　Paul Gilroy, 'Nothing but Sweat Inside my Hand', in *Black Film/British Cinema*, ed. Kobena Mercer, ICA Documents no 7, 1988; see also, Paul Gilroy, *There Ain't No Black in the Union Jack: The Cultural Politics of Race and Nation* (London: Hutchinson, 1987).

8.　　Gilles Deleuze and Felix Guattari, 'Rhizome,' *I&C* no 8, Spring 1981, reprinted as *Rhizome* (Minneapolis: University of Minnesota, 1984).

9.　　Henry Louis Gates Jr., 'Black London,' *The New Yorker*, April 28 & May 5, 1997, pp 194 - 205. See also, Gates's earlier account In, 'Hybridity Happens: Black Brit Bricolage Brings the Noise,' *Voice Literary Supplement*, October, 1992. The African American interest in trans-Atlantic exchange is further indicated by, Houston Baker, Manthia Diawara and Ruth Lindborg, eds, *Black British Cultural Studies: A Reader* (Chicago: University of Chicago Press, 1996).

10.　　Paul Gilroy, *The Black Atlantic: Modernity and Double Consciousness* (Cambridge: Harvard University Press, 1993).

11.　　*Newsweek*, May 5 1997, p 35.

12.　　See my, 'Busy in the Ruins of Wretched Phantasia,' in David A Bailey, ed., *Mirage: Enigmas of Race, Difference and Desire*, (London: Institute of Contemporary Arts/Institute of International Visual Arts, 1995) and also, Mark Sealy, 'Talking Hybridity: Interview with Kobena Mercer,' *Creative Camera*, no 34, March 1995.

13.　　Sonia Boyce in Manthia Diawara, 'The Art of Identity: A Conversation,' in *Black British Cultural Studies*, op cit. p 308.

14.　　Homi Bhabha, *The Location of Culture*, (London and New York: Routledge, 1994).

15.　　Yinka Shonibare, 'Fabric, and the Irony of Authenticity,' in Nikos Papastergiadis, ed., *Mixed Belongings and Unspecified Destinations*, INIVA Annotations no 1 (London: Institute of International Visual Arts, 1997), p 40. See also my, 'Art That is Ethnic in Inverted Commas: On Yinka Shonibare,' *frieze*, no 35, November 1995.

16.　　Gates, *The New Yorker*, op cit. p 198.

17.　　Stuart Hall in Caryl Phillips, 'Interview with Stuart Hall: The Bohen Series on Critical Discourse,' *Bomb* no 58, Winter 1997, p 40.

123

FIRST GENERATION REPRODUCTION

DAVID BARRETT

L et's look at the factors that affect all art students at the moment, factors that play in the backs of their minds, perhaps in a similar way that museum shops play on your mind, simply because you have to enter and leave the museum via them—they frame your experience. Broad cultural influences are the unavoidable backdrops for students, both in the art schools where we spend our days and in the mass culture, of which we are a prime target: Douglas Coupland's character Dag from *Generation X*, said that he achieved no small thrill of power to think that most manufacturers of life-style accessories in the Western world considered him to be their most desirable target market. It is true that virtually all mainstream media is aimed at the magical 18-49 age range, and that the most frenetic of this media attention takes the 18-29 group as its target. But this 'honour' is a double-edged Wilkinson's Sword. We are supposedly monied but free of responsibilities, and so we are encouraged to conform to this stereotype by being free of the responsibilities of money—and to do so in air-cushioned soles and blue jeans. But maybe this is not such a visible influence, perhaps we don't really notice this attention so much due to its omnipresence, and because we have never really been conscious of living outside of the target range. However, I imagine we most certainly will notice when we slip out the other end of capitalism's Most Wanted group.

First published in the *new contemporaries 96* catalogue.

So if it's not the hip hype of media bombardment, then I guess the most visible cultural influence has to be the fact that the 90s has finally achieved a positive, productive zeitgeist. Somehow—who would have thought it —we've stumbled across a milieu full of constructive possibilities. What combination of events could have produced this surprising situation?

The 60s. There, I said it. I didn't want to, but what could I do? It's the decade that never dies, just keeps coming over all retro: cool, uncool, cool, uncool. I wasn't even conceived in the 60s, and yet I still know more about it than I do the 70s. There's this whole generation who missed the utopia—and disaster—of the 60s, but all they've ever heard their whole lives from everyone, everywhere is how great it was. We've heard it, read it, and seen it, but never lived it. However, the belief that things can happen is spreading again; if our parents can do it, then we damn-well can too.

The 80s. Another ne'er-be-mentioned. That was when I grew up, and in those days there was something you could believe in, could trust in, aim for: money. But even that simple(minded) belief was lost in the darkest recesses of the deep recession. But all the ungodly shit that went on in the 80s, yes it's true that we're still up to our knees in it, though that's only because it's finally receded from our necklines.

However, the panic's over now because the worst has already happened, all that we're left with is this massive fall-out which, as it turns out, is the richest of pickings for artists. It may be a kind of cultural nuclear winter for everyone else, but it's definitely springtime for young artists. Why? Because in a way it's interesting to live in a country where the government is

RICHARD WRIGHT *UNTITLED* 1996
(INSTALLATION VIEW) WALL PAINTING,
GOUACHE AND ACRYLIC, DIMENSIONS
VARIABLE, COURTESY OF THE ARTIST

collapsing, where an entire ideology is failing, leaving only confusion. Without a centre, the collective consciousness has become a mass of undifferentiated peripheries. No one really knows what is of value since all values were levelled in the 80s. And with this, artists have suddenly discovered that they are as (un)important as everyone else. The situation that we find ourselves in is the interesting time when one thing has come to an end, but where that which will replace it has not yet arrived. (Perhaps this rich sense of collapse will be dissipated by the cocksure New Labour, which is worrying, since surely we all now understand that for 'New' we must read 'Not'.)

At the same time as the financial market's collapse, the overbearing influence of theory receded, simply because it went into orbit and finally became a discipline of its own. When it was claimed that artists made objects and critics made art, first year art students all over the land waved bye-bye to that particular spaceship. When the spaceship lands again then, sure, we'll all get on board, but until that time we're stuck here on Earth, more specifically the 'United'

Kingdom, in my case Hackney, and it's kind of difficult to ignore that. There simply can't be any more space-cadets Out There than there are Here already. So it seems more interesting, more stimulating, to ground the theoretical in the everyday. Experience, and trying to make sense of it, has once again become the fundamental reference point. Not that theory has been forgotten; we're devouring it faster than ever, but it has dawned on us that to begin a piece by choosing a theoretical reading that the artwork must then deliver has reached such a level of complexity that it can only end in a paralysing stalemate. The reading has to be done by someone other than the maker, otherwise nothing will ever get made.

GILLIAN WEARING **'CONFESS ALL ON VIDEO: DON'T WORRY YOU WILL BE IN DISGUISE. INTRIGUED? CALL GILLIAN...'** 1994

MAT COLLISHAW **BUTTERFLY TABLE** 1996

Perhaps it has always been true that young artists ground things in the everyday, perhaps it's just that they are now more visible than they ever were before. Art, it seems, is going the way of British pop: younger bands, higher praise, less time at the top. Everything is new and it's always the new-big-thing. Yeah, it leads to instant burn-out, but—as the editor of the *NME* once asked—who ever said it was about careers anyway? One problem of this, though, is that fashion then becomes the dictator as to how long an issue can be sustained in the public eye, so whatever progress can be made in an 'in' area, like multi-culturalism was, will be lost as soon as the issue is no longer 'fresh'. Fashion, by definition, can sustain nothing but itself, which means that as trends turn over faster, less will actually change—save for the packaging. Every generation will be the first generation, or as Tricky succinctly put it: 'Brand new, you're retro'.

As a comparison, this art/pop thing is hardly new, but recently the Brit Pop/Brit Pack phenomena has become rather hard to ignore. And it does enable us to look at a trend within another discipline which, at times, is fairly analogous to the visual arts. Certainly at the moment the coincidences are too strong to ignore, so let's take a look at one of the more interesting parallels, and that is the death of cool (by 'cool' here I mean 'distanced'). This was signalled in the pop-scene by the eventual triumph of *Oasis* over *Blur*, the underdogs finally taking the colours by indisputably succeeding in America in a way that *Blur* most definitely never will. The reason for this is that *Blur* are, essentially, a parochial band; their references, both musical and lyrical, are always sad, English-urban in origin. They are, at heart, an 80s band: ultra-knowing, self-conscious, clever-clever. *Oasis* are a 60s band of course, they look and sound like *The Beatles*—

JORDAN BASEMAN **BASED ON ACTUAL EVENTS** 1995

a 'real' rock 'n' roll band. You don't expect ironic lyrics from them, and you most assuredly don't get them; their words are effectively nonsensical phonetic musical additions. With *Oasis* you don't stand outside of the music, you are engulfed in it. *Blur* was the band that the critics with a theoretical bent loved, though it seems that listeners have finally reached the pinnacle of detached coolness: they are actually bored. People want to be inside the music again, mixed up in it all—they want to Roll With It.

So, finally, what can we say? We have two extraordinary decades, the 60s and the 80s, combining to potent effect: one positive, one negative; one force-fed, one lived through. Intensive self-promotion has given way to a sense of fun, a lightness of touch—which is not to say that professionalism has disappeared, it's just that we've noticed that things don't have to be so bloody serious. There is a sense that things can actually happen, those famous fifteen minutes are back again and—hey!—it could be you. Essentially, it's a confidence thing; young British artists have heard that Young-British-Art is where it's at and, not surprisingly, they want to be there too. Conspiring circumstances have dropped this situation into our laps, handed us a baton on the run. We're yet to slow down long enough to discover if it's ticking.

David Barrett is an MA Fine Art student at the Slade School of Art and a regular contributor to *frieze* and *Art Monthly* magazines.

BACK TO BASICS:
BRITISH ART AND THE PROBLEMS OF A GLOBAL FRAME [1]

NIKOS PAPASTERGIADIS

OLD AND NEW INTERNATIONALISM

Throughout this century, part of the definition of modern art has been the aspiration towards internationalism. Borders were there to be broken, ever since Apollinaire declared:

I am everywhere or rather I start to be everywhere.
It is I who am starting this thing of centuries to come.

For the avant-garde, the local was the place you left. The 'national schools' of art that dominated Europe in the late nineteenth and early twentieth centuries were seen as expressing discrete cultural values and reflecting the interests of the old aristocratic and landowning classes. The cultural field of modernism, and the avant-garde in particular, sought to challenge this connection between art and the dominant order. Avant-garde artists were never concerned simply with the authentic expression of national culture. Their formal experiments with the new technologies of representation, such as the camera, suggested the possibility of new 'ways of seeing', and their embrace of the rhetoric of revolution inspired new visions of social change. Art and politics found a new relationship, and together they expressed a hope of breaking out of a restrictive and nationalistic framework. The power of modernism was therefore invariably linked to both a reaction against the particularistic culture of the *ancien régime* and a projection towards a new internationalist culture.[2]

In the post-war period, the radical spirit of modernism was truncated as it was increasingly incorporated within the mainstream institutions of art. This institutionalisation within an aggressively nationalist framework, pitting West against East, was not only antithetical to its founding principles but also conducted in a selective fashion. At a time when there was an increased traffic between people from different parts of the globe, and a greater exchange in cultural symbols, the contributions to modernism made by artists in the peripheries or migrants from former colonies were excluded from the official discourses. Western modernist artists could lay claim to universal values and find global appeal. The populist image of Picasso, as the Western artist who could incorporate non-Western artforms, is the clearest example of the Eurocentric bias in the modernist sensibility.

While the Western artist could freely move across borders, the passage of non-Western artists was more problematical. Non-Western artists who embraced the modernist movement were routinely dismissed as 'mimic men'. Non-Western artists could, at best, aspire to reproducing static and closed traditions. Their representation of the local was no more than that. The suggestion that an intimate representation of the local may also be an allegory for the global was never extended beyond the boundaries of Western modernism. The Eurocentric construction of the universalism and internationalism of modern art escaped rigorous critique, precisely because it felt empowered to distance itself from those characterisations of nationalism that stressed an introverted mindset. At this end of the century, as the concept of the nation-state undergoes another crisis, it is the banner of internationalism that is once again raised as a possible site for cultural renewal.

VONG PHAOPHANIT **UNTITLED** 1995-96

However the notion of internationalism has never been an open or all-embracing concept. Meanwhile, colonialism was, by definition, always an internationalist project. How could we overlook the devastation and suffering that was ruthlessly executed in the name of a uniform and global modernization? Colonial rule may now be formally dismantled, but as Ngugi Wa Thiong'o reminds us, de-colonising the mind is far from complete. The notable lack of conviction given by successive British governments to the institutions formed under the umbrella of the Commonwealth is testament to its inability to explore a multi-racial vision of internationalism. While the indigenous élites of Africa and India may have expressed suspicion and distrust towards the Commonwealth in the immediate post-colonial period, this opportunity has been most crucially undermined by the shift from sentimental appreciation to outright disdain by the British Foreign Office. As Robin Cohen has argued, Britain turned its back both economically and culturally on the Commonwealth, but in doing so it scarcely embraced a new European internationalism.

In its new, uncomfortable union with Europe, Britain still insists, for instance, that it should retain an independent immigration policy on the grounds that 'it is an island'.[3] It is also worth noting that the current committee that discusses issues of migration for the European Union is the same group that is set up to advise on the threat of terrorism and drug smuggling. By keeping the issue of migration in the same frame as these other forms of violent transgression, it maintains a continuum with the so-called 'histrionic tendencies of social life'. The stigma of migration is deeply ingrained in the political imaginary. The ongoing complicity between globalisation and Eurocentrism only adds new levels of insecurity to the modes of inter-action and integration in the world economic and communications systems. Such challenges are inevitably at the forefront of the way we understand artistic production.

It would be naive to celebrate the fluidity of cultural exchange that follows from transnational capital, rapid telecommunications, and mass tourism, which in fact operates against a background of deepening economic divisions between the North and the South, and the ever-stricter policing of refugees and migrants along political borders. For while the idea of an authentic nationalism is the antinomy of modernism, the liberatory projects of the new internationalism have also threatened to homogenise cultural differences. The choices today should not be reduced to either local nationalism or global modernity. What we need to consider is how we can rethink the relationship between the axes of cultural contact and political equality, without reinscribing the exploitative models of centre and periphery.

GLOBAL VISIONS

In the past decade a growing field of cultural criticism has developed, that seeks to challenge many of the fundamental misconceptions in modernism, and to offer counter-histories of cultural exchange. The publication of Global Visions[4], which brings together papers delivered at the conference entitled 'A New Internationalism'—the first conference of the Institute of International Visual Arts held at the Tate Gallery, London, 27- 28 April 1994—is an index of this problem of examining the framework of contemporary art from a global perspective.

The contributors to the collection vary from critics such as Hal Foster, who commented on the utility of quasi-anthropological paradigms in the visual practice of representing other cultures, to the curator and writer Gerardo Mosquera, who cautiously mentioned that the precedents for a 'new internationalism' lay between a form of complicitous multicultural relativism and the axes of globalisation that divide and alter the zones of silence to satisfy the dominance of the West as a cultural centre. Such scepticism is also to be found at the centre of Jimmie Durham's essay, as he asks the deceptively simple question: 'how might we imagine internationalism without it being among nations?'[5] A distrust of nationalism may be healthy; but is the disavowal expressed by more complacent members of the artworld both premature and counter-productive? By pointing to dramatic shifts in the practices of geo-political administration, much of the discussion on globalisation presupposes the obsolescence of the nation-state. Therefore it may be more appropriate to think of the reconfiguring rather than the withering of the nation. Rasheed Araeen's comments on the shallowness and hypocrisy of earlier experiments with internationalism within the parameters of an ideologically divided British state, and Durham's reflections on the delusions of transcendence, are careful reminders of the gaps between the promise and the performance of a concept.

Global Visions provides a necessary reference-point for the rethinking of the legacy of modernism, as well as offering an indication of the issues that have come to preoccupy mainstream art institutions. This collection illuminates a number of new political and cultural trajectories. There has been a contestation over the term ethnicity, as it has been moved out of the political domain of anti-racism into the cultural field of identity. With the influence of psychoanalytic literature on the necessary, not simply negative, relationship between the self and the Other, and an increasing awareness of what Kobena Mercer calls the 'diasporic aesthetic', the status of difference *in* identity has also been re-evaluated. These new shifts have provoked many new questions. How will the traditional be cross-cut with the modern? What is the geo-political framework that will contain the trans-national pattern of cultural exchange? How valid is the national as a category for identifying a contemporary sensibility and identity? What capacity do mainstream institutions have for understanding and responding to the histories of exclusion and marginalisation?

The institutional responses to such radical questions are at best uneven; at worst, defensive. The forces pushing for change are conjunctural, a combination of activism and legitimation, creating an implosion. However such conjunctural energy is often diverted, and the sources blurred. A common trope for this form of misrecognition and diversion is found in the representation of the Other in the guise of the virginal origin. For instance, while speaking on the panel for the opening of the mega-exhibition *Les Magiciens de la Terre*, in Paris (1989), Gayatri Spivak pondered on the distance between this title and the expression, *artistes du monde*.[6] The separation was not innocent; moreover she suggested that this was consistent with a certain hesitancy in the way the institution of art can cede some of its ground.

By turning to face the problematics of the margin in the name of *terre*, the art museum was seeking to erase the preceding space of the *monde*. Spivak reminded us that the reception of other practices is often preceded by both inscription of their world as a 'virgin' territory, together with the hope of constructing an elevated plane for new forms of cultural interaction.

I would argue that the way the dominant institutions respond to the issues of cultural difference is also bound by their very conceptualisation of crisis. It has varied from recognition of the necessary re-negotiation of existing resources to a re-thinking of the very paradigms within which cultural practice is conducted. The first level is often conceived as *the crisis of culture*. The factors behind this approach can be clearly stated. Mass migration, decolonisation, emancipatory social movements, and feminism are routinely cited as the forces that have generated new levels of expectancy, stimulated further demands, heightened consciousness of the gaps between formal and substantive rights, and re-defined the horizons of the permissible and the desirable. In short, they have challenged the certitudes and order of the dominant culture.

However in a world of transition and rupture it is not just hierarchies that are contested; the rules of the game also come under scrutiny. For example, Terry Eagleton is right to claim that the current crisis is so deep that the very concept of culture cannot be introduced to reconcile or redeem material struggle. For culture itself is perceived as complicit with the construction of the struggle *in* the social. Culture

131

PAUL GRAHAM **TELEVISION PORTRAIT (YUKO, KYOTO)** 1992

and other transcendental values are no longer neutral concepts. 'Culture is now part of the problem rather than the solution.'[7] As we witness the breakdown of the conventional models for integrating and organising the question of difference—when both universalism and particularism are seen as inadequate, or when neither evolutionism nor relativism seem satisfactory—we can then twist the level of understanding crisis: modernity is *the culture of crisis*.

This crisis is most palpable in the difference between the rhetoric of inclusion and the practice of participation. The crisis is thus not confined to the process of assimilating a foreign entrant, but involves both re-structuring and re-orientation. Pragmatic switches and genuine reforms, while dominating the sensibility of the guardians of institutions, offer paltry compensation for the complex demands being imposed by a life-world of heterogeneity and the cultural dynamisms of difference. At the broad level of how an oppositional strategy is construed, Meaghan Morris has observed a shift in the left-leaning assumptions of solidarity and common struggle. The projected unity and essentialist identities that sustained the earlier ideological critique of a crisis in culture is being fragmented, and she notes that:

> Real dilemmas are emerging, some of which will make it more difficult in the future for the old 'left-liberal' and leftist cultures to maintain their political imaginary by identifying with a spectrum of causes once smoothly construed as coherent — feminism; anti-racism; gay activism; land rights; environmentalism; opposition to uranium mining.[8]

NEW ETHNICITIES

In his influential 1988 essay, 'New Ethnicities', Stuart Hall argued that black cultural politics in Britain were undergoing a significant transition. Hall distinguished two 'moments' in black cultural politics. The first was 'the moment when the term 'black' was coined as a way of referencing the common experience of racism and marginalisation in Britain'.[9] Notions such as the 'black experience' provided a unifying framework for building up a common identity across a variety of ethnic and cultural groups, and was instrumental in providing a coherent challenge to dominant conceptions of British national identity. This unified and unifying notion of black identity also informed the development of what Hall calls a cultural politics 'designed to challenge, resist, and where possible, to transform the dominant regimes of representation'. Critical in this struggle over the 'relations of representation' were questions of fetishisation, objectification and negative figuration, manifested in a concern 'not simply with the absence or marginality of black experience but with its simplification and stereotypical character'. The key demands of this struggle were for access (representation by black artists), and for *contestation* (the provision of positive images to counterpoint existing negative stereotypes).

The second 'moment' of black cultural politics that Hall identifies arises in the context of a struggle over the 'relations of representation', becoming a struggle over the 'politics of representation' itself. Through this, Hall points firstly to the increasing acceptance that representation

133

does not merely reflect culture but is constitutive of that culture; and secondly, to the increasing awareness of the limits of the 'essential' or unified black subject.

What is at issue here is the recognition of the extraordinary diversity of subjective positions, social experiences and cultural identities which compose the category 'black'; that is, the recognition that 'black' is essentially a politically and culturally *constructed* category, which cannot be grounded in a fixed trans-cultural or transcendental racial category and which therefore has no guarantees in Nature. What this history brings into play is the recognition of the immense diversity and differentiation of the historical and cultural experience of black subjects.[10]

At the forefront of this diversity is the recognition that the black subject cannot be represented without reference to the dimensions of class, gender, sexuality and ethnicity. Moreover, awareness of the complexity of affiliations which traverse subjectivity necessitates the recognition of the contradictory processes and investments which constitute identity. As Hall notes, racism is powered not only by the negative positioning of blacks but also by an 'inexpressible envy and desire'.

Just as masculinity always constructs femininity as double—simultaneously Madonna and whore—so racism constructs the black subject: noble savage and violent avenger.[11]

It is in this sense that Hall posits the emergence of a new ethnicity. Instead of operating as a form of closure in the name of purity of nation and race, Hall points to:

...what I think is the beginning of a positive conception of ethnicity of the margins, of the periphery. That is to say, a recognition that we all speak from a particular place, out of a particular experience, a particular culture, without being contained by that position as 'ethnic artists' or film-makers.[12]

Thus we see how, from the early 80s, there was a significant contestation over and shift in the representation of identity in British culture. In their last special issue for the journal *Ten 8*, David A. Bailey and Stuart Hall referred to the 80s as 'the critical decade'. As the nation-state struggled both to integrate the people into an homogenous collective with a uniform self-identity and to organize a socio-economic system that guaranteed the rights of labour and social dignity, and while the gap and contradictions between these promises were being exposed by everyday experiences, a series of critiques was being mounted that supplemented the traditional materialist perspective of the orthodox left. Feminist, postcolonial and ecological critics raised new questions about the definition and boundaries of the national culture.

Such a context of cultural and political contestation facilitated the emergence of new forms of artistic practice and critical discourse. During this period we saw the ascendance of a number of figures whose work was critical of essentialist national iconographies, and yet they were increasingly being promoted as exponents of the cosmopolitanism of British culture. At a conference in Berlin, I was once asked by a director of the Goethe Institute to explain 'why it was that Britain had attracted migrants such as Anish Kapoor and Salman Rushdie, while Germany,

meanwhile, with a much higher proportion of immigrants, had not produced comparable artists achieving international recognition.' He went on to answer his own question by suggesting that the immigrants in Germany were of 'inferior stock'. He then bemoaned the 'purely' economic motivation of the *Gästarbeiter*, and expressed an admiration for the cultural aspirants within the Commonwealth.

Although not sharing such a racialist ideology or unfounded nostalgia for cultural migrations, black American critics and artists, when visiting the offices of the journal *Third Text*, invariably asked us the question: 'How did such a publication get off the ground in London?' The subtext to this question was the contrast to New York, a city that is more self-consciously a city of immigrants; and yet according to their impressions, it would have been impossible to imagine such a journal getting off the ground there. As the 'Rushdie Affair' exploded in the late 80s, the price of success and the hard road ahead became even clearer.

A journal such as *Third Text* did not simply fall from the sky and land in London, just as the dynamic between migration and cultural practices does not always find a positive recognition in the mainstream. Why these things should have happened requires a complex historical understanding; and at this point, I can only furnish rather broad and crude explanations. First, we should acknowledge the initiative and insistence of key individuals. There have been people like Rasheed Araeen, the artist, activist, writer and founding editor of *Third Text*, who saw the omissions and distortions in the public discourse on the arts, and then not only pointed them out but proposed strategies to address them.

Second, these individuals must draw from a collective language of discontent and resistance. In the 50s and 60s London was a kind of haven for exiles engaged in the political struggles of decolonisation. By the 80s, the politics of colonialism had been substantially dismantled, but the vestiges of cultural and economic neo-colonialism were far from gone. In such a context the psycho-philosophical texts of Frantz Fanon proved more telling than the instructions on guerilla tactics from Che Guevara. Black radicalism began to move from the essentialist polarities that had fractured the uneasy alliances found in, say, the Black Panther movement, to a more complex and inclusive cultural politics of hybridity. The mediatory roles and translational skills of intellectuals such as Stuart Hall and Homi Bhabha were crucial in this move.

Third, there is the position from which the migrant or exile speaks. In the post-war period, all people from the colonies could claim the status of British subjects with the right to immigration and residence in Britain. This 'freedom' was a cause of considerable anxiety to successive British governments, and it was systematically withdrawn as soon as black subjects began to exercise it. Nevertheless, for a brief period of time, artists in search of a metropolitan modernism, students in pursuit of higher degrees, exiled revolutionaries and manual labourers, arrived in considerable numbers. Artists, students and revolutionaries mixed together, and this created a vibrant and confident intellectual and political community. They were in the mother-country; they had been educated in the best of British institutions; they had the right to stay, and it was time to 'strike back' at the ideas of Empire. But who would listen?

The fourth factor depends on the formation of a broader audience beyond the constituency of the disenfranchised or the community of the marginalised. Black activists forged links with feminist, libertarian and socialist movements. The 'rainbow coalition' that was formed by Ken Livingstone, which for a few years effectively ran the Greater London Council and had considerable influence in a number of arts boards, showed how exciting and unstable such experiments could be. However, alongside such political realignments, it was the dialogues and disputes between these groups that steered the shifts in the discourse on cultural boundaries and the responsibilities of the welfarist state.

Ultimately, it has been the *conjunctural forces* of individual agencies and social movements, within a specific historic and political context, that have extended the challenge to the constructions of British culture. This critique of the homogeneous national category, and the *subject* with a unified and exclusive essence, gathered further impetus from the philosophical perspective of postmodernism.

Attention now turned to the question of *difference* in culture, and to the fragmentation of the *subject*. From such perspectives black culture and subjectivity were not simply marginal, but expressive of the incontrovertible hybridity and dynamic creolization of all cultural identity. Art institutions such as the Institute of Contemporary Arts and the British Film Institute, as well as many of the art colleges, became heavily involved in sponsoring debates and encouraging cultural practices that articulated those histories and perspectives that were previously ignored or repressed.

All this might suggest that black art in Britain has now been established within the mainstream. Conferences at the Tate Gallery and survey shows at Southbank can be used to demonstrate such a tentative inclusion. However just as those who are already settled in Britain are getting their foot in the front door, the external gates are being locked even more firmly, and the house of culture is being dismantled and decentred.

It is crucial to point out that Britain is no longer an immigrant society. Since the late 60s mass migration has effectively ceased. The impact of migration on mainstream British culture is going to be increasingly mediated and abstract. Furthermore in the 90s we have witnessed what can only be called the backlash against cultural and sexual theory. The 'FUCK THEORY' approach that is evident in the so-called 'yBa' [ed. 'young British artists'] phenomenon, and which has been championed by critics such as John Roberts, is not simply a rejection of sophistry; it is also the licence for a more narcissistic and uncritical expression of 'Englishness'.

There is now a concerted effort to reclaim the cultural terrain that was for a moment being challenged by feminist, postcolonial and postmodern perspectives. It is a rearguard offensive which has as much credibility as the isolationist and anti-Europe movement in the Tory party. However the chauvinism is more duplicitous and unspoken in the artworld, and as a consequence, commercially far more successful. Those very artists who are concerned with the 'instinctual' practices and the 'banalities' of everyday life at home, are often proud to be called British abroad. The promotional literature of the yBa phenomenon says nothing about 'multicultural Britain'; it bypasses the sociological sensibilities of feminist theory; it accentuates a primordial construction of identity; and it suggests that the notion of the aesthetic as a pure and transcendent category has returned with a 'visceral' but 'dumb' vengeance.

THE GHETTO OF ETHNIC ARTS IN ARTS POLICY

The history of shifts in cultural policy is rarely in step with changes in British society, and this complex relationship is also in need of further research. Parethentically, it may be noted that while most of the research on cultural *practice* stresses the prevalence of an internationalist perspective, the research on cultural *policy* is nevertheless conducted on an almost exclusively national basis. Despite the increasing international circulation of institutional models, and the identification of parallels in the construction of the social world in various nation-states, there has been very little, if any, research which has been conducted on a comparative basis. It would be a valuable exercise to consider the relationship between the formation of arts policies and the broader processes of social negotiation and political contestation. Further research is needed to trace the peculiar ways in which ideas migrate *across* national boundaries, and how they are consequently institutionalised *within* specific state structures.

The concept of a new internationalism in the visual arts emerged primarily from the ideas and struggles of black arts in Britain. Throughout the 70s and the 80s black artists and critics in Britain critiqued the prevailing models and categories for representing cultural identity. They attempted to shift the debate on 'blackness' beyond either exotica or stigma, and to expand the political horizons that were set in the anti-racism discourse. This new cultural movement challenged the funding practices of the major government institutions, and was a crucial part of the groundswell that led to the formation of The Institute of New International Visual Arts (INIVA).

One of the earliest documents to specify the limitations in British cultural policies was written in 1976 by Naseem Khan. She was commissioned to write the first-ever report on the diverse nature of contemporary British culture, and to evaluate the access that 'ethnic minorities' had to state funding. Naseem Khan identified some of the glaring contradictions and failures in the financing of the minority arts. Her report was entitled *The Arts Britain Ignores*. Needed and well-intentioned as it was, this report was subject to immediate criticism.[13] Black artists and critics were quick to contest the very frame of reference and the validation that it lent to the term 'ethnic minority arts'. Such commentators felt that the state's ethnocentric cultural policies would not be revealed by merely identifying the gaps and flaws in the allocation of funds. They argued that black artistic production should not be defined by such patronising terms, which only further polarised cultural positions and reinforced an oppressive social hierarchy. The question repeatedly asked was: How will a dominant culture recognise the achievements and significance of individuals from other cultures, when their cultural traditions are being constructed as not just the origin, but also the limit of their creative potential?

By working on the assumption that multi-culturalism was an ideology that legitimised the status of all forms of cultural production, Khan failed to look into the power differentials that ghettoised specific practices, relegating them to the margins of the national culture. Thus from the beginning there emerged a very clear critique of a form of multicultural policy that confines black artistic practice to enclosed notions of community, or to an exemplification of static forms of tradition. Embedded within such a conceptual framework, the dominant discourse would inevitably continue to ignore the linkages between black art and other forms of contemporary artistic practice.

Following Naseem Khan's report, very few significant steps were taken to alter the frame of reference. The commissioning of the Roundhouse project, which promised to serve as a 'superstructure' that would accommodate and enhance a wide range of black cultural practices was a spectacular failure. Throughout the 80s the Arts Council of Great Britain commissioned various reports that tested the relationship between the rhetoric of cultural diversity and the allocation of funds. The emphasis was on evaluation of the commitment to funding, monitoring of attendance at events, consolidation of specific bases, and the possible outreach to new constituencies or sponsors. Most of these reports concluded by noting the double disadvantage that confronted black arts organisations; and they all called for long-term strategies that would tackle structural problems associated with racism that blocked the integration of hitherto neglected constituencies within a broad pluralist framework.

STAGING NEW INTERNATIONALISM

The publication of the report on *The Institute of New International Visual Arts* (INIVA),[14] in December 1991, was heralded by Sandy Nairne, then Director of Visual Arts, as 'a new stage in the development of the Arts Council's thinking about the visual arts and its support to cultural diversity.'

What is unique about INIVA is that it aims to develop a new kind of institute, which not only builds on the history of black arts but will also play an active role in shaping a plural cultural aesthetic. The intention is to challenge the prevailing Euro-American axioms in the discourse on contemporary culture, by giving particular recognition to the vitality of non-Western practices. INIVA proposes to tackle the limitations of the dominant views in two ways: firstly, by confronting the exclusion of the majority of the world's cultures; and secondly,

CRITICAL DECOR **ARROWS** 1995

hegemony. Cultural difference is no longer posited as an optional addition, but as a constitutive force in the dynamism of plural societies.

From this perspective, the frame work of 'new internationalism' cannot be defined by merely attacking the chauvinistic aggressivity that marks the re-emergence of nationalism(s). Neither can 'new internationalism' simply be implied as the congregation of those previously excluded from the institution of modernism. The concept needs to be defined in terms of its points of departure, the horizons that it sets out for, and the associations it seeks to encourage. The concept should be a frame for enabling connections in all the processes of engagement, rather than simply in the positive networking and unintended consequences that result for those who participate within its own structures. The concept needs to suggest a method which others can either adopt or reject.

However while the agenda for work to be done is rich and demanding, the broader cultural predicament in which the concept of 'new internationalism' is located is not so optimistic. Sandy Nairne has noted the poverty of cultural policy within the European Community.[15] The Treaty of Rome was concerned only with maintaining the heritage of national culture within its respective borders, and reinforced the priority of market principles so that contemporary art can be traded freely. The Maastricht Treaty was also no significant advance. There was a generalised acknowledgement of the responsibility for developing a common culture while respecting the

by addressing the marginalisation of minority cultures within western states. Thus the concept of a 'new internationalism' calls for a wider understanding of both global culture and the history of art. It also presumes that in this particular moment of ideological transition, and the rupture of social and cultural certitudes, the issues of difference and hybridity have to be given greater cultural value.

The cultural and intellectual promise of INIVA thus rests on establishing a critical negotiation of the cultural formations that are emerging as a consequence of the twin pressures of cultural diasporas and socio-economic globalization. INIVA not only offers the opportunity to excavate and 're-present' the works of significant artists who were repressed by the mainstream; it can also act as a spur for rethinking the criteria for institutional inclusion, and mount a critique against the ethnic patterning of cultural specificities of existing cultures. However, as Nairne observed, this policy is limited by two flaws: first, the absence of any detailed clarification; and second, the failure to acknowledge the role of minorities within the respective national cultures. The combined effect is to undermine the potential for establishing a diversity of reference points and pattern of interchange in a broader cultural formation.

The flaws that Nairne identified at the transnational level cannot be overcome by simply imposing models and practices within specific nation-states. For instance, who could dispute Anthony Everrit's claim that we need both a 'value-free space', and a broader framework than that which Eurocentric modernism established?[16] Yet, when it comes to defining the basis—the criteria and boundaries of the 'new internationalism'—the main initiatives and responsibility are invariably passed back to the cultural producers.

Gavin Jantjes, who is one of the key advocates of 'new internationalism' and the main consultant of the INIVA policy, has linked the shift in the Arts Council of Great Britain (ACGB) cultural policy to two phenomena: first, a step away from the paternalistic absolutism that was constitutive of the earlier 'ethnic arts policies', and a corresponding move towards a form of democratic accountability that is responsive to the specific needs of racial minorities; second, Jantjes suggests that just as the figure of *the* other has taken on new significance in the philosophical and cultural discourse of post-modernity, cultural policy should similarly be consonant with these broader shifts.[17]

Such a redemptive narrative is particularly transparent in the essay 'The Emperor's spectacles' by Anthony Everitt— the then-Secretary-General of the Arts Council of Great Britain. Everitt begins by graciously reversing the Thatcherite mania against the threat of 'swamping'. Instead, he characterises the arrival of migrant labour from colonies other than Ireland as the injection of vitality that has rescued a body from atrophy:

The country was set to dwindle into a marine Ruritania. But then an extraordinary thing happened. A gift from the Third World to an undeserving member of the First.[18]

Thus one of the unintended consequences of the reverse migration flows of decolonization was the emergence of a cultural surplus in the 'mother country'. The resulting challenge, Everitt implies, is what to do with the 'gift' of this surplus. Down-playing and often conflating the significant differences between assimilation and integration, he thereby considers the validity of multiculturalism as cultural policy. Everitt reasserts two fundamental critiques that have been directed against multiculturalism: first, that there was an inadequate application of the principles of equity; second, that the principles of tolerance were misconceived. Everitt admitted that, even on a crude economistic scale, the existing structures did not deliver adequate services or respond to the needs of their constituencies. Such marginalisation was also reflected in the values upon which notions of acceptance were defined. 'Multiculturalism is like an invitation a host issues to his or her guests: everyone is welcome to stay provided they obey the convention of the house.'[19]

How does one imagine INIVA going beyond the limitations of paternalistic multiculturalism? With a slight conceptual transposition of Everitt's mapping of the migrant's 'homeland', we discover that the 'surplus' is no longer in 'Gujurat, St. Lucia or Uganda', but in 'Brixton, Leicester and Liverpool'. The margin appears to be relocated, but the asymmetries of 'gift exchange' that sustain paternalism are far from shattered.

In contrast, I would like to suggest that INIVA be seen as a way-station rather than as a terminus. While embracing the future-oriented principles of initiating research into new methods for representing cultural expressivity that *articulates* the condition of itinerancy and transition, *heightens* the modes of syncretism and translation, *negotiates* the spaces between binarisms and *explores* new media, I would also stress that both the potential and security of INIVA rests on a broader historical consciousness. It is for this reason that, at this stage, we need to complement the principled promises of policy-makers with the counter-histories of INIVA. Faith that the turn towards Europe will facilitate an intercultural and relativist sensibility is not necessarily well founded when the British state has consistently disowned the informal and formal experiments in internationalism that emerged after the implosion of empire. In recent years we have not only witnessed the dismantling of institutions that were born of the integrative aspirations of the Commonwealth; the utilisation of multiculturalism at all levels of education and social welfare has also been targeted as the soft option. The political context for a 'new internationalism' is therefore still bound by xenophobic border-control and a parochial surveillance of cultural utility.

THE PROCESSUAL FRAME OF GLOBALISATION

For some time the term globalisation has been used as a starting-point for conceptualising the patterns of integration and destabilisation that have occurred in many aspects of everyday life. In more recent debates, this term has been shorn of its critical edge and simply used as a description of the way the world is! Globalisation has moved from being a concept for defining the context and pattern of forces that construct a socio-economic field, to an everyday term for rationalising patterns of domination.

In order to avoid the pitfalls of 'anything goes', so often pinned to nebulous terms like the 'global postmodern', I return to the question: how has the globalisation of cultural production affected the relationship between dominant and marginal cultures? Early in this essay I pointed to the shift in the discourse on art history from formalism and Primitivism to hybridity and 'new internationalism'; moreover it is tempting to construct this transition as a progressive movement from the cultural blindness of appropriation and displacement to the political insight of negotiation and compensation. However faith in such progress is qualified whenever a closer examination is made between the stated intentions and structural practices of the art institutions. When considering the levels of change that have been initiated, we must always consider: who initiated change and what are the axioms that mark change? This level of questioning now demands a further consideration of the broader frameworks in which such debates are situated.

Thinking globally is not the same as thinking of universals. Despite the ever-increasing evidence of global effects and processes, a critical analysis of globalisation still remains a difficult task. With the collapse of totalising schemas for explaining social change and cultural formation, there has been an increasing interest in the sphere of the social world that was previously considered as the underside of modernity. It is at this theoretical juncture that the symbolic status of the migrant is being re-evaluated. Such belated attention can encourage various forms of exaggerated claims. We can begin to note a certain perversity in the celebration of the migrant, as exemplifying modernity's potential either to liberate or to exploit through detachment. Three types of migrant dreamings seem to stake out the modernist quest. Can the migrant *stand in* for the history of the place of origin, *stand up* as an intimation for the future of the place of arrival, or figure instead as a *shuttle* between these temporal and spatial axioms?

Writing against the grain of recent debates in cultural studies that have elevated the status of the migrant, Gayatri Spivak has issued a firm warning against the strategies of false continuities: 'The trajectories of the Eurocentric migrant poor and the postcolonial rural poor are not only discontinuous but may be, through the chain-linkage that we are encouraged to ignore, opposed.'[20] With justifiable disdain, Spivak has poured scorn on the mobilisation of a homogenising heading like 'the other' to contain everything from the ethnicity of the migrant, the history of anti-slavery and the politics of decolonisation. The tactical strategies of oppositional politics, she judiciously reminds us, are not automatically transposable to the benefits of consolidating the parameters of minority discourse within academic and cultural institutions.

Spivak goes on to suggest a number of problematics in the representation of the transnational dynamics of culture. The transnational cannot be identified simply by extending the logic of comparative work—that is, by adding together or substituting categories of the national.[21] The identity of the transnational is always catechrestic, in the sense that original meaning can be secured only by reference to another place that is beyond its own borders. This tension between naming and ontology makes 'postcoloniality a deconstructive case', and heightens the utility of deconstruction in countering the reification of ethnicity in postcolonialism.[22] This implies that the multi-racial inflections in the dominant culture of plural societies like the United States and Britain cannot be raised as evidence of globality. Globality has no paradigmatic form; it is only found in the incessant process of 'negotiation between the national, the global and the historical as well as the contemporary diasporic.'[23] Thus, if globality is not just an extension of earlier forms of multiculturalism, and transnationalism is not only an extrapolation of internationalism, then the difficult task that lies before us is to grasp these new phenomena in their precise measure, and to define a conceptual language that can address such cultural shifts.

MAUD SULTER **CALLIOPE FROM THE ZABAT SERIES** 1989

IN CONCLUSION: LEARNING TO THINK GLOBALLY

In the past decade critical theory and cultural politics stressed the importance of addressing the specificity of the local while maintaining a vigilant eye on the global frame. This suggestion, which was underpinned by a polemical urgency, now seems under threat from a different angle. Homi Bhabha has noted that one of the consequences of the liberal discourses on multiculturalism is a shifting in the burden of who defines culture. Attacking Charles Taylor's dismissal of hybrid cultures and his inability to address the issue of belatedness within the terms of the 'politics of recognition', Bhabha thereby alerts us to the pernicious logic of conversion or deferral in liberal discourse when confronted by the partiality of minority culture.[24]

One of the tactics within liberalism for defusing the crisis of the *difference* in culture is the stress given to the putative tolerance and equality of diverse cultures. Yet if globalisation involves the increasing interconnection of social processes across time and space, then how will the discreteness of the local be sustained? Bhabha points to this difficulty when he reminds us of the necessary perils in what he calls 'simultaneous translations', whereby the compulsion to speak to others must face the dilemma of either elevating communication to a false universalism or being caught in a mute particularism. With some frustration he notes:

> The common coin of cultural exchange in modern societies, at the international level, is still the national community and the national culture, even though their representations may be more complex.[25]

ANDREA WILKINSON **GREEN RANGE** 1994

Even when the national is marked as hybrid, the representation of culture still proceeds as if all its mixtures still add up to a discrete and unique geo-political unit. In the liberal schema of negotiated congruence and continuity, the *difference* of cultural difference must always be presented in discrete and concrete terms. Like Spivak, Bhabha is concerned with the processual in cultural difference, rather than the products of cultural diversity. Their attention to the question of cultural difference is connected to a critique both of the legitimacy of the prevailing hierarchies, in which identities are inserted, and the construction of frameworks for evaluating respective positions. Part of the problem is that the symbolic and political institutions that have a formative role in our preconceptions of history, and which forge both concrete and abstract relationships to place, have yet to construct frameworks for either evaluating the 'new' cultural identities based on hybridity or imagining the tensions of globality.

Nikos Papastergiadis is a major contributor to the current debates on political and cultural theory. He is author of *Modernity as Exile — The Stranger in John Berger's Writing* (Manchester University Press, 1993), and editor of *Random Access I and Random Access II, Ambient Fear.* Currently he is lecturing in Sociology at the University of Manchester.

NOTES

1.   Once again I am grateful for the advice and direction of this essay from my friend Scott McQuire.

2 .   Peter Wollen, *Raiding the Icebox: Reflections on Twentieth-Century Culture*, Verso, London, 1993.

3.   Robin Cohen, *Frontiers of Identity: The British and the Others*, Longman, London, 1994, p. 30.

4.   *Global Visions: Towards a New Internationalism in the Visual Arts*, ed. Jean Fisher, Kala Press in association with the Institute of International Visual Arts, London, 1994.

5.   ibid., p. 113.

6.   Gayatri Chakravorty Spivak, *Outside in the Teaching Machine*, Routledge, London, 1993, p. 210.

7.   Eagleton's astute observation concerning the pitfalls of transcendentalism and relativism in contemporary culture is marred by his consistent conflation of deconstruction and an apolitical form of pragmatic relativism, which is inevitably an alibi for free-market capitalism. See T. Eagleton, 'The Crisis of Contemporary Culture', in *Random Access*, eds. Buchler and Papastergiadis, Rivers Oram Press, London, 1995.

8.   Meaghan Morris, 'Future fear', *Mapping the Futures: Local Cultures, Global Change*; eds. Bird et al.; Routledge, London, 1993, p. 37.

9.   Stuart Hall, 'New Ethnicites', in Mercer, K. (ed.) *Black Film, British Cinema*, ICA Documents, No. 7, London, 1988, p. 27.

10   ibid., p. 28.

11.   ibid.

12.   ibid., p 29

13.   See Rasheed Araeen, *Black Phoenix*, No 2, London, 1978.

14.   Gavin Jantjes and Sarah Wason, *Final Report: The Institute of New International Visual Arts (INIVA)*, London Arts Board and Arts Council of Great Britain, December 1991.

15.   Sandy Nairne, 'European Fusion', *Frieze: International Art Magazine*, No 11, Summer 1993, p 18.

16.   *Cultural Diversity in the Arts: Art, Policies and the Facelift of Europe*, Ria Lavrijsen, Royal Tropical Institute, The Netherlands, 1993, p. 57.

17.   ibid., pp. 59-66.

18   ibid., p.53.

19   ibid., p. 56.

20   Gayatri Chakravorty Spivak,' Scattered Speculations on the Question of Culture Studies', *Outside in the Teaching Machine*, Routledge, London, 1993, p. 257.

21   ibid., p. 262.

22   ibid., p. 281.

23   ibid., p. 278.

24   Homi Bhabha, 'Culture's In Between', *Artforum*, September 1993, p. 167.

25   Homi Bhabha, 'Simultaneous Translations: Modernity and the Inter-National', *On Taking a Normal Situation*, Museum van Hedenaagse Kunst, Antwerp, 1993, p.163.

BRITISH ART IN THE 1980S AND 1990S: THE SOCIAL AND POLITICAL BACKGROUND

PATRICK J. BOYLAN

In his now famous West Point Military Academy speech, the distinguished American diplomat and Secretary of State, Dean Acheson, launched the most widely-quoted modern aphorism about the United Kingdom when he argued that, 'Great Britain has lost an empire and has not yet found a role'. Three and a half decades on, this prophetic warning is as apt today as it was when Acheson first spoke the words in December 1962.

Despite (or could it be because of?) nearly two decades of growing kitsch nationalism and anti-European megaphone diplomacy by many government ministers, and even more stridently by the ruling Conservative Party as a whole, the British (or perhaps more accurately, the English) have not been feeling comfortable with themselves over recent years. Research published in May 1997 on the attitudes of substantial samples of older primary-school-level children in France and England has shown some truly remarkable differences. Barely one third of the English children felt 'proud to be English', and only 42% seemed to care much about what country they belonged to. In contrast, nearly two-thirds of the French children questioned agreed strongly with the statement 'I feel very proud to be French'; and even more agreed that 'it matters which country I belong to'.

Probing further, the researchers found that a high proportion of the French children rationalised their love of France with reference to what they felt their country had contributed to the wider world, recognising and expressing particular pride in France's role in the development and promotion of key universal values such as democracy,

freedom, and equality. In marked contrast, the English pupils typically identified their nation's gifts to the world as football and pop music. While French pre-teens can articulate their love of country in terms of 'because one is free and equal', or 'because France is a magnificent, democratic and welcoming country', their English counterparts offer 'Man. United' and the Spice Girls, coupled with a near xenophobic pride that the English language now dominates the world (with the clear subtext that hence there is no need to learn about other people's countries, let alone learn their languages).

These apparently disillusioned English nine-to-eleven year-olds are not merely Thatcher's children; the majority are arguably Thatcher's grandchildren as well, since in many cases their parents will have spent most, if not all, of their later teens and their adult lives during the 18 years of Conservative governments. Further evidence of this—at least in relation to a significant proportion of their mothers—is seen in the findings of a long-term, broadly feminist, sociological study of the attitudes and values of adult women across a dozen western European countries. This is disclosing that the United Kingdom has, by a factor of three or four times in excess of the European average, the highest proportion of women who fall into a type that the research team has distinguished by the shorthand term 'working girl'. These are defined as: poorly educated under-achievers, in badly-paid low status jobs (when they are working at all, otherwise subsisting on welfare benefits); they reveal very low self-esteem and equally low developmental ambition for themselves or their families. For these, the research showed, typical short-term and medium-term ambitions and priorities were disclosed as the hope of a 'laddish' girls' night out, and perhaps an annual package holiday of 'sun, sand, sangria and sex' in one of the cheaper holiday resorts of the Mediterranean or the Canary Islands.

If this is far from the expected picture of the United Kingdom at the end of the millennium, there is other, equally disturbing evidence of a troubled land, in which two of the last government's proudest boasts—of runaway successes in the economy, and law and order—are shown to be highly questionable.

There was much talk, especially in the run-up to the 1 May 1997 General Election, of an economic miracle—a recent economic performance that was portrayed as the envy of the developed world. If that was a true assessment, rather than based on some highly selective and tendentious statistics and arguments, why has the United Kingdom slipped at least six places down the OECD's global economic league table in less than 20 years, and is now firmly in the bottom half of the 15 European Union countries in terms of GDP per head of population? Arguably, if there has been a runaway economic success story in the British Isles in recent years it is the Irish Republic (still largely ignored if not actively despised from the British side of the Irish Sea). The truth is that traditionally backward Ireland is now within striking distance of the UK in economic terms, and could well overtake Britain within the next few years—as Italy, for example, has already done (despite that country's endemic and apparently intractable economic, social and political problems).

Similarly, it has been the constant claim of the Tory government of being 'tough on crime'—as evidenced by a torrent of new criminal laws and ever-tougher sentencing regimes, which have nearly doubled the prison population (now one of the highest per capita of any democracy in the world). However the 1997 international Crime Victimisation Survey, covering eleven major developed countries, showed that currently a third of UK families are victims of crime each year—the highest level found in the eleven countries studied. Indeed, the current level of violent crime against the person in the UK is, according to the survey, even higher on average than in the United States.

Of course, despite its official name, the United Kingdom is far from the 'unitary state' that Margaret Thatcher boasted about so strongly whenever she was in one of her many confrontations with our European partners. For example, its four distinct internal nations (England, Scotland, Wales and Northern Ireland), and five self-governing territories (the Isle of Man and the four Channel Islands), have between them five fundamentally different legal systems and six indigenous languages—plus of course well over a hundred other languages in regular use amongst the UK's many European and non-European minority communities. It is likely that a survey of 9-to-11-year-olds in Scotland, Wales or either of the two communities in Northern Ireland would have found a much higher proportion expressing pride in their traditional nations. Even more surprising may be the news that despite the popular image of the Province, because of the much-publicised 'Troubles' of the past quarter-century, the recent crime victim study shows that

Northern Ireland is actually the safest part of the United Kingdom, with the lowest levels of house-breaking, car crime and even of crimes of violence against the person.

No doubt it will take decades of debate and historical research before we see anything approaching a consensus on the reasons for the recent dramatic economic and social decline, but there are already some significant lines of enquiry for such eventual research. Central to these is the effect of the last government's unrelenting pressure to replace the broad post-War, all-party consensus on social issues—not least, the traditional values and policies of the Conservative Party itself—with an aggressive individualism at the expense of communitarian or any other collective responsibility. Indeed, in a particularly telling presentation of the new right-wing libertarian agenda, with which she intended to place unambiguously clear blue water between her administration and the consensus position of every previous twentieth-century government (whether Conservative, Labour or Liberal), Prime Minister Margaret Thatcher once insisted that there is no such thing as 'society'.

Of equal importance was her government's frontal onslaught on equality—which, it should be remembered, was one of the two things regarded as most precious by the majority of the French pre-teens in the recent survey. This began quite slowly, although the first Thatcher budget almost doubled the rate of Value Added Tax as the first step in a planned switch from direct taxes—such as a progressively structured income tax system, targeted on those considered best able to pay—to universal indirect taxes, levied on all. It was quickly followed by the breaking of the established link between average earnings and levels of pensions and other welfare benefits. Such regressive policies inevitably had a particularly serious effect on pensioners, students and the low-paid (a category which includes the great majority of those working in the cultural sector, including many tens of thousands who would be classified as professionals under any normal definition).

The first, fairly tentative, steps along the road of what soon became known as 'Thatcherism' were so universally unpopular by 1982 that the experiment seemed set to last just one parliamentary term of five years. However the wave of nationalist sentiment that followed the Falklands War contributed greatly to the unexpected electoral landslide of 1983, which gave Margaret Thatcher an overall majority of 147 in the House of Commons. This election was quickly followed by further major changes in policy, so drastic as to be little short of a *coup d'état*. The very legitimacy, let alone morality, of taxation of any kind—or of government expenditure on the most traditional public services—came under overt and sustained attack, not least because of their alleged re-distributive effects.

Moreover, it quickly became accepted government doctrine that pay-differentials should be greatly widened by both fiscal and other means. One senior finance minister memorably argued that senior management—whether in the private sector or in the military, judiciary or other public services (including the arts)—were under-rewarded, and therefore must be given very substantial pay rises and large

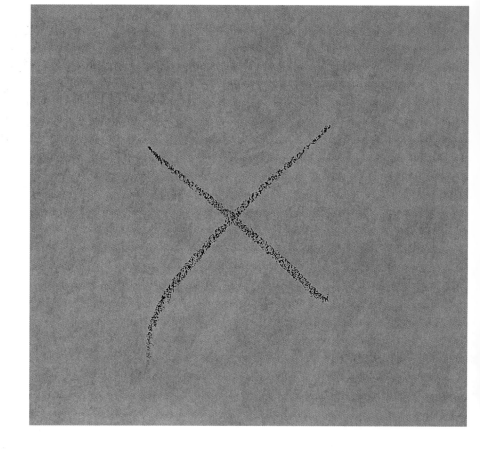

JONATHAN PARSONS **KISS** 1994

tax cuts in order to give them the incentive to work harder. On the other hand, he argued, basic pay scales for ordinary working people in both public and private sectors were too high, and therefore needed to be cut to give the necessary incentive for them to work harder. (Despite frequent questioning in Parliament and elsewhere, the minister concerned was never able to explain what he considered to be the crossover point between the seriously under-motivated, top staff needing the incentive of large pay rises, and the seriously under-motivated, already low-paid, requiring pay cuts as an incentive to work harder!)

Despite its dubious logic, this anti-egalitarian agenda was pursued with ever-increasing vigour through fiscal measures such as major cuts in the higher rates of income tax, and in capital gains, inheritance, property and corporation taxes. The consequential loss of what came to many billions a year of government income was effective in a number of ways: a doubling of indirect tax rates; continuing, year on year real-term cuts in public expenditure in almost all areas other than defence, police and prisons, and above all in local government (with especially serious effects on discretionary services, such as the arts and museums); together with rising government debt, and hence borrowing. Moreover, as independent calculations have shown year after year, cost inflation in the arts, museum and library sectors has consistently been averaging around 2% higher than the general Retail Price Index (RPI) used by Government as the benchmark for calculating permitted levels of public spending. What were claimed to be 'standstill budgets' (or even slight budget increases) on the basis of the RPI average, usually amounted to real, and cumulative, budget cuts in the arts.

The high point in the campaign against local government was Margaret Thatcher's forcing through, in the face of almost all independent advice and serious misgivings from many within her own government (let alone her party at large), of the so-called Poll Tax—a flat rate 'Community Charge' to finance local government, in place of the traditional (and graduated) local property taxes. The Poll Tax was levied on all adult citizens regardless of their ability to pay, with the openly admitted intention that it would force the electorate to vote in local elections for those candidates (assumed by the Prime Minister to be Conservatives) offering local government spending and service cuts, and hence a lower rate of Poll Tax.

CEAL FLOYER **SOLD** 1996 (INSTALLATION VIEW)
(PETER DOIG *BAKED* 1996)

One previous attempt to introduce a flat-rate Poll Tax of this kind, payable by everyone regardless of income or property, had led to the 1381 Peasants' Revolt. This time, the effect of the overwhelming opposition and resistance (particularly the 'Can't Pay, Won't Pay' campaign which almost immediately overwhelmed the local courts) was less dramatic, though ultimately more effective. When in 1990 the Prime Minister refused to back down over the Poll Tax, Conservative MPs, recognising that the government faced almost certain electoral disaster, in effect forced Margaret Thatcher out of office. Dismantling the hated Poll Tax was one of the first tasks undertaken by her successor, John Major, although the scale of budget and service cuts in local government (by far the largest source of UK arts, museums and heritage services provision) in fact accelerated rather than diminished in total under the new Conservative government.

Most seriously of all, during the 18 years of the Thatcher-Major governments, none of the capital receipts from the sale of privatised public assets and services totalling around UK £120 billion (Aust. $240 billion), or North Sea oil revenues and taxes of around UK £100 billion (Aust. $200 billion), were reinvested in any systematic way. Instead, the proceeds of these (by definition) irreplaceable—public assets—were used largely to subsidise current expenditure and tax cuts: a veritable Rake's Progress of deterioration. It was a distinguished former Conservative Prime Minister and Chancellor, Harold Macmillan, who (in what was one of his last appearances in Parliament) described what was going on as 'selling off the family silver'—asking, not at all rhetorically: what did the government intend to live on when the last teaspoon and family portrait had been sent off to the auction rooms? Needless to say he received no answer; merely the customary abuse heaped on those regarded as not 'one of us'.

The 1983 general election was equally pivotal in relation to a changing perception of basic concepts, both of governance and the management of public services—though there were deep, frankly puzzling, internal contradictions between the way in which these two were conceived and applied. On the first, governance, there was an increasing reluctance to recognise the legitimacy of government itself, echoing the anti-government stance of the growing number of radical neo-Conservatives in the United States. Government as a whole—not merely so-called 'big government'—should be shrunk, and got off the backs of citizens, especially the taxpayers. However in marked (and quite illogical) contrast, government control over the most specific aspects of operations of the remaining public services became ever more detailed and severe.

With such a fiscal agenda, a severe and continuing squeeze on public expenditure was perhaps to be expected, if only for financial reasons; and perhaps inevitably, this severely affected the cultural sector. With the exception of archive services and some limited obligations in relation to minimal maintenance of historic monuments and buildings, the UK's arts, museums and heritage services are not mandatory. Therefore they have little or no legal protection when public expenditure cuts are being allocated. The

151

situation has been most difficult of all among local government services, which in fact form the backbone of the cultural sector outside London.

As local authorities, especially those in the major metropolitan areas, became more exposed politically as among the last bastions of traditional public service values, they came under sustained attack from central government on several fronts. Compared with a post-war average of perhaps two substantial local government-related laws per year, in 18 years the Conservative-controlled Parliament passed an astonishing total of more than 150 government Acts relating to the powers of local authorities. Moreover the majority of these Acts was intended to constrain the authorities' discretionary powers over services and spending. For all practical purposes, the Secretaries of State for England, Scotland, Wales and Northern Ireland currently fix (between them) the budgets and local tax levels of every local authority across the country. Meanwhile there has been a wholesale transfer of local government powers and functions to unelected bodies, appointed by government ministers. (In the case of London and the six major English metropolitan regions, the local authorities were completely abolished when voters continued to elect councils unacceptable to the government, leaving London as the only major metropolis in the world with no regional or strategic public authority.)

In 1979, a mere 1,000 paid appointments were made directly by government ministers—mainly senior board and executive positions in the then-nationalised industries.

However according to estimates made by the respected Financial Times, by 1995 an astonishing 70,000 paid positions, on the boards of at least a thousand new 'quangos', were within the personal gift of ministers. Such ministerially appointed bodies nowadays control, between them, substantially more public expenditure than all the democratically elected councillors in the country. In the arts and museums sector, even the Regional Arts Associations— voluntary charities created and run by local arts organisations and local authorities to support and promote the arts in their regions—were simply closed down and replaced by appointed Regional Arts Boards. These are chaired by ministerial appointees, with the remaining members being appointed by the Arts Council, all of whose members are themselves appointed by ministers.

In addition, there emerged a clear and ever-increasing tendency to fill the boards both of established bodies—such as the Arts Council and national museum trustee boards— and the ever-growing number of new bodies, with prominent businessmen distinguished, in what became one of Margaret Thatcher's best-known phrases, as 'one of us'. In a memorable exchange in the House of Lords about the growth of overtly political patronage, breaking a century-old tradition of non-political or at least evenly-balanced appointments, the Trade and Industry Minister readily confirmed that she had never knowingly appointed a Labour supporter to any of the many hundreds of jobs within her patronage. Meanwhile another minister rationalised the politicising of public appointments by arguing that there was no point in appointing people who might be hostile to the

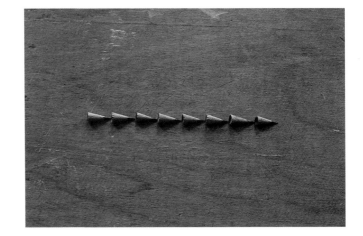

JUDITH DEAN **OF** 1995

government's objectives of a root-and-branch restructuring of the public services. The politicising of public bodies and their policies was particularly noticeable in the cultural sector, including the Arts Council, the BBC, and some of the trustee boards of the national museums and galleries, where key appointments went not just to businessmen known to be Conservative supporters, but also to high-profile Conservative politicians, including former ministers.

The most important of the mechanisms adopted to achieve political and organisational changes required by the new political agenda was to pass as many government functions, responsibilities and services as possible to the private sector: either by selling them off completely through privatisation; otherwise by contracting out service-provision to private-sector businesses. In those cases where privatisation was felt to be either economically or politically impossible (as with hospitals and the country's higher and further education colleges), the solution preferred was to turn these services (or in many cases the individual establishments) into quasi-independent businesses, each competing fiercely with each other for 'business' and 'market share', within a bewildering range of new internal markets.

Such an outcome was favoured for services as diverse as the Prison Service, the Historic Royal Palaces, national museums such as the Victoria and Albert and Science Museums, the Department of the Environment's historic buildings and archaeology services and responsibilities, and National Health Service hospitals. Even secondary and primary schools have been strongly encouraged, through offers of substantial financial incentives, to become independent of their local education authorities. Those that have refused to do so, and stayed within local government, now have fully devolved budgets. Such a situation has often had devastating effects on specialised services traditionally organised collectively, on an authority-wide basis—for example, art advisers; schools of music; museums and arts education services; and 'art for schools' commissioning and purchasing schemes. This is because the local education authorities no longer have the necessary central funds for such shared services.

Some hundreds of significant areas of the public sector, and in total tens of thousands of individual establishments (covering almost all public utilities, more than half of the national Civil Service and large areas of local government, for example), were nominally moved out of direct public control. However the reality was very different. Although ministers claimed that under the new systems and structures they were now responsible only for public service policy—but not for operations—the government's simultaneous demand for ever-greater 'accountability' and 'performance measurement', and for achieving the ubiquitous 'three Es' (Economy, Efficiency and Effectiveness), led rapidly to a degree of bureaucratisation, planning and control previously unknown—at least not in peacetime.

What ensued with such changes was the introduction into the public service of virtual caricatures of some of the worst models of American 'macho management' systems and styles—most of them already abandoned by the industries in which they were once popular. The 20s Fordist management model, satirised so devastatingly in Charlie Chaplin's *Modern Times* of 1936, and the demand that 'managers must have the right to manage', had been abandoned by the Ford Motor Corporation itself, in favour of employee participation and teamworking according to Japanese (and indeed continental European, Christian Democrat) models.

On the other hand, in marked contrast with the protestations of economic and managerial liberalisation, the reality of the government's demand for 'accountability' spawned an ever-growing paper-chase of corporate planning and reporting (using re-workings of American corporate and government models of the 60s, which had been discredited and largely discarded by the early 70s). Indeed it could be argued that the nearest parallels to British preferred options could be found only among the failed state planning systems of the Communist world; similarly, the enormous investment in staff and consultancy time seems to have been no more effective than those models.

By 1995, central government expenditure on management and other consultancies was running at an astonishing UK£700 million (Aust. $1.4 billion) a year—excluding the often huge consultancy costs of privatisations. There seem to be no estimates available of the figures for local government and the quasi-privatised public sector 'agencies'; however the total costs could well be of the same order of magnitude in addition.

In the first fifteen months after the transformation of the Office of Arts and Libraries of the Cabinet Office into a full cultural ministry for England—the Department of National Heritage in 1992. At least UK £7 million (Aust. $14 million) was spent on management and other consultancies in setting up the new ministry, and the establishment of its internal and external corporate systems. Meanwhile every one of the museum and arts sector organisations directly funded by the new Department had to set up their own parallel corporate planning and reporting systems, in the form of long-term, medium-term and annual business and corporate plans. This was at an estimated average cost of a further UK £100,000 (Aust. $200,000) per year—perhaps a further UK £4 million to 6 million (Aust. $8 million to $12 million) in addition, at a time when (at least on the basis of realistic inflation rates for the sector) there were real-terms cuts in public support.

In their turn, the smaller scale arts and heritage organisations receiving grant-aid from bodies such as the Arts Council and its Regional Arts Board subsidiaries—or applying to the Arts Council, Heritage, or Millennium Fund lottery boards—found that they, too, were expected to prepare and submit corporate plans along required lines for security and approval.

The value or effects of such a huge annual effort and cost are highly questionable. The Department of National Heritage's own corporate planning system was reported to allow an average of just four hours of senior staff time, per institution per year, to analyse, report on and incorporate into

CRITICAL DECOR **NIETZSCHE PIECE** 1992 (INSTALLATION VIEW)

the ministry's own planning and budgeting processes annual corporate plans of perhaps 100 pages or more each, and containing some hundreds of items of financial and other statistics. In practice, in the face of declining overall allocations, annual budget decisions continue to consist largely of across-the-board percentage changes—usually real-terms reductions. In consequence, such laboriously and expensively produced annual plans will simply gather dust in filing cabinets in the Ministry, until they are transferred to the Public Record Office in 30 years' time.

There was however a more sinister side to the new political framework: an interventionist or hostile arts minister, or indeed Arts Council or other funding body officer with his or her own political agenda, now had in place a potent mechanism for interfering in and indirectly controlling the artistic policies and practices of the funded bodies, if they chose to utilise this. Accordingly it became easy to protest that an apparently unconstitutional intervention with a funded body was no breach of the much-vaunted 'arm's length principle'—merely an impartial action to ensure proper financial control and accountability.

Some of the major national museums and galleries were amongst the first areas of the public service to be

MARK WALLINGER **HALF-BROTHER (EXIT TO NOWHERE - MACHIAVELLIAN)** 1994-95

hit by the new 'managerialist' agenda. This occurred first with the introduction of new, very limited, salary scales for professional staff, in place of the traditional longer-term career grades (paralleling those in the related employment areas of university and school teaching); it was followed by the widespread introduction of short-term employment contracts of just two years, or at the most five years. In February 1989, the Victoria and Albert Museum fired eight of its top staff, all of them heads or deputy heads of departments, in a major down-rating of the status (and pay) of senior curators within the Museum.

However this high-profile fracas paled to insignificance when compared with the combined effects of two decades of unfilled vacancies, redundancies and other abolished professional posts in almost every category of public museum, together with the ever-increasing demand for any incoming staff to carry out the demands of the new managerialist agenda. Perhaps the most telling statistic is that curators, in the traditional sense of high-level professionals responsible for museum collections, displays and exhibitions, have declined in numbers from over 35% of the total UK museum and gallery work-force thirty years ago, to a national average today of around 12%.

NICKY HOBERMAN **SWEET PICKLE** 1996

To some extent this change has been due to the emergence of specialised sub-professions, such as conservation and education; however that accounts for only a small part of this remarkable (and worrying) trend. Much more significant has been the growth in administration (in the narrow sense) and of marketing and fund-raising, all in direct reflection of the new political agenda. The National Gallery (in the honourable company of the British Museum and the Tate Gallery, amongst the major London national museums) has in fact been an unusual bastion of stability over recent years, in comparison with the succession of reorganisations, re-structurings and redundancy programmes at some of the other major nationals, such as the Science Museum, the Natural History Museum, and the Victoria and Albert. Nevertheless, over the past quarter-century, even the National Gallery has seen a more than 600% increase in its administrative staff; meanwhile a single public relations officer post, formerly, has grown into public relations and 'development' departments totalling more than 20 staff. In marked contrast, the doubling of the Gallery's curatorial staff—from five to ten positions—has barely kept pace with the near-doubling in size of its building and collections over the same period.

The declining importance and status of the professional curator has been even more marked in the local government sector, the traditional core of museum provision and arts support across the country. Fourteen central government departments—out of twenty ministries—have significant cultural sector responsibilities and: they spend between them around UK £700 million (Aust. $1.8 billion) a year (excluding the substantial funding that is starting to flow from the relatively new National Lottery). In contrast, annual local authority support of culture was around UK £1.4 billion (Aust. $2.8 billion) when it peaked two years ago, though there are clear signs that this is now in decline, because of the continuing government spending squeeze on local authorities.

The effects of consequential staff reductions, and the pressures of the new managerialist agenda, have been most serious in relation to the top leadership of museums (and, to be fair, to most if not all other specialised professionalisms). In particular, there has been a steep decline in the number of museums and galleries that have any professional representation in the top echelons of their governing authority. This has occurred as departments and services have been merged into ever-larger departments of recreation, leisure, planning and tourism; or even an all-embracing 'community services' departmen—perhaps extending to housing, social work and public health, as well as sport, recreation, libraries, arts and museums.

In such mega-departments, the head of museum and arts services may well be at third or even fourth tier in the managerial hierarchy; and hence for all practical purposes, completely outside of the senior policy and decision-making process. The number of local-authority museum or arts services with their own chief-officer-level director, and specialist governing committee, has fallen dramatically in the past half-dozen years to an almost negligible level. The recent history of the internationally important arts and museums sector in Birmingham—the largest local authority in England, and probably the largest museum and arts employer—is all too typical. Two directors, and three deputy- and assistant-directors, were 'let go' with little or no prior notice on a single day in 1995, as the service was merged into a conglomerate recreation department. These five top-level professionals were replaced—after a gap of eighteen months—by just one assistant director, inevitably drawn from a general and personnel management background, rather than any museum professional experience.

Overall, less than a dozen of the more than 600 British local authorities still retain a distinct museum and arts service under its own specialist officer, and fewer still now you have a specialist governing committee of the local authority. This trend, coupled with the downgrading of professionalism and promotion opportunities in the national museums and galleries network, has plainly very serious consequences for the survival of museum work as a distinct profession.

Such trends have been paralleled closely in the art education field—where, if anything, the implications of recent political and managerial trends for the status of the contemporary British artist have been even more serious.

The country's once rich network of specialist art colleges (an average of at least two per county) has almost vanished in successive waves of educational amalgamations and take-overs. Merged into the far larger and more bureaucratic structures of the ex-polytechnics—now the new universities—there are nowadays far fewer opportunities on offer for part-time teaching sessions by practising artists. Until recently this was a source of income for British contemporary artists.

Faced with declining financial resources, there have been ever-increasing pressures on purchase funds in both national and local institutions, especially concerning contemporary art purchases and commissions. For example the major museums and arts service of Leicestershire County Council had an exhibits purchase fund of around UK £70,000 (Aust. $150,000) per year in the financial year to March 1991; of this around 20% would typically be spent on contemporary art purchases and commissions. The county council had in addition typically spent around UK £25,000 (Aust. $50,000) a year, from the Education budget, for contemporary works of art and commissions for the county's schools and colleges. It also operated a 'percent for art' scheme, under which 1% of the capital cost of new buildings was allocated for art commissions and purchases. However by 1993, all such purchase funds had been totally eliminated.

In the case of local government, in particular, the absence of a professional voice at decision-making levels within the overarching department's senior management has also added greatly to the difficulty of ensuring adequate presentation of the case for continued development of art collections, especially for maintaining an allocation of funds for possibly controversial contemporary art. Nationally, the relatively small annual government grant to support local museums in their art and specimen purchases has been frozen in cash terms for more than ten years—equivalent to a real-terms cut of around 60% in their purchasing power.

The contrast with nearby France is particularly marked. During the decade of the 80s, British contemporary art purchase schemes appear to have supported acquisition of well under 500 works of art; meanwhile the parallel national and regional contemporary art funds in France have supported over 7,500 purchases and commissions (around 1,500 of which were actually of British contemporary artists).

By the early hours of Friday 2 May 1997, it was clear that the British people had taken a terrible revenge on the Conservatives in the previous day's general election. Not only was the New Labour overall majority of 179 seats its largest ever: the Conservatives had their worst electoral defeat since the foundation of the modern parliamentary system with the Reform Act of 1832. That very next morning there was already a remarkable feeling throughout much of the country, even among those who had voted for the re-election of the former government the previous day and now found themselves virtually voiceless, due to the way in which the British electoral system works. Many seemed almost elated at the scale and certainty of the coming change. Some prompt and forthright decisions of the new government are certainly encouraging for the arts—for example, the almost immediate return to membership of UNESCO; and the pledge radically to reform the National Lottery.

Perhaps most radical of all in terms of reversing the centralising trends of the previous 18 years has been the announcement that the Government is to sign the European Charter of Local Self-Government, which requires central governments to accept and then implement the principle of 'subsidiarity'—that is, that no higher authority should impose greater controls or restrictions on a subsidiary authority or other body that are genuinely *necessary,* rather than merely desired or convenient. It will be very interesting to watch to see whether this 'arms-length' principle is also restored in relation to the national arts and heritage funding bodies—such as the Arts Council—and by them in turn to the individual arts organisations.

However it must be recognised that the scope for action by any individual government (whatever its own instinctive priorities) is nowadays seriously constrained by the global commitment to what was once known in Britain as Thatcherism, and is now generally called 'economic liberalisation' in many countries—rigorously promoted and enforced by the World Trade Organisation, the International Monetary Fund and the World Bank. In such circumstances it would be foolhardy to believe that the arts in Britain (or anywhere else for that matter) will ever revert completely to what we now wanly view as the 'good old days' of the 70s.

Patrick Boylan directed major regional museums and art galleries for 22 years before his appointment as Professor of Arts Policy and Management in the City University, London, in 1990.

THE + ARTISTS

FIONA BANNER **THE NAM** 1997

JORDAN BASEMAN **UP, UP AND AWAY** 1995

RICHARD BILLINGHAM

UNTITLED 1995   **UNTITLED** 1995

UNTITLED 1994   **UNTITLED** 1995

UNTITLED 1995   **UNTITLED** 1995

CHRISTINE BORLAND **SHOES WITH 9MM HOLE** 1992

DAVID CHEESEMAN **CUT UP** 1996

MAT COLLISHAW **INFECTIOUS FLOWERS II (METASTASES FROM A MALIGNANT MELANOMA)** 1996/97

CRITICAL DECOR **BORING DEMOCRACY** 1994

NEIL CUMMINGS **DETAIL FROM THE COLLECTION: BLUE** 1996

JUDITH DEAN **INSTALLATION FOR A CHIHUAHUA: "ROUGH"
PATRIOTIC VERSION, WITH 25 OPTIONS** 1995

WILLIE DOHERTY **AT THE END OF THE DAY** 1994

ROTIMI FANI-KAYODE **UNTITLED** 1987-88

CEAL FLOYER **PROJECTION** 1997

JOHN FRANKLAND **OHNE TITEL** 1994

ANYA GALLACCIO **PRESERVE (SUNFLOWERS)** 1992 VERSION

RACHEL GLYNNE **LONG HAIR DRESS SHIRT** 1995

DOUGLAS GORDON **10 ms⁻¹** 1995

PAUL GRAHAM **TELEVISION PORTRAIT (DANNY, BRISTOL)** 1991

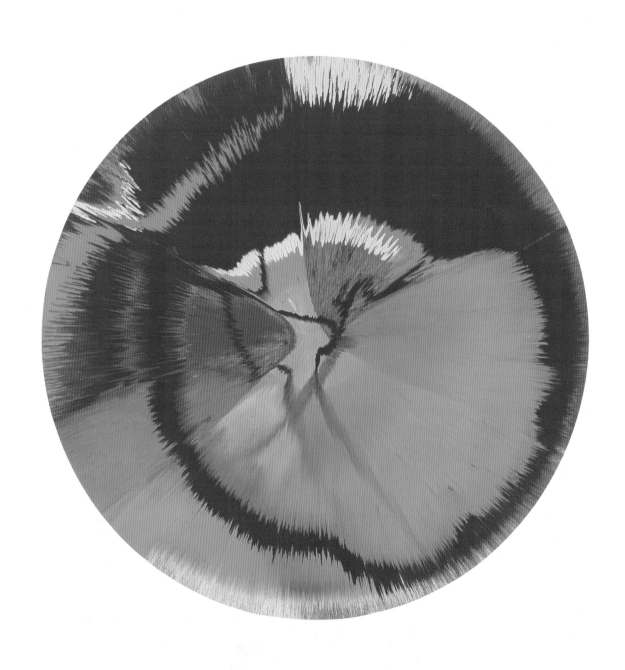

DAMIEN HIRST **BEAUTIFUL, MAD, CRAZY, SPINNING, PSYCHO'S, VORTEX PAINTING** 1994

NICKY HOBERMAN **MELTING CHERRIES** 1996

BETHAN HUWS **Y CWCH** 1983 - 1997

PERMINDAR KAUR **UNTITLED** 1995

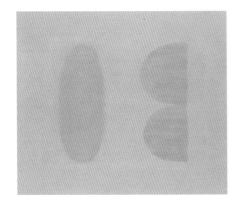  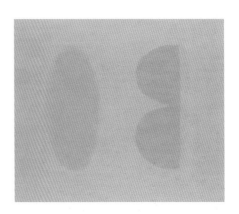

JOAN KEY

OB, BO, OB, BO, OB (OB/BO I—V) 1996

NOs 1, 2 & 5 FROM THE SERIES

TANIA KOVATS **VIRGIN IN A CONDOM** 1992

JOHN LATHAM

CONSTRUCTION (NUMBER 5)

FROM CLUSTER OF ELEVEN 1992

CHRIS OFILI **POPCORN SHELLS** 1995

RICHARD PATTERSON **MOTOCROSSER III** 1995

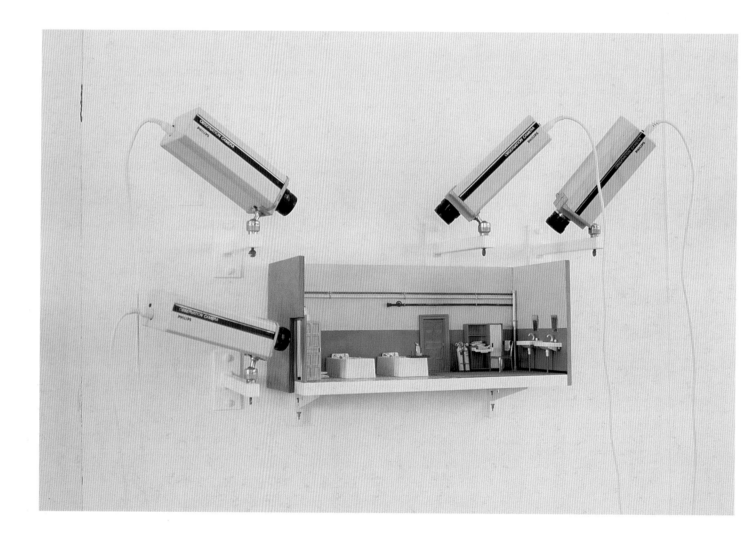

GARY PERKINS **CLEANLINESS NEXT TO GODLINESS** 1995

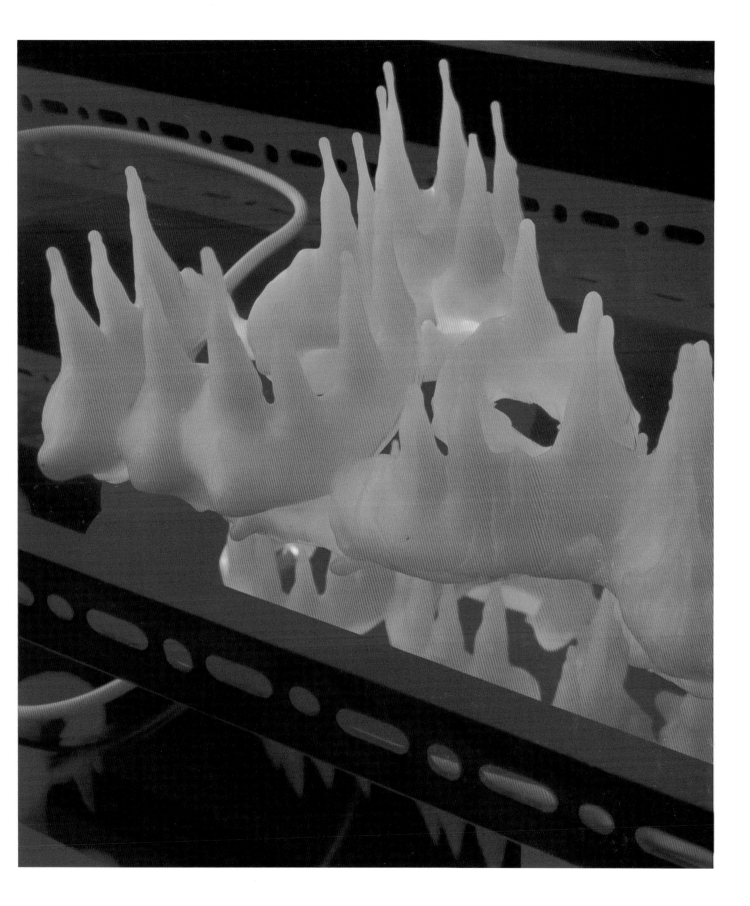

VONG PHAOPHANIT **UNTITLED** 1995-96 (DETAIL)

YINKA SHONIBARE **FIVE UNDER GARMENTS AND MUCH MORE** 1995

GEORGINA STARR **SO LONG BABE** 1996

KERRY STEWART **CAPE** 1996

JOHN STEZAKER **EXPULSION II** 1994

MAUD SULTER **TERPSICHORE FROM THE ZABAT SERIES** 1989

SAM TAYLOR-WOOD **WRECKED** 1996

MARK WALLINGER **ROYAL ASCOT** 1994

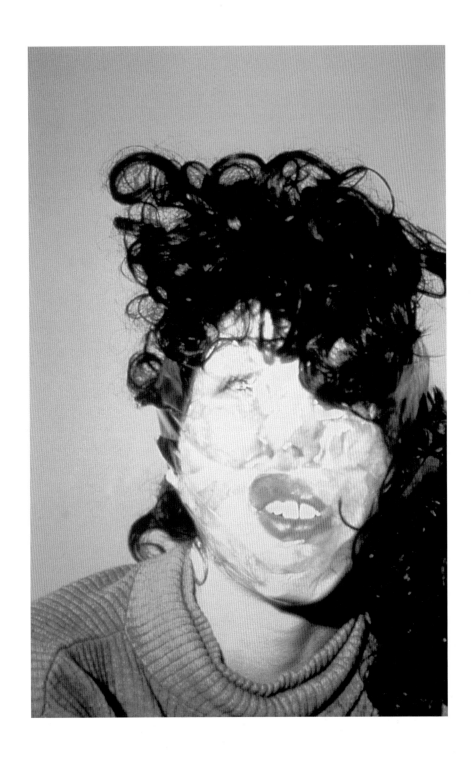

GILLIAN WEARING **'CONFESS ALL ON VIDEO. DON'T WORRY YOU WILL BE IN DISGUISE. INTRIGUED? CALL GILLIAN...'** 1994

ANDREA WILKINSON **GROUPS C4, B3, B1, D6** 1994 (DETAIL)

JANE & LOUISE WILSON **RED ROOM** 1995

HERMIONE WILTSHIRE **AAAAGH...!!** c1994

RICHARD WRIGHT **WALL PAINTING** 1997   CATHERINE YASS FROM THE SERIES **CORRIDORS** 1995

TEXTS ON ARTISTS

FIONA BANNER

Fiona Banner has just published a hernia-inducing handy paperback that all but needs a forklift to heft about. A thousand pages long, and written in a single paragraph, The Nam is a scene-by-scene description of Vietnam war movies...written in the present tense. Banner's promotional poster proclaims that her book is unreadable. This is a novel advertising ploy, and actually untrue...read at a stretch, Banner's simple, clear prose is hypnotic, and as exhausting as sitting through a Vietnam film all-nighter.

...Banner's book distils and replays the atmosphere of the war film in an alarmingly vivid way. It is frighteningly dramatic, and written in a high-pitched, unaltering tone. But the real point is the author's voice, and the sense of someone being there, not in the war, but at the movies, and experiencing the film. Banner the narrator is neither an eye, nor a camera, but a VCR racking up the images, the camera angles, the atmosphere, snatches of dialogue, the hectic backbeat of the choppers and the gunfire, the sickly sky behind the waving palm fronds.

Banner's treatment of the movies, and the experience of watching movies, is all about being overwhelmed and taken over. What she is really recounting is the visceral effect movies have on us as we sit there in the dark, trying to catch up with ourselves as the images bombard us. ...

Banner, the author, goes missing in the action. We read her, but we don't think of her as we read....[The] artist seem[s] to be part of a general shift towards narratives, stories, confessions and autobiographies in art, and they represent a blurring of mutually suspicious cultural genres, important though this shift might be, it is less important than the recognition that the stories we have to tell are all we have. There's no god-shaped hole for art to fill, just the space where we are, and this is enough.

This extract is taken from 'Me, me, me, me', a review by **Adrian Searle** of Fiona Banner's exhibition *Only the Lonely* (with Bridget Smith) at Frith Street Gallery, (2 May - 21 June 1997). Published in *The Guardian*, Tuesday April 22 1997.

JORDAN BASEMAN

There is often something disquieting about the familiar presented to us out of context. ...Jordan Baseman's work invites one to construct or establish meanings as much through a recognition of its visual structures and location within the gallery as through an understanding of the contexts from where its constituent parts originated. His appropriation of common signifiers intentionally seeks to access a universality of recognition that embraces both the meanings intrinsic to the objects' 'normal' situations and the new meanings that are brought to them in the interplay of associations established by their union. He uses elements that we already know, that we already have feelings about, evoking responses not through the strangeness of the objects' components but through their familiarity.

...*Based on actual events* and *Based on a true story* invite speculation on the relationships that we have with the domestic pets that we choose to have around us. In each piece, human dentures have been given dog's and cat's teeth respectively, indexing all that we associate with them— their role in feeding, their defensive, erotic and communicative properties (we bare them at our enemies, we flash them at our friends)—and their necessity for the production of the spoken language. ...*Based on actual events* and *Based on a true story* propose a series of elaborate similes that function not through concrete or established codes but through very personal readings and associations.

...The social aspects of our culture provide much of the material for Baseman's work. ...The re-appraisal of neglected societal tropes produces artefacts that in themselves provide material for cultural discourse. His works exist as complex visual synecdoches for society as a whole, seductive in both their appearances and their willingness to lend themselves to interpretation.

This extract is taken from 'Based on a True Story', a review of Jordan Baseman's work by **John Tozer**. Published in *Art Monthly* (Issue 197), June 1996.

RICHARD BILLINGHAM

...Richard Billingham is mostly an autobiographer: the confidence and familiarity with which he handles his subject matter are reiterated in dozens of photos which could be almost mistaken for neo-realist film stills, a cinematic genre similarly dependent on real-life experience. ...Billingham is not only a skilled image-maker but an eminent story-teller as well.

These pictures are so resonant with clues and atmosphere that all remaining questions seem thoroughly satisfied with the tiniest bit of additional information. Twenty-five year-old Richard Billingham lives at home with his parents in their Midlands council flat, has been taking these pictures for the past six years, and gets his pictures developed at the local chemist. The three characters we soon come to recognise are Liz, the artist's chain-smoking, thunderous mum; father Ray, an unemployed, chronic alcoholic; and younger brother Jason. ...Also figuring prominently is an assortment of cats, dogs and pet mice who seem to seep into any gaps not otherwise given over to ashtrays, furniture and innumerable glasses or jugs of something really lethal-looking called homebrew. The family seems somehow inordinately affected by gravity; spilt gravy and loose crumbs, thrown pets, tilted wall decorations and, finally, even Ray himself are perpetually dropping to the floor or slowly sinking, inevitably collapsing into the chaos which dominates the flat. We should be wary, however, of our willingness to assume so quickly that, with only a shred of background knowledge to guide us, we have a kind of omniscient foothold on what life in the Billingham household is really like. ...I am suspicious of our readiness to complete the narrative, to provide presumed answers as to why Ray's nose is bleeding, why Liz is sobbing, or why the couple is embracing in joyous abandon. I fear that our responses are generated by the worst sort of preconceptions, unfounded assumptions somehow confirmed by the pictures, and this would reduce such unforgettable work to something hardly eye-opening at all...

This extract is taken from a review by **Gilda Williams**, of Richard Billingham's exhibition at Anthony Reynolds Gallery (26 June - 3 August 1996). Published in *Art Monthly* (Issue 199), September 1996.

CHRISTINE BORLAND

...Many psychologists believe that in play we can explore violent impulses which would be worrying if actualised, but which in that transitional area can be...investigated in safety. While Borland's work is not content to rest at the psychological level, the consistency of her sculptural concerns with soft materials against the hard ones, of order versus the aleatory and the dispersed—these could all be seen as a moving out from psychological concerns towards collective ones, from play to society.

...The way one thing can pretend to be another has fascination for Borland, who has not only had things shot but has also made 'bullet holes' in a pair of shoes by hand. ...Another series of works has used the idea of protection. *Home-Made Bullet Proof Jacket* (1992) was made from cotton wool...and two pillow cases, and displayed on a mannequin. A later work...provided a counterpart to the 9mm hole in the neat black shoes. Slippers were made, like those heavy felt ones that are worn over shoes wherever marble or wood flooring needs to be protected from the pressure of visitors' feet. They were made, however, from bullet-proof fabric. Protection provided where it is least needed renders disquieting the whole nature of the journey about to be undertaken. But one could not say if the journey implied is negative or positive, or how directly it may be a rehearsal, an attempt to bring into life the point of death itself, that moment we are not given to experience: the negative we tarry with and live by.

...Borland calmly reassert[s] the value of certain brutal forms of objectivity. While her work's openness to feeling and to psychological patterns that are never fully complete is a strength, it is clear that this openness is no gush of sentiment. It has within it the ability to provoke reflection on the economy of compassion and projection, and on their continuing part in our understandings and our misunderstandings of our experience and perception of the most diverse phenomena.

This extract is taken from 'Serious Play', a review of **Christine Borland**'s work by Ian Hunt. Published in *frieze*, (Issue 26) January - February 1996.

DAVID CHEESEMAN

And what about little John Ruskin, with his blond curls and his blue sash and shoes to match, but above all else his obedient silence and his fixed stare? Deprived of toys he fondles the light glinting off a bunch of keys, is fascinated by the burl of the floorboards, counts the bricks in the house opposite. He becomes the infant fetishist of patchwork. 'The carpet,' he confesses about his playthings,'and what patterns I could find in bed covers, dresses, or wall-papers to be examined, were my chief resources'. This, his childish solace, soon becomes his talent, his great talent.

Quoted from the opening chapter of *The Optical Unconscious* by **Rosalind E. Krauss**. MIT Press, 1994.

MAT COLLISHAW

...In the course of the last seven years...Collishaw's thoughtful approach must surely have removed any apprehensions about his seriousness. He has used his art to discuss important moral issues, not least of which is the problem of what the term 'morality' might mean.

Photographic practice has its own unwritten code of decency. Collishaw decided to defy that code and see what happened. ...Photography, like sex, may involve nothing but a play on conventions. Bored by this, Collishaw reserves his fascination for areas where conventions break down or, indeed, where none exist. ...

Evident throughout Collishaw's work, the idea of seeing things for what they are seems to matter more and more. Nobility through abjection is part of his aesthetic, after all: of rule-breaking apparently for its own sake, of photographing women inserting tampons or lying dead, raped and headless. Punk attitude is the ideal prelude to a meditation on the futility of existence. In the same vein, for example, Collishaw made a video loop of a pet canary in a cage, referring to the famous painting by Joseph Wright of Derby, a bird, flapping its wings prettily in a bell-jar. Prettily but desperately: in an experiment, the air had been drained from the container and the bird was dying as a result. ...

Recently Collishaw has had less to do with truth than ever. Experiments with illusion led to works such as the images of flowers with fur petals: a model of decadence on the one hand, something resembling a superb fashion accessory on the other. It is something from a fairy story, the other side of the coin to the homeless and unemployed who converge on the centre of London everyday. ...In a country where the results of the National Lottery are felt to be more important than any other news, it makes some kind of sense.

This extract is taken from 'Forbidden Images', a review of Mat Collishaw's work by **Stuart Morgan**. Published in *frieze*, (Issue 26) January - February 1996.

CRITICAL DECOR

...A show of eight distinct pieces which were grouped together under the collective exhibition title, *Laughing in the Face of Tragedy*. Such a simple paradoxical engagement of the humorous and the tragic has, over the last six years of exclusively collaborative practice, become typical of the type of terrain that Critical Decor is most likely to occupy in order to contradict and collapse the distinctions between the chaos and control of comprehension. These discriminations are as important in the real world, which they resist, as they have become in the art world with which they enjoy an immediate but dislocated affiliation.

Within this fluid structure where nothing could be assumed to pertain to any single clearly defined logical policy, Critical Decor had surreptitiously inveigled the viewer into deciphering the duo's considerations about the ideologies of power and communication and, on a more specific level, ideas about the weight of tradition, the reality of nature and attitudes within society.

Since their earliest collaborative endeavours Critical Decor have been concerned with the notion of the void, infinitely empty of substance and consequently rich with conceptual innuendo....Many of Critical Decor's theoretical points are raised by the use and misuse of significant art gallery constructs and this show was no exception. *Melt* was a typical museum plinth constructed from MDF and painted bright white. As the title suggests, however, one corner of the structure had begun to liquefy, the substance of this simple reliable form had begun to flow down itself in a mock-Surrealist gesture which undermined the very nature of that which an art-work might depend on for support and added prominence. ...

...Ultimately it was the aphoristic gestures and intentions of Critical Decor that enable the artists continually to say one thing, mean another and do a third. This resistance to classification continues to prevent Critical Decor from being comfortably subsumed into the cultural situation that they assail. The final irony, however, is that the individual works maintain their insurgency in relation to the gallery context and never surrender their undeniable authenticity.

This extract is taken from a review by **Godfrey Worsdale**, of Critical Decor's exhibition at the Independent Art Space (IAS), London (5-28 September 1996). Published in *Art Monthly* (Issue 200), October 1996.

NEIL CUMMINGS

ARTIST'S STATEMENT:

Cummings continues to investigate the way we construct value—social, economic and cultural—through material things. This would include thinking about the 'institutions of display', galleries, museums and shops for instance, as well as the artefacts they contain. Imagine a 'museum' vitrine of neo-classical design, properly equipped with an interior light, in which plinths present vessels of immediate and luminescent elegance; works of art of obvious value and importance presented in the best contemporary manner. Approaching this seductive object across the gallery floor, the visitor discovers that not only does the vitrine lack the heavy plate glass to protect the contents, but that its mahogany was actually of a less solid order; merely found cardboard glued together to approximate the authority of museum display. Just as surprisingly, on closer inspection, the contents of this case turn out not to be important examples of Roman glass of inestimable value, but domestic plastic bottles, deprived of their labels and revealing beautiful shades of the palest to deepest blue. By a process of close attention to the conventions of display, Cummings has conjured from the discarded, a work of effortless glamour and sharp critique.
NEIL CUMMINGS, 1997

JUDITH DEAN

ARTIST'S STATEMENT:

These works are small things, intimate. They require close scrutiny in order to see what they are, close enough to be able to blow them away. They have to be remade in order to be seen, they don't exist in transit or in storage, only when exhibited.

Installations for a chihuahua *"Rough"*, all versions. Made of wax crayon sharpenings, they are the residue of another process and have an object (the crayon) which isn't present. Neither is the dog, its bark a ruff or rough. Like a drawing, the tool has got so close to the work and has left its mark. These pieces revel in coincidence; the individual parts maintain their identity, and rely on placing the naming to being to exist as anything besides themselves.

Of. Is more like a delinquent activity and a subsequent restoration—an attempt to put things right which I've destroyed, to put it back. It's like wanting to have all the points at once, to have no particular point.

These works are made of the outside and the inside of their material (object), respectively—just to one side of themselves. And some things are being presented which could have taken place anyway, elsewhere: there's a kind of temporal displacement going on.
JUDITH DEAN, 1997

WILLIE DOHERTY

At the End of the Day (1994), shot with a hand-held camera presumably from within a car, shows a view of driving down a country road at dusk and coming to an abrupt stop at a roadblock near the border. The incessantly repeated one-minute sequence is projected, floor to ceiling, onto a wall, accompanied by a male voice-over uttering a litany of cliché metaphorical phrases about the inevitability of progress:'At the end of the day there's no going back','we're entering a new phase','nothing can last forever','let's not lose sight of the road ahead','there's no future in the past','at the end of the day it's a new beginning'.

The work refers mainly to the peace process which got underway in late August 1994 when the IRA, through the efforts of Sinn Fein and the Catholic Social Democratic and Labour Party unilaterally declared a cease-fire, strongly supported at the time by the Irish and British governments in search of what the media then described as a 'permanent' peace settlement. The new media hype about an 'inevitable' peace, constructed by improper political appropriation of the philosophical notion of permanence is undermined by the continuously repeated drive up to the road-block, indicative of the frustrated desire to make progress and of a continuing level of conflict that cannot be permanently eradicated. In road movies the road is a metaphor of freedom, but here it is obstructed by six large cement boulders, so that the dual structure of the piece resides in the contrast between the idea of communications (the road, the telephone poles to the right of the road that continue on, even after the block, just as a flock of birds flies off towards the horizon) and the concrete facts of division and disruption.

This extract is taken from **Carolyn Christov-Bakargiev**'s text for an exhibition of Willie Doherty's work at the Kunsthalle Bern entitled *In the Dark, Projected Works* (17 July - 1 September 1996).

R O T I M I   F A N I - K A Y O D E

...In African traditional art, the mask does not represent a material reality: rather, the artist strives to approach a spiritual reality in it through images suggested by human and animal forms. I think photography can aspire to the same imaginative interpretations of life....As an African working in a western medium, I try to bring out the spiritual dimension in my pictures so that concepts of reality become ambiguous and are opened to reinterpretation. This requires what Yoruba priests and artists call a technique of ecstasy.

Both aesthetically and ethically, I seek to translate my rage and my desire into new images which will undermine conventional perceptions and which may reveal hidden worlds. I make my pictures homosexual on purpose. Black men from the Third World have not previously revealed either to their own people or to the West a certain shocking fact: they can desire each other....

An awareness of history has been of fundamental importance in the development of my creativity. ...In exploring Yoruba history and civilisation, I have rediscovered and revalidated areas of my experience and understanding of the world. I see parallels now between my own work and that of the Osogbo artists in Yorubaland who themselves have resisted the cultural subversions of neo-colonialism and who celebrate the rich, secret world of our ancestors.

...I feel it is essential to resist all attempts that discourage the expression of one's identity. In my case, my identity has been constructed from my own sense of otherness, whether cultural, racial or sexual. The three aspects are not separate within me. Photography is the tool by which I feel most confident in expressing myself. It is photography, therefore—Black, African, homosexual photography—which I must use not just as an instrument, but as a weapon if I am to resist attacks on my integrity and indeed, my existence on my own terms.

This extract is taken from 'Traces of Ecstasy', an essay written by **Rotimi Fani-Kayode** in 1987. Recently re-printed in *Rotimi Fani-Kayode & Alex Hirst Photographs*, published by Editions Revue Noire and Autograph (Paris, November 1996).

C E A L   F L O Y E R

Blind consists of a video monitor mounted on the wall of City Racing's main space. The tape playing on it is an unedited shot of a plain white blind pulled down over a window. Because, we infer, the window is slightly open, the gentle breeze blowing at the time of the filming causes periodic slight billowing of the fabric followed by its being sucked back against the window frame. If it remains impossible actually to see what is beyond the blind, it becomes clear nonetheless that there is something there - not least the source of the light that

214

illuminates it and the breath which animates its surface: the world outside. ...

Ceal Floyer's awareness of the fragility of the linkages that can be constructed between the real and its representations is evident with the other two works in the exhibition. *Untitled (Sculpture)* is a pull-cord light switch fixed just inside the door to the rear space. It hangs far enough away from the wall to announce itself as an object of attention, rather than as the functioning means of casting light elsewhere. In fact, what it casts in any direct sense is obfuscation since the four spotlights in the ceiling throw its shadow prominently onto the wall. A closer look reveals that the weight on the end is not plastic but wax, like the rounded top of a candle, and the cord is not nylon but a long length of cotton candle wick. *Untitled (Sculpture)* does not work, there is no switch mechanism inside the ceiling rose, but in the deliberate anachronism of its technology it focuses the mind on the reflective and critical operations of art in relation to the more habitual workings of things.

Upstairs a record sits on top of a chest-high white plinth. The plinth of *Carousel* is placed close to, but not right up against the far wall as you enter the room, inviting you to address the wall as it does: to look upon it at a distance. Playing on the deck is a record with a plain black label. Its content remans unannounced, although we can hear what is on it since amp and speakers are fitted into the plinth and throw the sound of a projector clicking through a carousel of slides against the wall. The sound itself...is the announcement of a content that one knows is already present without the need for Floyer to import and authenticate it for us. It will return endlessly, an ever-renewable problem.

The three works in this show cover a lot of ground. Confounding any divisions that might still exist between artistic categories - painting, sculpture, installation, or whatever - they constitute themselves as art in, as it were, the space for its proper recognition that they also help to confirm. This is a desiring space, not so much literal as one seen in the light of thought in action.

This extract is taken from **Michael Archer**'s review of Ceal Floyer's exhibition at City Racing (14 April - 18 May 1997). Published in *Art Monthly* (Issue 207), June 1997.

JOHN FRANKLAND

...John Frankland is best known for his glimmering gold corporate lift doors and wall installed in the entrance of the Saatchi Gallery. This stretched polythene membrane, of extreme fragility and thinness, belies both the weightiness of its appearance and the strength of its concept. *What you lookin' at?*, installed at Matt's Gallery, was a more complex and inscrutable development of similar themes. Here Frankland created a false wall just inside one of the gallery's large rooms. To anyone knowing the huge space it blocked off, the impact was highly disconcerting creating a windowless and claustrophobic corridor. Again using heated stretched polythene over a wood framework—with an effect of astonishing solidity.

Frankland had re-created a wall from the National Gallery, deep maroon with a dark, stepped skirting, all gleaming in tungsten light. It appears to have been based on gallery 42, one of the smallest rooms in the National Gallery and devoted to modestly-scaled mid-nineteenth century French pictures by Degas, Boudin, Carot and others. But is was not an exact replica and existed in its own right. The fact that no clues as to its origins were given in either press release or label severely curtailed the viewers' possible interpretations, if not their immediate responses. We were simply there to absorb the unsettling grandeur of the piece. But knowing other works by Frankland, one could take for granted an element of commentary, going beyond the question posed in the work's unsatisfactory title. I would lob a guess that some critique of the veneer of culture and the authoritarianism of display, how we perceive (as against how we understand) history, was intended. And the contrast of a wall meant for past art with the white minimalism of Matt's Gallery for new art would not have been lost on a viewer 'in the know'.

This extract is taken from a review by **Richard Shone** of John Frankland's exhibition *what you lookin' at?* at Matt's Gallery (17 April - 9 June 1996) entitled 'London and Edinburgh Contemporary exhibitions'. Published in *The Burlington Magazine*, July 1996.

ANYA GALLACCIO

Gallaccio predicates her work on change and transformation...Effects of time are of the essence and the common denominator of her materials is inconstancy. Flowers wither and rot or, drained of sap and colour, dry to shadows of themselves. ...Gallaccio explores fragility and evanescence in works that have no permanence but can only be repeated.

In the catalogue introduction to Gallaccio's Vienna show, Michael Archer nicely wrote of beauty being 'ushered in' rather than crafted or engineered in her work. She is an artist preoccupied by loss, change, mortality; her works have a personal, inward-turning melancholy about them like a bitter-sweet ballad or blues. Her tough attention to the most intractable materials and her sense of visual drama (she has often worked as designer and props-maker in the theatre) give her a distinctive place in her generation. Although she shares with some of her contemporaries several formal affinities (rectangles, repetition, layering) and uses similar commonplace materials as vehicles for her perceptions, she may well move to a more isolated position as experience deepens the metaphysical charge of her work. But to follow her progress is not an easy matter: impermanence is her *metier* and she 'leaves not a rack behind'.

This extract is taken from an adapted and expanded review by **Richard Shone**, of Anya Gallaccio's installation at Karsten Schubert Gallery (January - February 1994). Published in *The Burlington Magazine*, March 1994.

RACHEL GLYNNE

ARTIST'S STATEMENT:
Rachel Glynne was born in Llanelli, South Wales where she lived until she was 17, leaving to study Jewellery Design and Silversmithing in Manchester, England. Over the last fifteen years she has lived, worked and studied in a number of countries, including, Jerusalem, Israel; Galveston, USA; Barcelona, Spain; and most recently Northern Ireland.

Rachel's work demands a reaction. Materials selected from discarded fabrics and objects recycled and reused. Antique materials, childhood memories, fairy tales and emotions form the essence of the installations and sculptures the artist creates.

The significance of the work is the impact and reaction experienced by the viewer. Rachel is aware that the work she produces should connect visually and must be experienced to be fully appreciated. 'Making memory tangible' and engaging the viewer with tactile works that beg closer inspection.

The *Long Hair Dress Shirt* (1995) grew out of a series of works connected to conversations with the artist's mother.

Human hair and teeth are the discarded materials used to create these pieces of work. The hair is felted, sewn and manipulated into lengths of fabric enabling the artist to create larger- than-life garments.

Rachel often uses female forms and associated objects such as mannequins, basks, gloves, lace and ribbon to evoke a sense of the person as well as the past.

RACHEL GLYNNE, 1997

DOUGLAS GORDON

...Douglas Gordon, ...is now submitting himself to the acid test of his first one-person show in London.

...Here, propped with deceptive casualness against a black pole in the middle of a darkened space, leans a screen. ...this screen is the focus of a video projection, and the jerky images flickering here clearly derive from a silent film produced long before Gordon was born.

No attempt has been made to hide the ragged, blotchy grain of the original film-stock. It reinforces the desolate mood conveyed, in the opening seconds. Apart from an iron-frame bed, redolent of a hospital or an army barracks, the room is as empty and devoid of decoration as the gallery itself. But to start with, at least, a pair of naked legs occupies the centre of the screen. They move backwards, forwards and then stop. The camera reveals the whole figure, of a young man who looks sturdy and agile enough to have recovered from whatever ailment he once suffered. ...

Just as we are about to conclude that he is fit to leave, though, the man suddenly falls over. ...The man tries sitting up, only to fall back sharply on the floor. Then his head moves from side to side, as if to reassure him that he can still perform a simple feat. By this time, however, a horrible sense of paralysis afflicts this prone form. Well-muscled, he is nevertheless quite unable to make his limbs respond in a normal way.

...Using all the strength his arms can muster, the figure now tries to get up. He nearly succeeds, several times, before crashing back in a humiliating display of helplessness. The film leaves him lying horizontally, his body still twitching with spasmodic, unconvincing attempts to raise head and limbs.

It is, on one level, a gruelling film to watch. Whatever distress I felt, though, was increasingly countered by a sense of absurdity. As the figure's movements become more manic, so he sheds some of his humanity and begins to resemble a dummy. Lacking the strings that might restore co-ordination, the puppet is reduced to a permanent state of oscillation between striving and collapse. ...

The filming has clearly been carried out for medical purposes, ...Gordon has edited and manipulated the footage for his own ends, doubtless heightening the patient's air of futility. He must want us to become engrossed in the utter mortification of the figure's strivings—and to feel guilty about the perverse satisfaction involved in watching the man's pathetic manoeuvres so closely.

...Gordon does not involve the viewer in either mental or physical sensations, and that is why the tumbling man...impressed me... Oblivion...gives way in this shadowy chamber to a stubborn refusal to let go of the past. The writhing, toppling figure seems doomed to an eternity of remembering, years after the war itself has finished. I have a suspicion that his uncontrollable body will, in turn, haunt my mind for a long time.

This extract is taken from 'The naked and the undying', a review by **Richard Cork** of Douglas Gordon's exhibition at the Lisson Gallery (9 December 1994 - 21 January 1997). Published in *The Times*, 31 December 1994.

PAUL GRAHAM

...For the past fifteen years Paul Graham has...used the image of photographic objectivity as a tool so that the defining signs of contemporary life could be embodied within the structure of a corresponding re-evaluation of the place held by history. ...In his work...Graham has observed those isolated details and gestures which carry no exact definition and might hardly even deserve naming, but when viewed in a certain context hint at a wider condition that throws new light on the image of history that we all carry with us and which determines the way we think.

The linkage of disregarded everyday images with a momentous event of historical importance proposed a strategy that Graham has consistently enlarged and exploited in his work...Graham's project moves away from reportage towards an interrogation of the mechanics in which history and morality are treated within contemporary life, and how, at the same time, the single image could capture both polarities.

...This casual, everyday image has become, through Graham's eye, a hard and permanent symbol. ...Graham's concern may ultimately rest with history but his camera is arrested by its effect, primarily, on people. History to Graham is not an anonymous force. ...

...Graham's view of history shifted, from the all-encompassing landscape...to focus not on the 'incident' but on the effect the incident of history has on the individual...and how that history can be understood through their example. ...The *Television Portraits* which he started while in Japan in 1989 illustrate this point well. As images that might tell a story, they are so inconsequential as to be socially abstract. Although they are casually executed (he has described them as 'snapshots') their composition is formally considered. Each subject, caught in the act of looking, is held in profile by the camera, their eyes locked elsewhere. These photographs of close friends with their guard down are Graham's most personal photographs. The truths they present to us are so familiar that they can stand no naming, just as the photographs that make up *New Europe* and *Empty Heaven* are defined by a strategy in which disregarded accents are shown to hold a range of historical and metaphorical meanings.

...Ultimately what these photographs show, and what they are constructed from, is not something seen but that which is invisible: an iconography of thought as a response to history.

This extract is taken from 'History and the 'Thinking' Photography', an essay by **Andrew Wilson**, for the monograph *Paul Graham*, published by Phaidon Press Limited, London, 1996.

RICHARD HAMILTON

By chance in 1980, I was struck by a scene in a TV documentary about Irish Republican Army prisoners in the H block of the Maze prison in Northern Ireland. To the surprise of the British public, film was shown of men 'on the blanket' a term used to describe action taken by detainees in defiance of prison regulations. It was a strange image of human dignity in the midst of self-created squalor, and it was endowed with a mythic power most often associated with art. It manifested the noble spirit of Irish patriotism having retreated (or was it pushed?) into its own excreta.

Even in an environment of total deprivation humanity will find the means of protest. Violent reaction to physical and verbal abuse must lead to an escalation of force that no prisoner can hope to benefit from. Penned in, without the presence of inanimate objects to vent aggression upon, denied the tools of hostility, an individual has only what he can make with his own body; the IRA daubed the walls of their cells with shit. The strategy had two virtues, it kept the screws at bay and it was newsworthy. The 'dirty' protest, as the British called it (in a refined interplay of positive and negative concepts named 'no wash' by the Irish) lasted for some five years; more than 400 prisoners were involved. It was continued with hard determination until it became clear that the action was ineffectual. A decision was taken to move on to a mass hunger strike to death as a last resort to achieve the objectives.

What we had heard of the blanket protest, mainly through the propaganda agencies of Sinn Fein, could not prepare us for the startling photographic documentation on TV. The picture presented...was shocking less for its scatological content than for its potency. An oft declared British view of the IRA as thugs and hooligans did not match the materialization of Christian martyrdom so profoundly registered on film. One became acutely aware of the religious conflict that had resulted in the civil inequalities that gave a platform for IRA activity. The symbols of Christ's agony were there, not only the crucifix on the neck of prisoners and the rosary which confirmed the monastic austerity but the self-inflicted suffering which has marked Christianity from the earliest times.

...Having made a painting intended to summarize the image of Christian martyrdom contrived by Nationalist prisoners in the claustrophobic containment of their cells, it was appropriate to make a parallel representation of the Loyalist's vainglorious self-image in his free occupation of the streets.

An invitation to show in the Venice Biennale 1993 was accompanied with a request to produce a 'major new painting'. The seed was already in my mind to extend the diptych to a triptych for I had begun to think about the third component in the Northern Ireland conflict—the pig in the middle, the British army—*The state*.

This extract is taken from an essay by **Richard Hamilton**, previously published in *Rita Donagh and Richard Hamilton, A Cellular Maze*, for an exhibition of their work at The Orchard Gallery, Derry, 1983.

DAMIEN HIRST

...I always wanted to be a painter much more than a sculptor or an artist, but I was overwhelmed by the infinite possibilities of painting. I think it's got something to do with the void, the void of the blank canvas where anything and everything is possible beyond gravity, beyond life, in the realms of the imagination. ...

I often get asked about the spot paintings...They're about the urge or the need to be a painter above and beyond the object of a painting. I've often said that they are like sculptures of paintings. ...

In the spot paintings the grid-like structure creates the beginning of a system. On each painting no two colours are the same. This ends the system; it's a simple system. No matter how I feel as an artist or a painter, the paintings end up looking happy. I can still make emotional decisions about colour that I need to as an artist, but in the end they are lost. The end of painting. ...

I believe painting and all art should be ultimately uplifting for a viewer. I love colour. I feel it inside me. It gives me a buzz. I hate taste—it's acquired. ...

I once said that the spot paintings could be what art looks like viewed through an imaginary microscope. I love the fact that in the paintings the angst is removed. ...If you look closely at any one of these paintings a strange thing happens; because of the lack of repeated colours there is not harmony. We are used to picking out chords of the same colour and balancing them with different chords of other colours to create meaning. This can't happen, and so in every painting, there is a subliminal sense of unease; yet the colours project so much joy it's hard to feel it, but it's there. The horror underlying everything. The horror that can overwhelm everything at any moment.

I once said if you titled all the paintings *Isolated Elements for the Purpose of Understanding*, then it would be easier to relate them to the rest of my works. Not that there's a problem in making very different works. After all, whatever I make will be a Damien Hirst. I can't avoid that.

This extract was taken from an unpublished essay *On Dumb Painting* by **Damien Hirst**.

N I C K Y   H O B E R M A N

Nicky Hoberman was born in South Africa in 1967 and is currently resident in London. She read history at Oxford before going to the Parsons School of Design in Paris and Chelsea College of Art in London. The artist completed her studies in 1995 and the next year participated in two of Britain's most important open-submission shows (*New Contemporaries* and the *Whitechapel Open*), before having her first solo exhibition— at Entwistle in London. Recently Hoberman was included in *My Little Pretty*, an exhibition of images of girls by women artists at the Museum of Contemporary Art in Boston, where she showed alongside artists such as Judy Fox, Lisa Yusakavage and Inez van Lamsweerd.

Since her graduation Hoberman has produced a series of images of young girls, including two cycles of work entitled *Sweet Nothings* and *Chrysalis*. The artist starts by taking Polaroid photographs of her models, works freely from these in a wet-on-wet oil paint technique, and creates images which combine photorealism with the incidental distortions of drawing. Certain aspects of the artist's work, including her choice of titles and her use of colour, evoke sentimental ideals of childhood. However, the unshrinking gaze suggested by the images, and the expressionistic insights which they contain, give Hoberman's work other implications. The result is that her paintings have a disturbing quality, reflecting the complexities of actual childhood experience.

This text was written by **Mark Sladen**, Contemporary Director at the Entwistle Gallery, London, 1997.

L O U I S E   H O P K I N S

Louise Hopkins'...paintings dramatise how decisions about procedure can tentatively indicate their place in wider discussions of freedom and contemporary rhetorics of freedom. ...The recent series of paintings is made on the reverse of stretched furnishing fabric, which is prepared with...translucent gesso. Areas of the pattern are worked up in oil with small brushes, in shades varying from off white to dark sepia. ...Some works on paper [are made by] whiting out the staves, notes and lyrics of sheet music, still just legible by the sheen of paint I CAN'T STOP LOVING YOU. I KNOW. I LOVE YOU SO MUCH IT HURTS. Neither an ironic nor a sentimental gesture but a push-pull of avowal and disavowal, having and not-having, which changes according to the light. ...Louise Hopkins' procedure is bound by what looks like an extreme specialisation of labour, a willed curtailing of freedom, possibly a love of negation. But it has within it the ability to ring suddenly true of what freedom can be like (within a difficult love, perhaps, or within what used to be called a vocation, a notion preserved in the curious tasks artists invent for themselves). The eye returns to these works, looking for a way through, confident that one will be found though hesitating to proclaim what it is. ...

This extract is taken from a review by **Ian Hunt**, of Louise Hopkins' exhibition at 33 Gt Sutton Street, London (9 October - 7 November, 1996) and Tramway, Glasgow (16 November - 22 December 1996). Published in *Art Monthly* (Issue 202), December 1996 - January 1997.

BETHAN HUWS

Bethan Huws' artistic practice does not aim for a structure or construct which, clearly outlined, represents itself like any other object, and has a meaning as such or can assume a meaning according to its context. ...

The paradox and uniqueness of Bethan Huws' works seems in fact to lie in the concept of a spatial and hence a non-representational totality. It is paradoxical in that the space is, by definition, the precondition for the possibility of the presence of bodies, which rules out the totality of the work (physically possible though it may be). The specific non-representational nature of the work (which should not be confused with any forms of 'objectless' art) also brings about the unique vagueness or extension (if not absence) of its boundaries. ...

Bethan Huws' practice is to a very great extent guided by memory, particularly memory of the region where she grew up. She herself refers to this when speaking of her only 'representational' piece, which she has, in conversation, sharply differentiated from her 'works', and has not even allowed the status of 'art' (but which were included in the publication of the 'Works'), when she writes about the 'Boats' made out of rushes: 'The boats underline all the work and are important for the work...They function while being made as something that puts me back in my place. Their significance...lies in how they were made, by whom they were made, how they relate to the place they were made, and how that place relates to their function.'

...In the case of Bethan Huws, the construction of a work is also the linguistic recording of phenomenal details, the duplication of a thought, the thinking of a place. But without this duplication even the thought never occurs.

This extract is taken from 'Bethan Huws: Works - Thinking up a Place', an essay by **Ulrich Loock**, from the book *Mixed Doubles*, published by EA-Genrali Foundation and Wierner Secession, Wien (1992).

PERMINDAR KAUR

Permindar Kaur's new body of work continues to be as enigmatic as ever. What references to Sikh/Indian identity and culture should we read into her sculpture? Or should we set such readings aside, for fear of misreading or erroneously locating some of the most powerful sculpture currently on offer...

And yet, specific, highly charged cultural and religious symbolism has often been a feature of Kaur's work. ...We may be tempted to view such potent symbolism as a form of literal referencing of 'identity', 'religion', 'culture' and so on. But such limited readings would leave us distinctly short-changed because such symbolism takes its place alongside (but not above, or ahead of) other equally dramatic devices and elements central to Kaur's sculpture. Perhaps the most consistent dramatic device she employs has been her extraordinary use of scale. ...But the scale of the sculpture is not always expansive. There are a number of works that are reductive or undersize, creating further disquieting effects on the viewer. ...

Kaur's work relentlessly plays on our feelings of vulnerability, and effectively questions our attitudes towards power. She obliges us to reconsider our notions of childhood and adulthood, of the protector and the protected; what is safety, where we are safe, what demons or calamities might overwhelm us? What protects and what might harm us? She obliges us to consider these questions by re-presenting domestic objects that we have learnt to identify with 'home' and the protection afforded by 'family'. ...

Despite the magnitude of the emotions thrown up by Kaur's work, despite the potential within the viewer for feelings of despondency, her voice is not shrill or alarming. Nevertheless there is melancholy. There is sadness. ...

Perhaps ultimately, Kaur's work points towards the futility of 'protection'. ...But quite possibly, it is this point that makes Kaur such an important sculptor. By using material, be it glass, felt or whatever, in ways that go beyond the conventional or orthodox, she is able to animate a whole range of emotions and to oblige us to reconsider notions and attitudes that might otherwise lie dormant.

This extract is taken from 'Cold Comfort', a review by **Eddie Chambers**, of Permindar Kaur's exhibition *Cold Comfort* (at the Ikon Gallery, Birmingham, 18 May - 22 June 1996 and the Mead Gallery, University of Warwick, 25 May - 29 June 1996). Published in *Third Text* (No. 36), Autumn 1996.

JOAN KEY

...*BO.OB,BOO,OO.DO,DO.OO* are titles given to various works [by]...Joan Key. Say these titles and you will be on the edge of hearing the sound of language, yet see these paintings and you will become involved in a process of transformation where what is heard can be seen and what is seen can be thought and felt. Here I could speak of the work of transformation; indeed, the art of transformation.

With this body of work it is not the 'one off' painting which produces and stands for the work of art; rather, it is always the 'more than one'. The artist uses the term 'sequences' to speak of this production but, it must be insisted, these sequences continually throw into question the constitution of the sequential.

Sequences; here let me suggest another term: multiplicities. I suggest this term not in order to refer to what is always more than one but rather to speak of a production which is always *between*. I take my cue from the philosopher Gilles Deleuze. It is not the number of things which define a multiplicity; what defines it is the production of, and the productions made by, the between. ...

I am between something, on the edge of something, yet this something isn't well defined; on the contrary, it shimmers. ...

Shimmering with the production of a space of variable variation, these painting sequences make it impossible to settle or focus upon any part of their constituents. No review can produce an overview. No single image can be drawn. Something has happened to optical space. Indeed, no image can be settled upon and described by a viewer, or reviewer, of these paintings.

...Yes, these paintings get my ideas moving. ...Indeed, with these paintings I find myself asking what it means to think. What image of thought do I hold?

I meet simmering edges yet I also meet an artist who (like the philosopher prompting me) resists the separation of conceptual and sensual life. Yes, these paintings make me want to look, think and speak.

This extract is taken from 'Shimmering: An Act of Transformation', a review by **Yve Lomas**, of Joan Key's exhibition *An act of transformation* at the Richard Salmon gallery. Published in *make* (Iss ue 72), October 1996.

TANIA KOVATS

...Since 1985 Tania Kovats has explored metaphors for the constructed notion of female identity and iconography, often condensing it into various configurations of the Virgin Mary. ...She is aware that the formal content of her art paved the way for exploiting the anecdotal, particularly with reference to feminist art production. The work of Marina Warner, Julia Kristeva, Hélène Cixous and Luce Irigaray has influenced Kovats and inspired the creation of pale, skin-like clay pieces representing parts of the Virgin's body. For example, the ear was represented as a vagina (referring to the conception of Christ by the word of the angel Gabriel) and another sealed vagina referred to the Virgin's unbroken hymen. ...

...In practice, her modes of expression appear diverse, but in fact they express a clearly defined aim. This could be described as the desire to communicate an exploration of the relationship between mental and physical experience....Kovats works with a variety of media by which she achieves the ultimate artistic aim - expressing the conceptual in tangible form. ...

Kovat's use of the Virgin could be considered fetishistic - particularly when she dresses it in a condom. The combination of the two originated as a formal accident but has subsequently acquired more intrigue via anecdote. The piece has emerged as a controversial talisman, eloquently encapsulating issues surrounding Catholicism, contraception, abortion and sexual identity. The divine female, swathed in multi-layered, vagina-like robes is made phallic. It is suffocated beneath a temporary, delicate, but nevertheless loaded symbol of male potency, rendering the object reminiscent of the crucifix-cum-dildo in *The Exorcist*. However, to suggest that it is merely blasphemous limits its potential as an art work. Kovats reproduced the piece as a multiple, the Arts Council bought one and now refuses to exhibit it. She was shocked and amused to realise she had created what amounts to a piece of political propaganda. ...

This extract is taken from a review of Tania Kovats' work, by **Libby Anson**, published in *Art Monthly* (Issue 190), October 1995.

JOHN LATHAM

ARTIST'S STATEMENT:

prehistory:

1950 the mark as the Work

1951 No mark as the Work

Discovering FLAT TIME

1954   "Unit of Mark" via atomising paint instrument extends the idea, post zero action Work:"formation". Used in the presence of a transdisciplinary team of scientists, it kickstarted an Institute for the Study of Mental Images (ISMI); the artist as honorary founder member.

1958   Use of books, within "unit of mark" constellations, initialises black/white **sculpture** as physical **in-formation**. This affords an architecture and

dimensionality of "event", counterposing mass/ energy, spacetime et cetera.

1959   Exploration of film machinery potential: a '**Change-of-State**' medium, **time-engineering**. Book reliefs in use. **Time-based dimensionality**.

1960   "Observer" series and SkoobBox for a **Reflective Intuitive Organism**.

1967   Eventstructure board: Make- and Spectator-Events connected.

1972   **_Least Event as OI-IO_**. Project undertaken at Gallery House London **Time-Based Roller** constructed, representing 3-component point/ line/ plane (hence "FLAT TIME") "evenometry". (See Basic (T) diagrams).

1975   **Time-Base & Determination in Events** published, Dusseldorf.

1975   Steveni-negotiated APG appointment with the Scottish Office to attend to Urban Renewal, Graphics and Derelict Land as Work.

1977   Kunst als Soziale Strategie: APG address to Bundesrepublik. Helmut Schmidt administration. Bonn (public platform discussion).

1981   Paper, **Event Structure** published by Syntax, Calgary.

1983   **RIO**: 17-panel construction in Apollohuis Eindhoven summarises FLAT TIME Universe. Glass as an event-structural element (representing State O).

1984   **Report of a Surveyor** published Stuttgart

1991   Steveni reconstitutes APG as O + I.

1987-96 **Glass/Books**

1996   Installation in Mattress Factory, Pittsburgh Cosmic Blood series in Life/Live, Paris and Lisbon.

1997   FLAT TIME papers given at American Society for Cybermetics, Cyberfest97, Urbana Illinois.

JOHN LATHAM, 1997

LUCIA NOGUEIRA

One undercurrent within the writing which stems from Nietszche...is the recognition that one of the characteristics of a modern literature, as much as of art, is that it is unfinished—if not even unfinishable—and, as such, resists definition. ...Both what is produced and the process of its production come from something hidden, out of sight—as an attempt to represent that which is unrepresentable. As such, it is framed by a continuous failure within a desire to succeed. ...

These properties—of being unmappable, a traversal rather than an object or a referent, of straying from a straight route, of a disorientation where potential openings could be for either entry or exit—are present in the new work of Lucia Nogueira. Although taken together this work is resolved, there is also an air of incompleteness, of something that is perhaps waiting to happen; the disturbing menace found from doors left slightly ajar. ...

In an interview...Nogueira talked about her sculpture as having been produced by someone living in a foreign situation and the effect that this has had on her treatment of objects and the places in which they are positioned; just how a Gordian knot arises. 'I sometimes think that my work is all about gaps. For instance, you have routine in your life that carries on and then suddenly something happens, and that breaks the line. I think my work is very much connected with what happens when that line is broken, and the 'what happens then'. What happens in that gap.' ...Nogueira's language has been formed out of a feeling for these disruptive fissures between things. ...

What is the significant factor in her strategy is not so much the physical bringing together of those different sorts of objects, but rather her recognition of what she finds and what she creates as 'traversals' rather than objects. ...What imbues Nogueira's work with the resonance we find is not the result of an act of juxtaposition itself, but rather of an act of recognition in the bringing together. It is an act defined by the displacement of a search for representation in favour of its concealed energy in the creation of its meaning. ...

This extract is taken from a catalogue essay by **Andrew Wilson**, published by the Ikon Gallery, Birmingham, to accompany Lucia Nogueira's exhibition (6 November - 24 December 1993).

CHRIS OFILI

Data: SBM age: 27 Nigerian from Manchester
The ex-altar boy arrived. He came bearing gifts: gold, frankincense and elephant shit. To place at the feet and at the breast of his Holy Virgin Mary.

Canvases: *Someone described them as being like an African front room. Yes. A wealthy Nigerian front room in the decadent late seventies. Flocked wallpaper. Fitted shagpile carpets. Plastic covered velour furniture. Smoked glass coffee tables and gilt framed photos of ancestors that stared down at you sombrely.*
And the room full of your parents' friends, glamorously dressed in every colour and fabric you've ever seen: textured brocades, ornate lace, jacquard, decorative damask, dazzling gold jewels and fuschia pink lipstick. Drinking gin and laughing at jokes you didn't understand.

Like the smell of palm oil, Dax and Omo. Like old, torn pieces of Ebony, Essence, Black Hair and Beauty and Hustler.

The journey: was long. The search intense. The descent to London arduous. Strolling briskly through the Green Channel of Her Majesty's Customs, Heathrow airport, he feigns confidence and a sense of belonging, whilst carrying a suitcase stuffed with illegal elephant doo-doo.

Like space dust in your mouth and Super Trooper lights. Like game show sets and Saturday night TV.

He has presented himself at the table of High Art, but will he partake of the pork? Will he engage in the debate?

"Excuse me sir but where are you coming from? What was the weather like there? Where are you going to? How will you get there?" "Er......... dunno"

Like fireworks in the night sky. Like the intrigue of orifices.

Customs official No. 667, so busy busy busy scrutinising this Briton's passport for forged truths and illegal entries, forgets to check the case. From the corner of his eye, the ex-altar boy watches. It seems to glow, radioactive, and the faintest waft of fetid shit seeps through the zip.

This text by **Akure Wall**, was originally published in the exhibition catalogue accompanying *About Vision*, at The Museum of Modern Art (MOMA), Oxford (10 November 1996 - 23 February 1997).

JONATHAN PARSONS

Appearances can be deceptive. Jonathan Parsons knows this and he wants us to share in his vision. ...His concern is to make sense of the world about us—not least the world of signs and symbols—signifiers of human activity and intervention.

...For Parsons, every tiny element of the observed world possesses the power of a narrative painting. ...It is impossible...to ignore the unpretentious wit and wisdom that permeate such works as *Cuttlefish*—a large, faded Union Jack. Like all of Parsons' work, this piece operates on diverse levels. A flag, hung on a pole in an interior, might seem a metaphor for meaninglessness; a sad, futile declaration of pride and allegiance. Take a closer look and you will discover that this is no ordinary Union flag. It is not faded at all—but sewn together from carefully graded pieces of brown and white polyester. Whereas a faded flag would have made one point—by his intervention and his express intention to deceive—Parsons distances himself from the concept of found objects, locating himself within an older tradition of artifice. ...

...Parsons is an important link between the long-established ascendancy of the gestural abstract and a too-neglected symbolic formalism. Thus, the simple chalk 'x' of his *Kiss* is both a question as to why a cross should represent an embrace and an examination of its power to convey such a meaning.

Parsons is at the start of what will hopefully be a long mission to debunk art—to rid it of the superfluous cultural baggage accumulated over 500 years of post-Renaissance paralysis. Looking perhaps to the tradition of such artists as the hard-edge abstractionist Ellsworth Kelly, Parsons attempts to make his art as good as the original that inspired it, and, in so doing, to point up the things we miss as we blunder from day to day—the inevitable invisibility of reality.

This extract is taken from a review by **Iain Gale** of Jonathan Parsons' exhibition at the Richard Salmon gallery (4 - 23 July, 1996). Published in *The Independent, Section Two*, 16 July 1996.

RICHARD PATTERSON

...Richard Patterson's *Motocrosser*...ostensibly shows a life size model of a figure riding a motorbike, covered in paint, 'moving' from right to left. And yet this image is as arbitrarily conceived as the background—a sprayed and out-of-focus abstract. The tension that is set up within this painting is, however, not so much that of the figure-ground but between different levels of signification, given that the painting as a whole is conceived as a form of abstract. The meaning does not wholly reside in the image, nor in the process of the image's formation, but in a third place which is both dense and slippery where thought must constantly be rethought...

This painting...explicitly signals that a gap has decisively opened up within painting today, between subject, as a painting's capacity for self-definition, content or meaning that such a painting can hold, and the effectiveness by which the two co-exist between what can be seen and ways in which it can be apprehended. It is not so much the image of the motorbike that works as a metaphor here but the paint itself, in occupying a number of representational spaces, of which one actually holds the image.

Similarly, there is no absolute 'what you see is all there is' appeal to tangible facticity...not in the sense that the work is just an arrangement of paint that configures into an image of one sort or another, nor in the sense of being a defined sign that stands to be simply read. The work...comes alive through the ways in which it can be approached by both artist and beholder, so that the arbitrary and the transient can be fixed within this encounter, without actually being found.

This extract is taken from a review by **Andrew Wilson** of Richard Patterson's exhibition at the Anthony d'Offay Gallery (1 June - 4 August 1995). Published in *Art Monthly* (Issue 188), July-August 1995.

GARY PERKINS

Gary Perkins was born in Manchester in 1967. A member of the first European TV generation, his work imagines a childhood fantasy bordering on adult nightmare, a depersonalised world, psychotically dissolving distinctions between reality, fact, fiction and the imaginary. Constructed of playthings but arranged in a way which strips them of innocence, his scenes suggest an imagined future event which in some way will break rules.

In *The Kind of Prizes Money Just Can't Buy* the collision of household and terrorist paraphernalia insinuate threat and violence as a domestic norm, a complete breakdown of so called traditional values—a case for the 'authorities'.

Cleanliness next to Godliness on the other hand implies a situation which has already seen the intervention of a disciplining power. Four CCTV cameras peer inwards and dominate a traumatic space with two baths, two sinks and institutional decor, where any sense of privacy is lacking and is again further removed by the camera. The presence of what looks like Oxyacetylene cutting equipment offers the possibility of escape, but maybe it's a trap, a conspiracy. After all, any attempt at release would be caught on camera and doomed to failure.

These and other possible scenarios are relayed live and via the technology of the screen and enter another order of reality, which highlights the way the screen levels the real. Fictional models become strangely more real than before, while dysfunctional behaviour becomes a potential media event. In Gary Perkins' work a major event is that nothing ever happens, here are worlds where we look, watch and wait, and where the dark imagination of both the observer and observed is perhaps the one thing which exceeds any attempt at containment or control.

This text was written by **Michael Marshall**, and originally published in the catalogue accompanying the exhibition *Station Deutschland*, at the Kunstlerhaus Belthanian, Berlin, 1995.

VONG PHAOPHANIT

Writing on Vong Phaophanit's work is inevitably a somewhat paradoxical enterprise in as much as the work itself consciously plays at the borders of what is and is not accommodated by language. One could go further; it is perhaps a pursuit which is both spurious and ill-advised in that the work is always irretrievably superfluous to that which can be said of it. ...Notwithstanding this, an effort can be made to attend to the work's own terms, its own materiality, over and above any impulse to define and fix it within the ready-made categories of language and beyond any anecdotal narratives that may temptingly offer themselves in a process of 'reading' and 'understanding' the work. ...His is an art that, through its heterogeneous cultural resonance, calls directly on the senses. It is a sensuous art, making meaning at the level of the material as well as the discursive.

...If you name something, bring it into the terms of language, you control it. ...If something refuses to be named, if at each attempt at naming, its resonance moves elsewhere in a kind of perpetual circulation, it cannot be controlled by this inimical naming process of language. It can begin to move in the direction of creating new and different meanings, or as Phaophanit puts it, 'possibilities of meanings'. Perhaps the most frequent strategy of control has been the East/West dichotomy which has repeatedly been foisted onto the work. Appealing to these imagined fixed polar points to ground and explain the work presupposes that there is some sort of binary to be adhered to. Clearly, however, there is not and never has been for Phaophanit in his practice. As early as *Rice bed* (1987) and *Fragments* (1990), he was showing that it was where two images merge and form a third image which is where the work really began. The surface juxtapositions he has repeatedly set up may seem to invite this kind of dualistic interpretation, signifying as they do, at their most connotative level, cultural oppositions and differences (rice/neon, bamboo/lead, rubber/neon, ash/silk). But scratch the surface and it is clear that they gently mock the very notion of a simple East/West polarity and undermine the terms it rests upon. The cultural associations the materials carry and in turn the cultural allegiances we might imagine them to hold are much more complex and problematic than an easy dualistic reading allows for.

This extract is taken from an essay by **Claire Oboussier**, for the exhibition catalogue entitled *From Light*, accompanying the exhibition *Phaophanit and Piper*, which toured to Nottingham, Sheffield, Cambridge and Colchester. The catalogue published by Eddie Chambers, Bristol (1995).

YINKA SHONIBARE

African fabric: signifies African identity, rather like American jeans (Levi's), an indicator of trendy youth culture. In Brixton, African fabric is worn with pride amongst radical or cool youth. It manifests itself as fashion accessory with black British women in the head wrap form and it can also be found worn by Africans away from the home country. It becomes an aesthetics of defiance, an aesthetics of reassurance, a way of holding on to one's identity in a culture presumed foreign or different.

African fabric, exotica if you like, is a colonial construction, as its origins can be traced from Indonesia to Holland (hence Dutch wax), to Manchester and then sold to Africa where indigenous variations on the fabric have been appropriated for local use. The appropriation of Dutch wax, ironically is an indicator of modernity in the urban African setting, the new Africa after 'independence'. These fabrics carry with them a freedom of expression in the urban African setting, a freedom to be different (not European). ...Modern Africa celebrates its freedom in the excessive patterning of these industrially produced fabrics. ...

In this exhibition canvas has been replaced with African fabric and the aforementioned baggage which African fabric carries, to engage questions about the possibility of a modern African identity in the contemporary *postmodern* setting. Here questions are being asked about painting, its narrative, the possibility of a contemporary African engaging with the medium. What is at question is purloined seduction. Purloined fabrics from Brixton Market, purloined identity or notions of this, purloined authenticity or 'pretend authenticity' as it was once said to me. The primary aim of Airport Art (popular 'African' Art sold to tourists) is to seduce. Here the viewer is seduced by paint, the very primary vehicle of expression/seduction of male abstract expressionism—or is it white male as it is written in the official version? The denial of the single image/painting manifests itself in small non-heroic, non-authentic paintings/objects in this most seductive and self-indulgent of games, which carries the viewer simultaneously between clichés of centre and margin, as constructed to engage its contemporary site, its destined space, the gallery space.

This extract is taken from an essay by **Yinka Shonibare** for the catalogue accompanying the exhibition *seen/unseen* at the Bluecoat Gallery, Liverpool (18 June - 23 July 1994).

GEORGINA STARR

The Nine Collections of the Seventh Museum...is essential Starr. She began it in 1994 in The Hague...supposedly creating a project for a local arts group, she claims she hadn't a clue what to do. So she sewed a doll, Junior...and videotaped herself doing so; she took photos when she went walking...and she just lived...and then collected her photographs and videos and bits and pieces, together with clothes...writings...and the general accumulation of her stay, and made them into an installation in her hotel room. Then she took a photograph of the installation; then she left town...and then she wrote a long dissertationlike exegesis of the photograph, reading its mundane and peculiar images as art objects and organising them carefully into "collections" —*The Nine Collections of the Seventh Museum*.

...*The Nine Collections* doesn't excoriate, though, in the way of satire proper—there's no hate in it. The creator of a system as intricate as this one, ...is too involved in this kind of complexity to want to see it all levelled. Indeed, in one sense *The Nine Collections* aims as high as the art history it parodies: it proposes a model of artmaking.

All art does this implicitly, of course, just by being whatever it is, but Starr makes artmaking her subject. And the artmaking she enacts seems to be one of makeshift invention...using whatever comes to hand, including her own moods and memories...The piece does seem like some kind of record of a few lonely weeks...Starr's mode here is expressly personal; titles like the 'Seven Sorrows Collection', or the 'Allegory of Happiness Collection', seem to name her own emotions and experience. On the other hand, though, the whole thing is framed as an art-history thesis topic - is framed as fiction. The emotions and experience recede. ...

...One effect of Starr's combinations of video and installation is a feeling of absence: where you sit and stand...[where] Starr herself once played the parts you're watching on TV, but she's not there anymore. Similarly *The Nine Collections* now exists as a poster, a text, a set of photographs, and a CD-Rom; the installation itself has dematerialised. This recurrent bodilessness...gives a haunting undertow to Starr's humour, but also supplies another metaphor for her work: magic.

This extract is taken from 'Now You See It Now You Don't', a review by **David Frankel** of Georgina Starr's exhibition at the Barbara Gladstone Gallery, New York (27 April - 25 May 1997), by David Frankel. Published in *Artforum*, November 1996.

JOHN STEZAKER

...Indeed, his collage is as much a work of subtraction, division, and multiplication as of addition and combination. Its first act is excision, or outcut, and then suspension. The image is cut out of passing currency and then hung up in limbo, neither dead nor alive but submitted to indefinition. A second cut then redefines it, but this time as image, not as meaning. The simplest kind of second cut takes the form of cropping, a reframing which directs the gaze to a sector or detail of the scene. Some works consist of a single image cut into: perhaps with the head removed so that the rest is bereft of an 'absent limb' yet relieved of the burden of norm, whole, and integrity. In a way, losing *capot* is like losing caption, but the head is of the same order as the image itself, and its excision alters the conditions of outline and frame, so that they become active and visible agents of

imaging, rather as in the field painting of Newman or Stella. But for Stezaker, structures and formats achieve significance only in relation to the specific character of the imagerial fragments. All pictorial work is out of and upon the image.

...Or perhaps we should say cutting into nothing, for in the midst of all its endless possibilities, collage will always be next to nothing. The blade cuts into a surface and there is nothing there beneath it when removed. If this is so, it seems to be in John Stezaker's collage a nothing made for images, images that have a greater depth than that which they are made of.

This extract is taken from 'Cutting into Nothing' by **Brian Hatton**, a preview of John Stezaker's exhibition of new collages at Salama-Caro Gallery (10 January - 2 February 1991). Published in *Artscribe*, January - February 1991.

KERRY STEWART

...[Kerry Stewart's work] is informed by a consistent preoccupation with human isolation.

She first defined her own peculiarly unsettling vision in 1993. Still at Chelsea [School of Art]...Stewart made a work called *The Boy from the Chemist is Here to See You*....Barely visible behind a semi-opaque glass door, the boy is based on an old-fashioned charity figure of a cripple. He evokes memories of dusty shopfronts where donation-box effigies waited plaintively for coins to be pressed through their head-slots. But Stewart implies that the boy has somehow returned from the past, miraculously mobile and ready to disrupt our privacy with his uncomfortable nagging presence.

...[A]ll her work deploys humour as a counter to fear and sadness....So however damaged and defenceless her figures may be, they are stiffened by a curious spirit of obstinacy as well. ... Unlike most adults, she finds that the emotions of childhood still seem to play an active, nourishing role in her imagination. ...[Stewart] sees humour in her work as a subversive and liberating agent which acts, at times, with the force of an explosion.

A vein of coldness runs through Stewart's art, helping to ensure its freedom from sentimentality....Whether exuberant or forlorn, phantoms or outcasts, her versatile cast of figures stirs buried memories in a naive yet complex way, implying that the legacy of childhood impinges on adult experience at every turn.

This extract is taken from 'All Figured Out', a review by **Richard Cork** of Kerry Stewart's work. Published in *The Times Magazine*, September 16 1995.

MAUD SULTER

Maud Sulter's work has always been about exploring history through visual and literary means to create an impact of elements which continuously ebb and flow into and amongst each other, dovetailing; inextricably linked.

Text and image play equal but often different roles within the overall theatre of the work. ...

ZABAT...achieved in its nine works a multitude of aesthetic, political and historical agendas. ...Each muse a black contemporary artist/activist filled the space combining ancient creativity with contemporary practice. The writers, painters, musicians, strategists took on the roles and brought their own lives to the work. ...Each woman held the stage, singing her own aria while at the same time interweaving her story with that of her sisters. Back and forward across a geographical triangle negotiating a political force field each muse presented possibilities for the viewer. Possibilities, magical, spiritual and creative.

...The inspiration for *SYRCAS* has haunted Maud Sulter for many years. Politically the power of fascism in the 20th century, spiritually the rememory of the holocaust of slavery for the African diaspora, and personally the Holocaust of the 1930s and 40s, which once again tore people from the psychic and physical homelands, robbed people of their dignity, their lives and their families.

The aesthetic springboard for *SYRCAS* is twofold. The writings of Primo Levi, both prose and poetry, and the photographs of August Sander, were crucial to the development of the work. ... In this Europe where 'ethnic cleansing' is being tolerated, indeed policed even, by the West, the echo of Levi's words is loud and mournful.

What fascinates Maud Sulter about Sander's magnum opus is the wide inclusion of people of African descent...she found important...images of young black women who were obviously also part of the [circus] troupe.

Maud Sulter has no easy answers to our predicament at the end of the 20th century but she does offer a voice to our souls, an opportunity to give voice to our personal anxiety and traumas.

This extract is taken from 'A Brief Introduction to the Magical World of Maud Sulter's Photoworks', **Lubaina Himid**'s catalogue essay for Maud Sulter's exhibition *SYRCAS*, which toured to Manchester, Wrexham, Munich, Edinburgh, Dublin, Aberystwyth and Swansea between March 1994 - Spring 1995.

SAM TAYLOR-WOOD

Sam Taylor-Wood's work is distinguished by the potent image of the human figure isolated in the film frame. In almost all her film and video pieces we are confronted by solitary human subjects in various physical and emotional states. They are lethargic, bored, angry, pained; they sing, argue, dance and mime —but they are all united in their fragmented isolation from the world, from each other and from us, the spectator. Whatever the stance or mood, the viewpoint is always singularly objective, establishing an uncomfortable distance achieved by the camera's relentless, austere gaze. ...

...For Taylor-Wood, the self is always an opaque impossible entity that remains in the shadow of its need to express itself. Voice, gesture, mannerism and facial expression are, in the end, inadequate signifiers of self-authenticity. Thus, Taylor-Wood is not concerned with the moral dilemas of film melodrama but rather with the gesture of emotion itself, as an element of representation.

Taylor Wood's fascination with the elongated landscape format photograph is wittily used in *Wrecked* (1996), a reconstruction of Leonardo's painting 'The Last Supper'. Placing it in a contemporary setting using friends as apostles and modern-day props implying a booze-up more than a sedate supper, ...Christ is portrayed as a woman, but Taylor-Wood shuns the obvious tactic of inserting a woman in a 'feminist' stance, instead Christ becomes something between a naked 'angel' and a stripper. She stands, arms outstretched, behind the seated 'apostles' who ignore her, suggesting that she lies outside their space. The effect is similar to that of adding opera in some of her other works, that is to say, a high art moment is ambiguously grounded in an image of more mundane characteristics....Again, what seems expressive of emotion and joy even, is out of reach, lying beyond the shadowed space of the drunken revellers, but nevertheless at the centre of the image, and as such, suggesting some kind of redemption.

...Taylor-Wood's rendering of the 'Last Supper' denotes her wide-ranging approach to Western culture. Gangster movies, method dramas, avant-garde films, cinema stills, opera, documentary photography, and pop stars alike are all susceptible to her pillaging. But it is not a form of bricolage that simply hijacks glamour. On the contrary, it is her sensitive recognition of the ways in which popular images embody dichotomies, paradoxes and ambivalences, marking the subject as a self committed to forms of disclosure which are at the same time forms of concealment.

This extract is taken from 'Dear God, how much longer do I have to go?', an essay by **Michael O'Pray** in *Sam Taylor-Wood*, published by Chisenhale Gallery, City of Sunderland and Jay Jopling, London to accompany an exhibition of work by Sam Taylor-Wood at Chisenhale Gallery, London (11 September - 27 October 1996) and at Third Floor Gallery, City Library and Arts Centre, Sunderland (15 January - 22 February 1997).

MARK WALLINGER

Mark Wallinger runs risks. The risk to be negotiated in unearthing more and more about class and race in British society is what you might find. Take, for example, his *Royal Ascot*, (1994) a video installation. Four screens, packed tight in a row, show the Queen and other beaming members of the Royal Family arriving on the race-course at Ascot in their horse-drawn open carriages. They are being paraded by for the public, the Queen particularly resplendent, her varied hats and summer-coloured outfits signalling the fact that each video...is from a different day. So ritualised, however, is the royals' approach, and so ritualised the BBC approach to it, that the degree of synchrony between the

four videos is quite hypnotic, blurring the distinction between one day and another....In the flow, the four videos, bumping along together like four royals in a carriage, or like the four horses in each team, get caught up themselves, it seems, in the colour and heat of the scene they are recording. In the melting of boundaries, a shudder is released....

The work is, of course, ironic, Royal Ascot as meaningless farce. The risk is in the power, that the archaic material induced could buckle the irony fencing it in....

Mark Wallinger's work seems to be rooted in residual material from just before, or during, Industrial Revolution. The activities which interest him tend to be ones which survived, while resisting integration into the new industrialising order. Horseracing and country life prospered on the margins.

If the rise of science and the Industrial Revolution were connected, for reasons given above, with an expulsion from the collective unconscious of the mother figure in England, then identifications may well have surfaced in her place which were more archaic, perhaps identifications which were not with human beings. Wallinger's work can be seen as containing such identifications....

It seems to me that the political radicalism of Wallinger's work, ie the desire to facilitate social and political rebirth, leads to a conflict which lies in the historical material itself. His attempt to integrate the realities of sex, class and race within a critique leads not to their integration, but the opposite: to their expulsion. And where are they expelled to? Further into consciousness, it seems. The archaic material grows in strength. It becomes more difficult to master.

...Wallinger's works do not in fact tell you anything particular about class, sex or race in Britain at all, ie they do not give analysis....This is not to make a criticism of Wallinger. Analysis involves description. Wallinger's works do not, it seems to me, describe anything. What they do is dig up a buried layer of the English unconscious which has successfully resisted analysis.

This extract is taken from a review by **Conor Joyce** of Mark Wallinger's retrospective at the Ikon Gallery, Birmingham (25 February - 1 April 1995) and the Serpentine Gallery, London (10 May - 11 June 1995). Published by *Third Text*, (Issue 31), Autumn 1995.

GILLIAN WEARING

...Recently, Wearing placed an ad in *Time Out. Confess all on video. Don't worry you will be in disguise. Intrigued? Call Gillian.* They called, and here they are on screen, these few anonymous men who trouped, briefly, through Wearing's life with their delusions, their incomprehensible pain, their boasts and their weirdness. They face the camera in fancy dress masks (chosen from Wearing's collection) and stumble through their guilty secrets. Some are sad, some creepy, some ridiculous: sometimes all these things. A man in a rubber Neil Kinnock mask, who broke into a school and nicked some computer equipment; a guy with a Pinocchio nose who once (only once) betrayed his girlfriend; a very boring transvestite who talked at length of the joys of cross-dressing; a chap who became the willing butt of a trivial sexual humiliation game.

Wearing has her own routines and strategies for getting strangers to talk about themselves, to display and reveal a little of themselves to us. In the past she's handed blank placards to people on the streets and photographed them posing with the slogan of their choice. ...

She gets in close, with her charm and her guile, and people just spill, they show off, they chat her up, and sometimes they come apart. Yet she can be conspiratorial too, and encouraging, as in a recent sequence of photographs of herself in bed with a series of transsexuals. ...

The viewer looks and listens as though to a play, a Mike Leigh monologue or an Alan Bennett vignette. But this is real, the product of a one-woman Mass Observation team, done partly in fun...but mostly for reasons no less complex than those that drove her subjects to collude with her. These people exist. Wearing's work could be seen, with its behavioural games playing on our vicarious voyeurism, as a kind of smart exploitation of the unwary: but one must remember that all these people have offered themselves willingly to our gaze, there's nothing covert in Wearing's activities. She's putting herself at risk too. It pays off.

This extract is taken from a review by **Adrian Searle** of Gillian Wearing's exhibition at Interim Art, London (12 June - 13 July 1994). Published by *frieze*, September - October 1994.

RACHEL WHITEREAD

Rachel Whiteread's sculpture deals with things close to hand: the house, the room, the stair and the floor. Tables, baths, sinks, closets and mattresses; the bookshelf and the mortuary slab. Her works are death masks of the solid world.

...[O]ne might think that Whiteread's work is concerned only with solidity, the mass and volume of familiar objects in the physical world. Yet it is necessary to remind ourselves that what faces us are not simple re-cast versions of...the timeless furnishings of the ordinary life, but the spaces around and within these things. We are confronted with displaced volumes, the traces of objects which have disappeared, hidden emptiness made both visible and tangible.

Commentators on Whiteread inevitably end up focusing on her intimations of death and mortality, but seen *en masse* her sculpture is enormously alive. Though Whiteread's work has been necessarily indebted to earlier artists and innovations, her subject is both universal and her own. As her work has progressed, she has come more to understate her subject...

Whiteread's show is filled with ghostly familiars, the traces of a vocabulary of silences. ... With each fresh encounter one is struck by both the familiarity of the objects she has worked with and by their strangeness, their mute authority. What, in the hands of a lesser artist, could be seen as a glib though technically demanding exercise, becomes in Whiteread's grasp an encounter with tragedy.

Her work retains its power and its presence after many viewings. She recognises that art is neither decoration nor commodity, and her work does what art, at its best, has always done: it makes us see the world afresh. The fact that the world she is scrutinising is the most familiar of all makes her sculpture all the more impressive. We become re-attuned to what we know so well that we have come to disregard. ... If the words used to describe her works have become too familiar, it is because they are the only words that fit. Sculpture goes beyond words, into the real, and that is where they find their home.

This extract is taken from 'World of Interiors', a review by **Adrian Searle** of Rachel Whiteread's retrospective *Shedding Life*, at the Tate Gallery Liverpool (13 September 1996 - 5 January 1997). Published in *The Guardian*, 17 September 1996.

ANDREA WILKINSON

Andrea Wilkinson sometimes has trouble talking about what she has made, or where ideas come from. Startle her out of a daydream...and you will get close to it because this is the state in which much of the work exists—somewhere between the known and the unknown, the experienced and the only dreamt of—conceived and comprehended in a fleeting moment of lucidity.

The work emerges from an almost subconscious dialogue with the stuff of everyday life: bleach, detergent, coffee, sugar, pepper, water, pot plants, sand, ribbons and rosettes, discarded plastic bottles, malfunctioning strip lights, frosted glass. Wilkinson combines these humble substances and objects to create a disturbingly poetic critique of our unthinking activities. The familiarity of the material belies the multi-layered potential of the objects.

Where a more specialised material is used (like Perspex...) it is introduced in order to exploit what might be seen as fleeting phenomena or ephemeral characteristics. The fact that Perspex acts in some situations as a 'light gatherer or intensifier' when seen edge on is utilised with subtle wit. ...Perspex as traditional display support, but now the glowing neon-bright edge serves to underlie the mountains like magma or some schematic tectonic plate. Ideas of orogenesis are curiously complete.

Geological associations occur repeatedly..The use of natural material is deliberate and points to one of Wilkinson's underlying concerns—the fragility of our tenure on earth. ...

The observation and re-presentation of peripheral occurrence and coincidence between unexpected and seemingly unrelated activities or objects is what Wilkinson's work is about. Whilst the rest of us madly rush around, she moves at her own pace. ... she'll say 'See what I've found, find what I've seen', presenting something else which everyone looked at but nobody saw. It's time to open our eyes ...

This extract is taken from an unpublished review by **Hadrian Pigott** of Andrea Wilkinson's exhibition at the Heber-Percy Gallery, Leamington Spa, (March - April 1995).

JANE & LOUISE WILSON

The quiet, insidious power of Jane and Louise Wilson's photographic and video installations builds like a dark threat or a secret promise, only to evaporate in a non-climax, leaving the subject of their investigations as complex as it ever was. Their approach is a flirtation, a torture and a denial, one that explores altered states of consciousness, either through LSD, hypnosis or psychodrama, with themselves as subjects.

...[In *Crawl Space*] the conventions of the horror genre are mapped onto the interior of a house which denotes the feared female body - the body that can reproduce, the body whose messy bleeding signifies terror. Drawing on references to *The Exorcist, The Shining, Whatever Happened to Baby Jane, Repulsion* and *The Tenant*, we are spun down the corridors of a disturbed psyche, where doors slam in the protagonist's face, a bloodied lump bashes against a wall and dilapidated ceilings threaten to implode on the characters. The blood red walls and floors do not connote a bloodbath, but suggest dangerous fluid female sexual and reproductive power. The noise pressure is like an industrial pump, a mechanised heart.

The film calls on horror conventions only to dissolve them. ...Memory of fear and memory of filmed fear of women's bodies collude and collide as the body erupts in the flesh-written words, 'crawl space', which appear across a woman's belly. Our fear of invasion, of incapacity, of violation, are summoned and then critiqued as the adrenalin rush subsides: we find the heroine safe and the film ends in comic parody.

A recent survey concluded that while boys prefer to watch action thrillers, girls overwhelmingly choose to view horror movies. As Cindy Sherman suggests: 'I love horror films because they function in the same way fairy tales do in allowing society to see something very gruesome and hard to deal with, which somehow psychically prepares us for our own deaths. Or prepares us for the potential of any violence in our lives. Or reassures us that our lives are okay because we don't have that threat in them'. (Cindy Sherman, interviewed in *Art Papers*, July/August 1995.)

...The Wilsons' densely packed, beautifully composed work lies at the forefront of attempts by women artists in the nineties to mark out new territories of the female body. Evoking and subverting the discourse of criminal anthropology, sociology and psychoanalysis which have defined the female deviant, and referencing cinematic representations of the female body, theirs is an art of subtle, provocative retaliation. Their cool practice never resorts to easy irony but teases around notions of non-release, with a private humour, playing on the tensions between women as victim and...strong subject.

This extract is taken from an essay by **Cherry Smyth**, for the exhibition catalogue accompanying the exhibition *Normapaths*, at Chisenhale Gallery, London (22 November - 22 December 1995) and at Berwich Gymnasium Gallery (19 May - 23 June 1996).

HERMIONE WILTSHIRE

Whether she uses ready-made photography as a quotation from the world, or takes her own, photography has been a way for Hermione Wiltshire to deal with both the object and what it represents. Transferring the three-dimensional to the two-dimensional is not only a formal fascination, but a way of exerting a wider control. She has increasingly used her particular combination of medium and message with greater singularity of purpose, making it more concrete and physical.

Working with photography has made Wiltshire, of necessity, think about its framing. Her work of the last three or four years has focused on glass, and how it affects the image it protects. She has given glass a more active role than is usual, experimenting with curved and domed glass, and with glass that is integrated into the sculpture.

Wiltshire's work increasingly engages us not only with its imagery, but also by pushing insistently into our field of vision. While some leap forwards more or less wildly, others press slowly but unremittingly towards us. These works are neat because everything knits together formally; their subjects are both internal and external, of art and of the body. They play on the engagement or interface between the subject and its spectator. The subjects have both been open (of the body's openings and their exhalations—the mouth, the breath, the shout, the ejaculation) and closed....

As glass in Hermione Wiltshire's work has steadily acquired a life of its own, she has looked at how it can bring life to the image underneath, combining their forces. Making art-works that are generally displayed on the wall has focused her attention on ways of making them reach out towards the viewer. Amalgamating the forces of the body with the forces of her own work has led her to create analogies between bodily exhalations or expansions and those of her sculptural fields. ...

This extract is taken from an essay by **Penelope Curtis**, in the exhibition catalogue *The British Council Window Gallery Prague, Selected exhibitions 1993-95*, edited by Andrée Cooke.

RICHARD WRIGHT

ARTIST'S STATEMENT:

It is remarkable, that when it comes to speaking about work, how quickly you can find yourself making a leap from an isolated position of uselessness (of the material being out of control) to one in which it is already possible to invoke the whole of history and everything else into the bargain, as the background of your actions.

In this sense it is very easy to be confused into believing that painting is predetermined by thought, when often I can find that it is my thoughts which are determined by painting. This sounds senseless, but it is rather like saying I have arrived at thinking about history through action instead of thinking about action through history.

RICHARD WRIGHT, 1997

CATHERINE YASS

These images were made by Catherine Yass during 1994 at Springfield Hospital, a Victorian psychiatric institution in London...The work is a response to Springfield's photographic tradition dating back to the work of a certain Dr Diamond in the 1840s and that of the better-known Francis Galton in the 1880s, both of whom pioneered photographic research into mental health in the name of 'scientific investigation'. After asylum inmates had been ushered in front of the camera to have their portraits taken, Galton would layer together several of the resulting negatives to produce a composite photograph which, he claimed, represented a generic image of madness, or the face of the archetypical 'lunatic'. ...

The dynamics between institutional and personal identity are central to Yass' work. What is intriguing about *these* images is that though the artist is best known for her portraits, Yass has made a conscious decision to exclude the sitter in favour of what was originally intended merely as a backdrop. The background claims a higher significance than that which we would normally expect to find in the foreground; in so doing, Yass turns Galton's, and her own, photographic practice inside-out, shifting the viewer's gaze away from the lens-pinned specimen to the immediate environment. Architectural interiors have a subliminal impact, and none more so than the corridor, a transitory zone with a beginning and an end. It is a picture embedded deep within the human psyche, the stuff of dreams and nightmares. ...

Yass employs a process of layering together positive and negative colour films within the same image, with further enhancement taking place during the printing process. The result is ghostly; the images are filled with a peculiar resonance as positive and negative meet in symphysis across the surface, causing a semi-X-ray quality or suggesting architectural dissection.

It is the subtle shifts in our perception of nuances within architectural space that Yass explores through these interiors. ...[S]ome appear comforting while others hold a certain dread. We are stuck in the middle—mid-corridor—neither here nor there, somewhere between entrance and exit. ...

This extract is taken from a review of Catherine Yass' work by **Nick Hallam**. Published in *Art & Design, Photography & the Visual Arts*, (9 October 1995)

ARTISTS' BIOGRAPHIES AND LIST OF WORKS

UNLESS OTHERWISE STATED, MEASUREMENTS ARE IN CENTIMETRES, AND HEIGHT PRECEDES WIDTH PRECEDES DEPTH

FIONA BANNER
Born 1966, Merseyside
Lives and works in London

The Nam 1997
1,000 page, 280,000 word book
28 x 21 x 6
Published by Frith Street Books,
London

Full Metal Jacket 1996
diptych
typeset electrostatic print mounted
on 0.5 plyboard
each 194.5 x 194.5
Courtesy of the artist and Frith
Street Gallery, London

JORDAN BASEMAN
Born 1960, Philadelphia, USA
Lives and works in London

Based On A True Story 1996
cat's teeth, dental acrylic
dimensions variable
Private Collection, London

Based On Actual Events 1995
dog's teeth, dental acrylic
dimensions variable
Saatchi Collection, London

Up, Up And Away 1995
mouth braces, wisdom teeth
dimensions variable
Saatchi Collection, London

Call Me Mister 1995
man's shirt torso, child's shirt sleeves,
necktie, human hair, wooden hanger
dimensions variable
Saatchi Collection, London

RICHARD BILLINGHAM
Born 1970
Lives and works in London

Untitled 1995
SFA4 colour photograph on
aluminium
80 x 120
edition of 7 plus 1AP, AP
Courtesy of the artist and Anthony
Reynolds Gallery, London

Untitled 1994
SFA4 colour photograph on
aluminium
80 x 120
edition of 7 plus 1 AP, AP
Courtesy of the artist and Anthony
Reynolds Gallery, London

Untitled 1995
SFA4 colour photograph on
aluminium
120 x 80
edition of 7 plus 1 AP, AP
Courtesy of the artist and Anthony
Reynolds Gallery, London

Untitled 1995
SFA4 colour photograph on
aluminium
50 x 75
edition of 10 plus 2 AP, AP
Courtesy of the artist and Anthony
Reynolds Gallery, London

Untitled 1995
SFA4 colour photograph on
aluminium
80 x 120
edition of 7 plus 1AP, AP
Courtesy of the artist and Anthony
Reynolds Gallery, London

Untitled 1994
SFA4 colour photograph on
aluminium
80 x 120
edition of 7 plus 1 AP, AP
Courtesy of the artist and Anthony
Reynolds Gallery, London

Untitled 1993
SFA4 colour photograph on
aluminium
105 x 158
edition of 5 plus 1AP, AP
Courtesy of the artist and Anthony
Reynolds Gallery, London

Untitled 1995
SFA4 colour photograph on
aluminium
105 x 158
edition of 5 plus 1 AP, AP
Courtesy of the artist and Anthony
Reynolds Gallery, London

Untitled 1994
SFA4 colour photograph on
aluminium
158 x 105
edition of 5 plus 1 AP, AP
Courtesy of the artist and Anthony
Reynolds Gallery, London

CHRISTINE BORLAND
Born 1965, Darvel, Ayrshire
Lives and works in Glasgow

*Home-made Bullet-proof Vests -
Cotton Wool and Jewellery Collection*
1995
two dummies, vest with cotton
wool, vest with jewels sewn inside
each 80 x 44 x 36
Collection of Marvin and Elayne
Mordes, Baltimore, Maryland, USA

Shoes with 9mm hole 1992
pair of black, ladies, size 5 shoes
right shoe contains a hand made
hole corresponding to bullet
calibres
series of 8
Private Collection, courtesy Sadie
Coles, London

DAVID CHEESEMAN
Born 1960, London
Lives and works in London

Cut Up 1996
glass, sellotape and carpet
152 x 214 x 12
Courtesy of the artist and Richard
Salmon, London

MAT COLLISHAW
Born 1966, Nottingham
Lives and works in London

*Lustre, held by his Groom and Jenison
Shafton's Racehorse Snap with
Thomas Jackson, his Trainer & Jockey*
1990
photocopies, glass, bulb and rubber
bolts
a pair, each 20 x 23 x 13
Courtesy of the artist and Richard
Salmon, London

Butterfly Table 1996
wooden table, glass jar, video
projection and fishing net
dimensions variable
Courtesy of Art + Public, Geneva

Infectious Flowers II 1996/97
*Zoster of Supravicular Dermatomes
Metastases from a Malignant
Melanoma
Melanomic Orchid*
3 light boxes with photographic
transparencies
each 50 x 50 x 10
Courtesy of the artist and Thomas
Dane Limited, London

CRITICAL DECOR
David Pugh and Toby Morgan
Live and work in London

Boring Democracy 1994
blue neon and panting
20 x 60 x 5
Courtesy of the artists

Arrows 1995
wood, feathers and paint
dimensions variable
Courtesy of the artists

Nietzsche Piece 1992
photograph on canvas
2 panels, each 91 x 137
Carl Freedman Collection

NEIL CUMMINGS
Born 1958, Aberdare, Wales
Lives and works in London

Detail from the Collection: Blue 1996
found cardboard and plastic bottles
89.2 x 12.3 x 30.5
Courtesy of the artist and Richard
Salmon, London

JUDITH DEAN
Born 1963, Billericay
Lives and works in London

*Installation for a Chihuahua: "Rough"
17th century version* 1995
wax crayon sharpenings
5 x 0.3
Courtesy of the artist

*Installation for a Chihuahua: "Rough"
Party version* 1995
wax crayon sharpenings
5 x 0.3
Courtesy of the artist

*Installation for a Chihuahua: "Rough"
Patriotic version with 25 options* 1995
wax crayon sharpenings
5 x 0.3
Courtesy of the artist

*Installation for a Chihuahua: "Rough"
Undercover version* 1995
wax crayon sharpenings
5 x 0.3
Courtesy of the artist

"Of" 1995
pencil
14 x 0.6
Courtesy of the artist

WILLIE DOHERTY
Born 1959, Derry, Northern Ireland
Lives and works in Derry

At The End Of The Day 1994
video installation
dimensions variable
Arts Council Collection, Hayward
Gallery, London

ROTIMI FANI-KAYODE
Born 1955, Nigeria
Died 1989, London

Milk Drinker 1983
black and white photograph
51 x 41
Collection Museum of
Contemporary Art, Sydney,
purchased 1997

*Nothing To Lose I (Bodies of
Experience)* 1989
cibachrome print
51 x 41
Collection Museum of
Contemporary Art, Sydney,
purchased 1997

Untitled 1987-88
cibachrome print
51 x 41
Collection Museum of
Contemporary Art, Sydney,
purchased 1997

*Nothing To Lose IX (Bodies of
Experience)* 1989
cibachrome print
51 x 41
Collection Museum of
Contemporary Art, Sydney,
purchased 1997

Untitled 1987-88
cibachrome print
51 x 41
Collection Museum of
Contemporary Art, Sydney,
purchased 1997

*Every Moment Counts (Ecstatic
Antibodies)* 1989
cibachrome print
51 x 41
Collection Museum of
Contemporary Art, Sydney,
purchased 1997

*Every Moment Counts (Ecstatic
Antibodies)* 1989
cibachrome print
51 x 41
Collection Museum of
Contemporary Art, Sydney,
purchased 1997

*Nothing To Lose XII (Bodies of
Experience)* 1989
cibachrome print
51 x 41
Collection Museum of
Contemporary Art, Sydney,
purchased 1997

Untitled 1989
cibachrome print
51 x 41
Collection Museum of
Contemporary Art, Sydney,
purchased 1997

Untitled 1987-88
cibachrome print
51 x 41
Collection Museum of
Contemporary Art, Sydney,
purchased 1997

CEAL FLOYER
Born 1968, Karachi, Pakistan
Lives and works in London and
Berlin

Sold 1996
cadmium red oil paint
0.7 diameter
Courtesy of the artist and Lisson
Gallery, London

Projection 1997
35mm slide projection
Courtesy of the artist and Lisson
Gallery, London

Carousel 1997
10' vinyl record, hi-fi system, MDF
Courtesy of the artist and Lisson
Gallery, London

JOHN FRANKLAND
Born 1961, Rochdale, Lancashire
Lives and works in London

Right Here, Right Now 1997
polythene and wood
dimensions variable
site-specific installation at the
Museum of Contemporary Art,
Sydney, 1997

Ohne Titel 1994
tree trunk, gloss paint
dimensions variable
Saatchi Collection, London

ANYA GALLACCIO
Born 1963, Glasgow
Lives and works in London

(Untitled) 1997
site-specific installation at the
Museum of Contemporary Art,
Sydney, 1997

Preserve (Sunflowers) 1992 version
100 sunflowers and glass
150 x 150
Courtesy of Barbara Gladstone
Gallery, New York

RACHEL GLYNNE
Born 1962, Llanelli, South Wales
Lives and works in Belfast, Northern
Ireland

Long Hair Dress Shirt 1995
human hair, teeth, steel pins
427 x 61 x 25
Courtesy of the artist

DOUGLAS GORDON
Born 1966, Glasgow
Lives and works in Glasgow

10 ms-1 1995
video projection
dimensions variable
Collection Tate Gallery, London,
purchased 1997

PAUL GRAHAM
Born 1956, Stafford
Lives and works in London

Television Portrait (Danny, Bristol)
1991
SFA3 framed colour photograph
112 x 91
edition of 5 plus 1 AP, AP
Courtesy of the artist and Anthony
Reynolds Gallery, London

Television Portrait (Yuko, Kyoto) 1992
SFA3 framed colour photograph
112 x 91
edition of 5 plus 1 AP, 5/5
Courtesy of the artist and Anthony
Reynolds Gallery, London

Television Portrait (Jack, Bradford)
1989
SFA3 framed colour photograph
112 x 91
edition of 5 plus 1 AP, 5/5
Courtesy of the artist and Anthony
Reynolds Gallery, London

RICHARD HAMILTON
Born 1922, London
Lives and works in Oxfordshire

The citizen 1982-83
oil on canvas
2 canvases: each 200 x 100
Collection Tate Gallery, London,
purchased 1984-85

DAMIEN HIRST
Born 1965, Bristol
Lives and works in Devon

*beautiful, mad, crazy, spinning,
psycho's, vortex painting* 1994
gloss household paint on canvas
155 diameter
Private Collection, London

Dead Ends, Died Out, Explored 1993
MDF, glass and cigarette butts
153 x 243 x 12
Courtesy of Jay Jopling, London
Private Collection, London

NICKY HOBERMAN
Born 1967, Cape Town, South Africa
Lives and works in London

Melting Cherries 1996
oil on canvas
240 x 150
Courtesy of the artist and Entwistle,
London

Sweet Pickle 1996
oil on canvas
91.5 x 91.5
Saatchi Collection, London

LOUISE HOPKINS
Born 1965, England
Lives and works in Glasgow

2/5 1996
oil on reverse of patterned
furnishing fabric
diptych, each panel: 91 x 130
Courtesy of the artist

Untitled (2) 1996
oil paint on reverse of patterned
furnishing fabric
56 x 45
Private Collection

Songbook 2 1997
white gouache on song book
45 x 31 x 2
Courtesy of the artist

BETHAN HUWS
Born 1961, Cymru
Lives and works in Malakoff, France

Y cwch 1983-97
rush boat in vitrine
20 x 22.5 x 14
Courtesy of the artist
©Bethan Huws, ADAGP 1997, Paris

PERMINDAR KAUR
Born 1967, Nottingham
Lives and works in London

Untitled 1995
copper bed with red fabric
110 x 70 x 67
Courtesy of the artist

Untitled 1996
window and birds
104.5 x 104.5 x 12
Courtesy of the artist

JOAN KEY
Born 1948
Lives and works in London

OO,OO (OO/95) I - II 1996
two paintings, oil on canvas
each 166 x 244
Courtesy of the artist and Richard
Salmon, London

OB, BO, OB, BO, OB (OB/BO I-V) 1996
Nos. 1, 2 and 5 from the series
oil on canvas
each 76 x 91.5
Courtesy of the artist and Richard
Salmon, London

TANIA KOVATS
Born 1966, Brighton
Lives and works in London

Virgin in a Condom 1996
resin and latex condom
10.5 x 4 x 3
Collection Museum of
Contemporary Art, Sydney,
purchased 1997

Fatima 1992
clear polyurethane, steel brackets
33 x 41 x 13
Courtesy of the artist and Laure
Genillard Gallery, London

JOHN LATHAM
Born 1921, Africa
Lives and works in London

Moral High Ground 1988
glass, books, light bulb
83 x 25.5 x 33
Collection of the artist, courtesy of
the Lisson Gallery, London

*Construction (number 5) from Cluster
of Eleven* 1992
plaster, fragments of books
35 x 30 x 28
Courtesy of the artist and Lisson
Gallery, London

LUCIA NOGUEIRA
Born 1950, Gioiania, Brazil
Lives and works in London

Step 1995
oriental carpet, broken glass
285 x 152
Courtesy of the artist and Anthony
Reynolds Gallery, London

CHRIS OFILI
Born 1968, Manchester
Lives and works in London

The Chosen One 1997
oil on Canvas
9 x 7
Collection Museum of
Contemporary Art, Sydney,
purchased 1997

Popcorn Shells 1995
paper collage, oil paint ,polyester
resin, map pins, elephant dung on
linen and 2 elephant dung
183 x 122
Arts Council Collection, Hayward
Gallery, London

Them Bones 1995
oil paint, polyester resin, elephant
dung on linen and 2 elephant dung
183 x 117
Saatchi Collection, London

JONATHAN PARSONS
Born 1970
Lives and works in Farnham, Surrey

Herma 1990
graphite on paper
44.5 x 81
James Moores Collection

Kiss 1994
chalk on black paper
49.5 x 46
Courtesy of the artist and Richard
Salmon, London

Cuttlefish 1995
sewn polyester flag with wall
mounted flagstaff
250 x 290
Courtesy of the artist and Richard
Salmon, London

RICHARD PATTERSON
Born 1963, Leatherhead, Surrey
Lives and works in London

Motocrosser III 1995
oil and acrylic on canvas
Collection Vicki and Kent Logan, San
Francisco

GARY PERKINS
Born 1967, Manchester
Lives and works in London and
Liverpool

Cleanliness next to Godliness 1995
CCTV cameras, 1/20 scale washroom,
MDF, 12" picture monitor
Courtesy of the James Moores
Collection

VONG PHAOPHANIT
Born 1961, Savannakht, Laos
Lives and works in London and
Berlin

Untitled 1995-96
Laotian words in clear blue neon,
glass, painted steel
242 x 26 x 140
Courtesy of the artist and Stephen
Friedman Gallery

Untitled 1995-96
Laotian words in clear red neon,
wax, glass,
painted steel
154 x 28 x 160
Courtesy of the artist and Stephen
Friedman Gallery

YINKA SHONIBARE
Born 1962, London
Lives and works in London

Five Under Garments and Much More
1995
African fabric, Rigilene, fishing line,
interlining
tailored by Sian Lewis
each 95 x 130 (circumference
dimensions)
Courtesy of the artist and Stephen
Friedman Gallery

Untitled 1996
emulsion and acrylic on textile
diptych
each 50 x 50
Collection Museum of
Contemporary Art, Sydney,
purchased 1997

GEORGINA STARR
Born 1968, Leeds
Lives and works in London

*The Nine Collections of the Seventh
Museum* 1994
mixed media
7 colour photographs, poster and
book
Collection Museum of
Contemporary Art, Sydney,
purchased 1996

So Long Babe 1996
wooden plane and video projection
dimensions variable
Courtesy of the artist, Anthony
Reynolds Gallery, London and
Barbara Gladstone Gallery, New York

KERRY STEWART
Born 1965, Paisley
Lives and works in London

Cape 1996
fibreglass, resin and polyurethane
rubber
181 x 160 x 128
Courtesy the artist and Stephen
Friedman Gallery

JOHN STEZAKER
Lives and works in London

Expulsion I 1994
oak framed iris print
84 x 119
Courtesy of the artist

Expulsion II 1994
oak framed iris print
84 x 119
Courtesy of the artist

MAUD SULTER
Born 1960, Glasgow
Lives and works in Preston

*Zabat: poetics of a Family Tree,
Calliope* 1989
cibachrome print, gilt frame
152 x 121.9
Arts Council Collection, Hayward
Gallery, London

*Zabat: poetics of a Family Tree,
Terpsichore* 1989
cibachrome print, gilt frame
152 x 121.9
Arts Council Collection, Hayward
Gallery, London

Duval et Dumas diptych 1993
matt laminated C-type colour prints,
raw oak frames
each 76.2 x 101.6
one of an edition of five
The British Council Collection,
London

SAM TAYLOR-WOOD
Born 1967, London
Lives and works in London

Wrecked 1996
C-type colour print
artist's proof
framed photograph
183.2 x 417.2
Courtesy Jay Jopling, London
Private Collection, London

MARK WALLINGER
Born 1959, Chigwell
Lives and works in London

*Half-Brother (Exit To Nowhere -
Machiavellian)* 1994-95
oil on canvas
2 canvases, each 230 x 150
Collection Tate Gallery, London,
purchased 1995

Royal Ascot 1994
television monitors, flight cases,
video tape
dimensions variable
Courtesy of the artist and Anthony
Reynolds Gallery, London

GILLIAN WEARING
Born 1963, Birmingham
Lives and works in London

*'Confess All on Video: Don't Worry You
Will Be In Disguise. Intrigued? Call
Gillian...'* 1994
video for single monitor
Courtesy Maureen Paley/Interim Art

RACHEL WHITEREAD
Born 1963, London
Lives and works in London

Untitled (Twenty-Five Spaces) 1995
resin
25 blocks
each 43 x 30 x 30
Queensland Art Gallery Foundation,
Brisbane, purchased 1996

ANDREA WILKINSON
Born 1967, West Yorkshire
Lives and works in London and
North Wales

Green Range 1994
fluorescent perspex and loose
modelling turf
approx. 2.5 x 196.5 x 4
Courtesy of the artist and Richard
Salmon, London

Groups C4, B3, B1, D6 1994
acrylic paint, photographic paper
and pins
approx. 50 x 2 x 1.5
Courtesy of the artist and Richard
Salmon, London

JANE AND LOUISE WILSON
Born 1967, Newcastle
Live and work in London

Attic 1995
C-type print on perspex
180 x 180
Courtesy of the artists

Red Room 1995
C-type print on perspex
180 x 180
Courtesy of the artists

HERMIONE WILTSHIRE
Born 1963, London
Lives and works in London

AAAAGH...!! 1994/5
23 diameter x 19 depth
glass with photograph
Courtesy of the artist

RICHARD WRIGHT
Born 1960
Lives and works in Glasgow.

Wall painting 1996
dimensions variable
site-specific installation at the
Museum of Contemporary Art,
Sydney, 1997

Wall painting 1996
dimensions variable
site-specific installation at the
Museum of Contemporary Art,
Sydney, 1997

Wall painting 1997
dimensions variable
site-specific installation at the
Museumof Contemporary Art,
Sydney, 1997

CATHERINE YASS
Born 1963, London
Lives and works in London

three works from the series,
Corridors 1995
3 photographic transparencies and
light boxes
each 86 x 70 x 14
Courtesy Public Art Development
Trust and
Laure Genillard Gallery, London

Published by the Museum of Contemporary Art, Sydney, on the occasion of the exhibition:

Pictura Britannica Art from Britain

22 August — 30 November 1997

Museum of Contemporary Art, Sydney: 22 August - 30 November 1997
Art Gallery of South Australia, Adelaide: 19 December 1997 - 1 February 1998
City Gallery, Wellington, New Zealand: 27 February - 26 April 1998

Curator: Bernice Murphy

Catalogue Editor: Bernice Murphy

Artists' biographies and short texts compiled and edited by: Sarah den Dikken and Raegen Kennett

National Library of Australia Cataloguing-in-Publication entry:

Pictura Britannica

ISBN 1 875632 53 0

1. Art Modern - 20th century - Great Britain - Exhibitions. 2 Art, British - Exhibitions. I. Museum of Contemporary Art (Sydney NSW)

709.42074

© Museum of Contemporary Art Limited, the artists and authors

Circular Quay, Sydney, Australia; PO Box R1286, Royal Exchange, Sydney, 1223; Tel: 61 2 9252 4033; Fax: 61 2 9252 4361

ACN 003 765 517

Catalogue Design and Production: Peter Thorn Design

Printing: National Capital Printing, Canberra

Photographers (other than artists): Chris Davies (John Latham); Paul Green (Fiona Banner); Paul Green (Judith Dean); Andrew Holligan (John Frankland); Jay Jopling, London (Sam Taylor-Wood); Cheryl O'Brien (Georgina Starr); Sue Ormerod (John Latham); Simon J. Starling (Louise Hopkins); John A. Walker (John Latham); Stephen White (John Latham, Yinka Shonibare, Vong Phaophanit) and Steve White (Fiona Banner)

Project credits:

Director: Leon Pariossien

Chief Curator - Deputy Director: Bernice Murphy

Assistant Curator: Sarah den Dikken

Exhibition and tour management: Louise Pether, Barbara Maré, Raegen Kennett of the MCA, and Clarrie Rudrum of The British Council

Exhibition installation: Marc O'Carroll, Kyle Ashpole, Jay Balbi, Michelle Beevers, Kevin Bray, Mark Brown, Peter Cerneaz, Darryl Chapman, Adam Clarke, Tania Creighton, Catherine Fogarty, Simon Ingram, Allan Giddy, Jules Gull, Stephen Hamper, Josef Mallard, Anneliese McAuliffe, Tony Mighell, Laurence Page, Emile Rasheed, Stephen Stocks, Torben Tilly, Finch Van Sluys, John Webb, Peter Woodford-Smith and Stephen Zepke

Museum education: Nicholas Baume, Thérèse Burnett, Ben Curnow, Louise Katz, Lyndall Phelps, Sue Saxon, MCA Guides; additional text proofreading: Ben Curnow

Vodafone mobile gallery guide: Written by Sarah den Dikken; edited and managed by Nicholas Baume; music selection by Colin Hamilton

Marketing and Sponsorship: Rachel Dibsdale, Stephanie Sims, Christopher Snelling and Fiona Hartley

Exhibition merchandise development: Jane Duff

Exhibition graphic design: Peter Thorn

The Museum of Contemporary Art was established by The University of Sydney through the J W Power Bequest with the assistance of the Government of New South Wales. The Museum also acknowledges the financial assistance of the Australian Film Commission, the Australia Council, the Commonwealth Government's arts funding and advisory body, and the NSW Ministry for the Arts.